COOPERATION WITHOUT COMPROMISE

JAMES DEFOREST MURCH

Cooperation without Compromise

A History
of the National Association
of Evangelicals

1956
WM. B. Eerdmans Publishing Company
GRAND RAPIDS, MICHIGAN

COOPERATION WITHOUT COMPROMISE
by James DeForest Murch
Copyright 1956 by
Wm. B. Eerdmans Publishing Company

LIBRARY OF CONGRESS CATALOG CARD NUMBER: 56-12876

PRINTED IN THE UNITED STATES OF AMERICA

INTRODUCTION

In inter-church circles, the word "ecumenicity" has received a great deal of publicity in recent years. This word has the general meaning of "universal" or "world wide." In the ecclesiastical sense, it means "pertaining to or representing the whole Church."

Since the New Testament compares the Church to a building, a body, a bride, or a branch, there is certainly a sense in which the ecumenical movement must be recognized as scriptural.

Before we can endorse any kind of ecumenical movement, however, we must clarify two very important factors which the dictionary definition does not take into consideration: First, what do we mean by the word "Church"? Second, is the whole Church to be represented by a coercive ecclesiastical machine, or, conversely, is it to be represented in activities and agencies depending entirely upon the unity in and leadership of the Holy Spirit?

This book regarding the history and functions of the National Association of Evangelicals reveals the proper answers to these questions. Dr. James DeForest Murch, with his keen analytical approach, shows that scriptural ecumenicity is the basis for the existence of the National Association of Evangelicals.

This organization, uniting in its various commissions and agencies some 10,000,000 evangelicals, is based upon a sound biblical confession of faith that accepts the Bible as the only infallible and authoritative Word of God. This confession also states a belief in the deity of the Lord Jesus Christ, His virgin birth, His sinless life, His miracles, His vicarious and atoning death, His bodily resurrection, His ascension to the right hand of the Father, and His personal return in power and glory.

The NAE believes that any institution calling itself a "church" must subscribe to these biblical truths. It also believes that anyone joining such a church must accept

12834

these biblical truths as a heart experience and, through the Holy Spirit, be "born again."

The NAE further believes that the only ecumenicity authorized by the Bible is that ecumenicity in which the Church is led and guided by the Holy Spirit in cooperative evangelical action at home and abroad.

The purpose of this book is to portray the only kind of ecumenicity in which evangelicals can cooperate without compromise.

H. H. SAVAGE
President of the
National Association of Evangelicals
(1954-56)

FOREWORD

Millions of American Protestants find in the National Association of Evangelicals their most satisfactory channel for inter-church cooperation.

Prior to the beginnings of the Association in 1941-42 these advocates of the historic evangelical Christian faith were divided and impotent. Many found themselves by reason of faith and conscience unable to work with existing agencies. They were an "unvoiced multitude" yearning for some adequate medium through which they might present their evangelical testimony to the nation and work together for the accomplishment of common purposes.

These dedicated millions found in the NAE "cooperation without compromise" of their doctrinal convictions and are making a tremendous impact for "the faith once for all delivered to the saints."

The necessity for the organization of the NAE and its continued existence separate from other media of inter-church cooperation can be understood only in the light of certain fundamental biblical and historical principles and the story of the "Great Apostasy" of the twentieth century.

We have endeavored to give that background in the opening chapters of this book and then to move on into the thrilling story of the organization of the NAE; its development through its various functioning commissions, agencies and affiliates; its achievements by the grace of God and its future prospects.

This book is a pioneer work. In it, for the first time in a more or less comprehensive and definitive form, we have endeavored to write the history of the NAE. We have drawn on many sources of information and employed the views of many of our evangelical leaders for which we have given due credit. We have plotted our own course, since there was no trail to follow. We trust that others, following, will be able to achieve a more adequate presentation of one of the greatest Christian movements of our times.

It is our conviction that in a very real sense the National Association of Evangelicals has "come to the Kingdom for such a time as this." Through its spirit-filled members, manifesting the love of their one Lord and seeking His enabling grace, it is advancing the Kingdom of Christ and is being used to accomplish the ultimate purposes of God.

JAMES DEFOREST MURCH

CONTENTS

COOPERATION WITHOUT COMPROMISE

I

EVANGELICALS AND COOPERATION

Unity, fellowship, and cooperative action are "hallmarks" of true evangelical,[1] biblical Christianity.

The Church, as pictured in the New Testament, possessed all these elements. Its Founder, the Lord Jesus Christ, established them as implicit in it. "For by one Spirit," declared the apostle Paul, "are we all baptized into one body" (I Cor. 12:13). Despite the human weaknesses of those who composed the apostolic institution they were "one in Christ," they belonged to one another and they worked together to achieve a common goal.

For some time there existed a happy blending of spiritual and temporal unity in the Church but with the advent of worldliness and apostasy divisions appeared. Greek and Roman Catholicism then sought to preserve outward unity in the pattern of an ecumenical ecclesiasticism. Church conformity became more to be desired than unity in spirit, life, and doctrine, resulting in a degenerate and apostate church.

1. The term "evangelical" has been in common usage since the Reformation and has been used to designate theological parties claiming that their doctrinal views constitute "the gospel." Webster's dictionary defines an evangelical as one who "holds that the essence of the gospel consists mainly in the doctrines of man's sinful condition and need of salvation, the revelation of God's grace in Christ, the necessity of spiritual regeneration and participation in the experience of redemption through faith." Dr. James A. Murray, in *A New English Dictionary on Historical Principles,* says: "From the eighteenth century, the term evangelical has been applied to that school of Protestantism which maintains that the essence of the gospel consists in the doctrines of salvation by faith in the atoning death of Christ and denies that good works or the sacraments have saving efficacy. . . . Other features . . . are . . . the sole authority of the Bible in doctrine, the denial of any power inherent in the church to supplement or authoritatively interpret the teaching of Scripture. . . ." Dr. V. R. Edman, in *United Evangelical Action,* Dec. 15, 1945, says: "Evangelical Christianity implies belief in the great essentials of divine revelation contained in the Scriptures, namely, the fall of man, the necessity of the new birth, the atonement of Christ, and justification by faith, with emphasis on presenting these truths to all."

13

Evangelical, biblical Christianity did not die, but insofar as its visible state was concerned it became a remnant flock under the one Shepherd. It was not until the period of the Reformation that it again began to take a significant place in the thought and life of the world.

The Church of Christ now began to manifest itself in many places and under many leaders often far removed from one another. These leaders found their visible unity in societies and denominations though recognizing that the church universal is essentially, intentionally and constitutionally one. They saluted one another as brethren on the basis of their faith in Christ and obedience to Him according to the Holy Scriptures and the manifestation of the Spirit of Christ in their tempers and conduct.

These people, denominated Protestants or Reformers (to distinguish them from Greek and Roman Catholics), gradually assumed certain distinguishing characteristics which marked them as the finest flower of Christianity.

They recognized Christ as the sole and supreme head of the Church and Lord of all.

They acknowledged the Holy Scriptures as God's infallible revelation of His will and the ultimate authority for the church in doctrine, ordinances and life.

They taught salvation by the justification of the individual soul through faith in Christ.

They practiced the universal priesthood of all believers and believed in the right of private judgment.

They required individual piety and practiced social righteousness.

They emphasized evangelism as the chief task of the Church and sent missionaries to the ends of the earth.

In its purest form, Protestantism insisted upon the separation of church and state.

Protestantism had become the bulwark of universal education, freedom of speech and worship, and all the larger human freedoms which are the fruit of obedience to God.

Wherever there was a common acceptance of these distinguishing characteristics there was a measure of cooperation between denominations in matters of common concern.

The emphasis upon basic and essential Christian doctrine was deemed of primary importance. There was wide acceptance of the "Apostles' Creed." Protestants were unwilling to compromise doctrine for the sake of cooperation. The least common denominator of Christian doctrine among Protestants might well be summed up as belief —

In the Bible as the inspired, the only infallible, authoritative word of God.

In one God, eternally existent in three persons: Father, Son and Holy Spirit.

In the deity of the Lord Jesus Christ, His virgin birth, His sinless life, His miracles, His vicarious and atoning death through His shed blood, His bodily resurrection, His ascension to the right hand of the Father, and His personal return to power and glory.

In the salvation of lost and sinful man, regeneration by the Holy Spirit is absolutely essential.

In the present ministry of the Holy Spirit by whose indwelling the Christian is enabled to live a godly life.

In the resurrection of both the saved and the lost; they that are saved unto the resurrection of life and they that are lost unto the resurrection of damnation.

In the spiritual unity of believers in Christ.

The first broad adventure of Protestants in the field of interdenominational cooperation occurred in the 1840's.

Roman Catholicism was enjoying a new ascendancy, evidenced in England by the Oxford Movement and the apostasy of Newton and Pusey from the Church of England. Religious intolerance in Esthonia, Latvia, Lithuania, Turkey, Persia, Spain, and Portugal had resulted in imprisonment and death to many Protestants. There was a universal demand for some sort of cooperation which would put an end to these threats and offer a channel for future action.

In the United States of America Protestants were becoming increasingly aware of an extreme fragmentization which had divided their ranks into over two hundred denominations and sects and rendered them impotent in the face of Romanism's rising power. Theologically there were the basic differences of Calvinism, Arminianism and Lutheranism; organizationally there were such varied polities as congregationalism, presbyterianism, and the episcopacy. Differences of language, race, nationality, provincialism, creeds, disciplines, confessions and traditions were being emphasized to the detriment of the Church universal. Politics, pride, selfishness, personal ambition, fanaticism, bigotry, and intolerance all played their part in what had become almost a public scandal.

Godly denominational and undenominational leaders on both sides of the Atlantic, who had upon their hearts the highest and best interests of the cause of Jesus Christ and the accomplishment of the ultimate purpose of His Church, began to pray for a way out. Under the leading of the Holy Spirit these men were brought together. They agreed that the time had come for some kind of cooperative effort that would provide for united and aggressive action in meeting common problems and that might bring a better spirit of fellowship among the churches themselves.

A preliminary gathering was held in Liverpool in 1845 which issued invitations to Protestants in all parts of the world to come to London in August, 1846, for united counsel and action. From the United States went such leaders as Lyman Beecher, S. H. Cox, L. M. DeWitt, Stephen Olin, and William Patton. In response to the invitations, over eight hundred gathered in Freemason's Hall (now the Connaught Rooms) and unanimously adopted the following resolution:

> That the members of this conference are deeply convinced of the desirableness of forming a confederation, on the basis of great Evangelical principles held in common by them which may afford opportunity to the members of the Church of Christ of cultivating brotherly love, enjoying Christian intercourse, and promoting such other objects as they may hereafter agree to prosecute together; and they hereby proceed to form such a Confederation under the name of The Evangelical Alliance.[2]

They immediately drew up and adopted a statement of the principles which they deemed essential to cooperation:

1. The divine inspiration, authority, and sufficiency of the Holy Scriptures;

2. The right and duty of private judgment in the interpretation of the Holy Scriptures;

3. The unity of the Godhead and the Trinity of Persons therein;

2. Data concerning the World's Evangelical Alliance was gleaned from *Goodly Fellowship, the Centenary Record and History of the Alliance* by J. W. Ewing (1946), *The World's Evangelical Alliance and Vital Unity in Christendom* (1946), Files of *Evangelical Christendom*, official quarterly publication of WEA, *Toward a United Church* by William Adams Brown (1946), and other sources.

4. The utter depravity of human nature in consequence of the fall;

5. The incarnation of the Son of God, his work of atonement for the sins of mankind and his mediatorial intercession and reign:

6. The justification of the sinner by faith alone;

7. The work of the Holy Spirit in conversion and sanctification of the sinner;

8. The immortality of the soul, the resurrection of the body, the judgment of the world by our Lord Jesus Christ, with the eternal blessedness of the righteous and the eternal punishment of the wicked;

9. The divine institution of the Christian ministry and the obligation and perpetuity of the ordinances of Baptism and the Lord's Supper.

While the extent of the statement and some of its phrasings were not pleasing to the Americans they accepted them in principle and came home eager to set up a national Alliance. The rumblings of the Civil War hindered their desires, however, and it was not until 1867 that the American phase of the work began. Mr. William E. Dodge, a prominent and philanthropic merchant of New York City, was chosen president and held that office for sixteen years. In 1873 the International conference was held in America. In 1886 a full-time American general secretary, Dr. Josiah Strong, was employed and the Alliance gained wide support. Dr. Philip Schaff, noted theologian and writer, speaking in Chicago in 1893, declared that the Alliance offered the hope of the reunion of Christendom.

At the height of its influence the Alliance succeeded in bringing the tremendous influence of Protestantism to bear in behalf of religious liberty, the observance of the Lord's Day, temperance, evangelism and human freedom. It sought to apply Christian principles in government and the social order. It established a worldwide Day of Prayer. It succeeded in breaking down the barriers of denominational intolerance and bigotry. It gave Protestantism a new vision of the *"Unum Corpus in Christo."*

The "fly in the ointment" was "liberalism." German rationalism and the social gospel had begun to penetrate America. Leading liberals at first tried to streamline the Alliance to fit their new ideas, but they found both here and abroad an adamant stand for the fundamentals of the faith. As one British leader put it:

We cannot countenance Rationalistic efforts to water down the Scriptures of truth by casting doubts upon the miraculous element in the Gospels and on the true deity of the Son of God. So-called Rationalism has always had a paralyzing effect on the work of the ministry. As evangelicals we are set for the defense of the Gospel. We have a message that is supernatural; a Saviour who is the Eternal God manifest in the flesh; and a Book that is divinely inspired as no other book. We have a Gospel to proclaim which is the power of God unto salvation to everyone that believeth.

Finding themselves in the minority such liberals as Charles L. Thompson, Elias Sanford, Josiah Strong, Washington Gladden, Walter Rauschenbush, Harry F. Ward, and Frank Mason North at first set up the Open Church League[3] (1894) and the National Federation of Churches and Christian Workers[4] (1900). Not all of those associated in these organizations were liberals but the directing spirits were definitely liberal and there is every evidence that they were but forerunners of a new agency which might supplant the Evangelical Alliance. It is interesting to note in this connection that it was the liberals, not the conservatives, who raised the first organized impediments to cooperative effort in America.

3. *Origin and History of the Federal Council of the Churches of Christ in America* by E. B. Sanford (1916), p. 34.
4. *Ibid.*, p. 146.

II

THE GREAT APOSTASY

The student of evangelical Christian cooperation in America cannot adequately comprehend or understand the events from 1900 to 1950 without the background of the Great Apostasy. Against this background all evangelical thought and action may be seen in its true perspective and significance.

We pause, therefore, in the delineation of the history of cooperation to deal with the theological crisis into which Christendom was plummeted at the opening of the twentieth century. A new interpretation of Christianity commonly known as "liberalism" challenged the "faith once for all delivered to the saints." It refused to accept the authority of the Holy Scriptures and the historic creeds of Christendom, and began to project its heresies into every root and branch of the Christian Church.

Two thousand years of history verify the fact that Christianity is a historical phenomenon. It is not an esoteric type of mysticism. It has existed and still exists in many different forms but it has a basic unity and substance without which it becomes purposeless and futile. If we are to know what Christianity is, we must examine its origin and see it in its purest form. In the Holy Scriptures we have the unquestioned authentic historical data by which we can determine what Christianity truly is.

Christianity is a great movement originated by Jesus Christ. It had its roots in His Messianic ministry in Judea and Galilee, but prior to His death on the Cross it existed only in embryonic form. In His death, His resurrection and His ascension into glory a basis was laid which eventuated in the birth of the great world movement which is commonly called Christianity. On the day of Pentecost A.D. 30 in the city of Jerusalem a strange new beginning, attended by the miraculous outpouring of the Holy Spirit, stirred Christ's apostles to unprecedented action and the evangelization of humanity began.

19

What were the elements inherent in this movement which have made it the marvel of history? They are summed up in the fifteenth chapter of the First Epistle to the Corinthians, in which the apostle Paul gives a summary of what he "received" from God and the first disciples of Christ in the Jerusalem Church. He puts it in brief: "Christ died for our sins according to the Scriptures; He was buried; He rose again the third day according to the Scriptures." Each one of these assertions is a historic fact — facts with meaning and far-reaching implications wrapped up in the personality of Jesus the Christ, Son of God and Saviour of the world. To deny a single one of them was to deny Him.

The propagation of this faith was characterized by the bold assertion of these facts and in their demonstration in the lives of those who accepted them.

Christianity is both a doctrine and a life. The common modern concept that it is "a life and not a doctrine", that it is an experience which has doctrine merely as its intellectual expression, is founded on shifting sand. The valid Christian life which characterized the early Church was produced by complete and unwithholding surrender of every area of life to the Christ who was God manifest in the flesh, who died for man's sin according to the Scriptures, was buried and arose again the third day according to the Scriptures, and who was capable of changing and transforming sinful men into new creatures after His own likeness. Without acceptance of these facts and their implication for mankind, acceptance of Christ is meaningless mysticism or crass humanism. He becomes either the figment of man's imagination or a good man who said some wise things and died a hero's death.

Wherever the Christianity of the first century has been proclaimed, believed, accepted, and demonstrated there has been a living, vital Church with an impact on society little short of miraculous. It is this sort of Christianity which has "turned the world upside down" and caused men to speak of the times in which it has lived as the Christian Era.

At the beginning of the nineteenth century there arose a new interpretation of Christianity. The apostle Paul characterized a similar apostasy in the first century of the Christian Era as "another gospel" and branded it with his anathema.[1] This new interpretation had its origin in scientific naturalism.[2] Following a period in which the world had been largely influenced by the rationalistic philosophies of David Hume, Immanuel Kant, Georg Wilhelm Friedrich Hegel, and August Comte there emerged a new secularism and scientism. The former produced Karl Marx's *Humanist Manifesto* and World Communism. The latter gave new impetus to the study of the natural sciences with many salutary benefits to humanity, but unfortunately, also to a tragic contempt for spiritual things. In the great universities of Germany scientific objections to the basic doctrines of the Christian faith gained such credence in intellectual circles that theologians were forced to reexamine their traditional views. Since many of them were pure professionalists in the field of religion they lacked the faith and conviction to meet scientific criticism with biblical truth. Such men as Schleiermacher, Ritschl, and Troeltsch abandoned to the new culture the inspiration of the Holy Scriptures, the unique deity of Christ, the atonement for sin, the personal resurrection of the saints, the second coming of Christ unto final judgment, heaven, hell, and every vestige of the supernatural elements of the Christian faith. These "German rationalists" then attempted to accommodate Christianity to scientific naturalism.[3] As a result so-called "liberalism" was born and soon spread to England and the United States.

Dr. Harold John Ockenga, the first president of the National Association of Evangelicals, has in contrast well characterized the two opposing views of Christianity[4] which battled each other "to the death" in America in the first half of the Century:

The Liberal View.[5] "Liberal" comes from the Latin word *liber* meaning a free man. Liberalism is the con-

1. Galatians 1:6-9.
2. *A History of Philosophy* by W. Windleband (1926), *Science and Religion in Contemporary Philosophy* by Emile Boutrous (1909) and *Protestant Thought Before Kant* by Arthur Cushman McGiffert (1911) give important background.
3. *The Problem of Religious Knowledge* by Douglas Clyde Macintosh.
4. Dr. Ockenga's views concerning "liberalism" and "orthodoxy" were well expressed in the presidential address delivered before the 1944 Convention of the National Association of Evangelicals in Columbus, Ohio, and printed in *United Evangelical Action*, June 1944.
5. Cf. "What Is Liberalism?" by Harold J. Ockenga in *United Evangelical Action*, Jan. 15, 1954 and "What Is Orthodoxy?" *Ibid.*, Feb. 1, 1954.

sciousness of liberty and the resistance to any attempt on the part of constituted authority to exert artificial pressure or regulation on the individual. Against such imposition on personality and initiative of the individual, whether in morals, religion, intellectual activity, social relationships, economics, or politics, liberalism must array its forces. The anomaly today is that whoever is a liberal in political economy or theology is contending against the protection of the rights of the individual, a complete reversal of position. The liberal today has sold out lock, stock, and barrel to regimentation and control in church and state. Whoever fails to fall in line and wishes to exercise liberty is today called a Troy or a reactionary, but liberal is the term chosen by the movement in theology to describe their wish to be free of the historic creeds. They do not wish to be free from theology, for they now have a theology which is even more dogmatic than the theology of orthodoxy in the form of their required belief in the Fatherhood of God, the brotherhood of man and naturalistic evolution. Their creed is even more rigid than the orthodox and their objection to theology is merely objection to the theology of orthodoxy. Therefore they disparage the creeds and the confessions of the church.

Liberalism has it origin and root in scientific naturalism. Liberalism denies the entrance of the creative power of God in the origin of Christianity, whether it be in the Virgin Birth, the miracles of Christ, the resurrection of Christ or the inspiration of the Word of God. Liberalism is an attempt to accommodate Christianity to modern scientific naturalism. Wherever scientific objections may arise from the details of the Christian religion, liberalism abandons to modern culture the inspiration of the Bible, the unique deity of the Person of Christ, the atonement for sin and a personal resurrection. On the other hand, liberalism retains the general principles of Christianity in "the good life," "the aspirations of the soul" and "the struggle for a better world."

It is not possible because of space limitations to analyze the various teachings of liberal theology today, but we can give a few suggestions as to landmarks in recognizing the liberal. No two liberals are really alike, but their general principles are the same. They all act upon the application of evolutionary naturalism to Christianity. The Bible, according to the liberals, is the historical record of the developing religious consciousness of one people. That is a far cry from the Christian teaching concerning the Bible as the Word of God and the record of that revelation as inspired.

Concerning Jesus, the liberal does not want to have a religious relationship. He does not accept Jesus as one to be worshipped. He does not accept the subjective-objective view of man in his relationship to Jesus. He merely accepts Jesus as an example, a prophet, a teacher and a moral pioneer. He is willing to accept the religion of Jesus so that he can come to God as the man Jesus came to God, but he is not willing to accept the Biblical revelation about Jesus, namely, that Jesus is the Son of God, and Saviour, and the object of our worship. What the liberal fails to recognize is that this same teacher and moral leader claimed to be sinless and that He also had a Messianic conscience in which even in the Sermon on the Mount He said, "In that day I will say unto you: depart from me ye workers of iniquity." He also said, "Hereafter ye shall see the Son of Man sitting on the right hand of power, and coming in the clouds of heaven." Caiphas declared that He was guilty of blasphemy when He made this claim, yet that claim cannot be expunged from the narrative.

The cross, as a substitutionary sacrifice for the liberal, is merely the thought form of that generation in which the truth of the love of God was expressed. The liberal claims that the same truth was expressed in dialectic by the scholastics, by doctrine in the age of the reformers and will be expressed differently in our age, probably by the sacrificial life. The liberal says that the eternal thing is the truth and that the category or form of expressing that truth changes with different generations. Hence the New Testament interpretation of the cross of Christ is not the final one for the liberal.

Miracles, for the liberal, are merely the legendary clothing of a great man. They are the age's high estimate of one who left a tremendous impact upon his contemporaries. In order to express the greatness of his personality they clothed him with miracles, but the miracles really did not occur.

The gospel, for the liberal, is utterly changed from the means of reconciliation with God, or the redemption of the soul from sin, or the liberation of man from the bondage of evil to a sense of filial piety, or brotherhood, of mutual understanding and of betterment. In the gospel, for the liberal, there is no mention of the cross or if it is mentioned it is only as a way of sacrificial living.

The church, according to the liberal, is an organization for human betterment. It is no longer the assembly of called out people who are redeemed, the body of Christ, the organism of which He is the Head and, which enjoys mystical union with Him. The church becomes a movement akin to a radical party in the historical destiny of social development. The Communist Party is the vanguard of the social revolution. So the church is the vanguard of the spiritual betterment of mankind. One can easily recognize the difference between this and the Christian gospel.

The doctrines of the church and of Christianity as revealed in the incorporation papers of Christianity are utterly repudiated by the liberals and new doctrines are substituted for them.

The Orthodox View. The nature of positive Christianity is set forth by Paul in I Corinthians 15:3, "For I delivered unto you first of all that which also I received, how that Christ died for our sins, according to the Scriptures, and that he was buried, and that on the third day he rose again, according to the Scriptures." Paul emphasizes four things here: First, the written Word; second, the atonement of Christ; third, the resurrection of the dead; fourth, the knowledge of salvation. These four things are the basis of orthodox Christianity.

First, *the written Word*. Paul said twice, "According to the Scriptures." Orthodox Christianity from the beginning has believed that the Bible is the Word of God. That does not mean that there is no revelation except in the Bible, for the Bible contains confirmations of revelation given elsewhere, namely in nature and conscience. The Bible strengthens such general revelation. The Bible says, "The heavens declare the glory of God and the firmament showeth his handiwork. Day unto day uttereth speech and night unto night showeth knowledge. There is no speech nor language where their voice is not heard." There is a revelation of God in the stars. Whether one looks at the microcosm or the macrocosm he is able to recognize order, design, intelligence and law. When he looks at the mind of man he finds a logical structure in which thought is able to be communicated. When he looks into conscience he finds a work of God written upon the human heart, but all this is not the unique revelation of God — of the Bible.

The Bible contains an absolutely new and exclusive revelation from God found nowhere else. It tells how a sinful man may become right with God. This constitutes the uniqueness of Christianity over against all other religions of discovery.

The Bible revelation is of an event which is the essence of redemption, namely God's giving of His only-begotten Son to be offered up on the cross for our sins. This was an act of God. Salvation is something that happened, an event of history. To this event, the whole Old Testament looks forward and in it the whole New Testament finds its center. Without the offering up of the eternal Son of God for our sins humanity is lost under the burden of its sin. What an effect this revelation has had upon humanity!

Christianity has always believed that the Bible is an inerrant record of that revelation and in its writing, through the Holy Spirit, men were preserved from error, despite a full maintenance of their habits of thought and expression. The human element may be found in the Bible in thought form, language, expression, and personal background. Therefore inspiration does not involve dictation, but superintendence, guidance, suggestion, and preservation by the Spirit of God over the minds of men. Therefore we believe that the Bible can be defended from all attacks and we declare it to be "an infallible rule of faith and practice." The Christian finds the seat of authority in the whole Bible which is no mere word of man, but the very Word of God. Not the mind which accepts or rejects, not the general Christian consciousness, not experience, and not the authority of the church, but the Word of God is the authority for the individual Christian believer.

Therefore Bible theology is orthodox theology and it is the practice of orthodox Christians to study the Bible systematically to determine what the doctrines of the Bible are. Greater emphasis must be given upon such exegesis to diminish the difference between evangelical Christians for there are important differences concerning the second coming, the sacraments and the priestly order of Christian service, but debate ought to determine those differences within the realm of Christian authority. Out of our study of the Word we come to the principal doctrines of God, man, salvation, the witness of the Spirit, immortality, and others, which are the certainties for the Christian faith. It was that Word which broke the power of Rome in the Reformation and it is that Word which is the power of Christianity today.

2 The second basic element in orthodox Christianity is that *Christ died for our sins.* That is a statement of a

vicarious satisfaction. Christ is our Saviour not only because of what He was and said, but because of what He did. He took upon Himself the dreadful guilt of our sins and bore it on the cross. Christ endured the positive wrath of God, the pains of hell and death, and the second death, in our place. The Lord Jesus because of His love tasted eternal death for us on the cross. Thus it is that Christ's cross, His shed blood and His exhibited love constitute the message which breaks the heart of man, changes sinful lives and constitutes a new loyalty in one's obedience to God. The example of the moral teachings of Christ will never do that, but the blood of His cross will.

This substitutionary satisfaction is the plain teaching of the Word of God. God's Word knows of no other kind of atonement. It says, "Behold the Lamb of God which taketh away the sin of the world." It is "redemption through his blood." It is "one died for all." It is "washed by his blood." To this end the pre-existent God became man by the Virgin Birth, lived a sinless life, performed miracles, made stupendous claims, suffered upon the cross, died, rose again, and intercedes at the right hand of God. All of that was that He might make atonement for our sins.

Other theories are only attacks upon the Word of God. That Christ died for our sins is no theory but is a fact interpreted by the early church and the apostles under the impact of Christ and the inspiration of the Holy Spirit. It is upon this doctrine that the scorn of liberals is cast more than on any other, but of this cross and of the crucified Christ the church preaches and of it the redeemed will sing forever.

3 The third element of orthodox Christianity is the *resurrection*. Paul said, "And rose again the third day." Imagine what the church would be without that belief. It would be like the disciples during the three days of Christ's burial. If you have a dead Christ today no matter how excellent a moral teacher or example, your church will be powerless as were the disciples during those three days. The resurrection is the apologetic doctrine of Christianity and the missionary message of the book of Acts. It cannot be dissociated from primitive Christianity. For this reason attacks have been centered upon the resurrection to explain it away, for it is God's seal upon the claims of His Son.

Yet the proofs of the resurrection will always stand before the minds of thinking men. Historically we can never get these records out of the narrative. No kind of criticism can expurgate them from the original Christian facts. They are part of early Christianity. There is the record of the eleven appearances of the resurrected Christ. Psychologically there is no explanation for the changed condition of the disciples from discouraged, disillusioned men to powerful preachers of the Word unless it is their belief that Jesus rose from the dead. Logically there is always the open tomb, and if the disciples themselves would not have investigated it their enemies would have, and thus have put an end to their preaching about the resurrection of Jesus Christ in Jerusalem where the tomb was located.

Here is the one attestation of the supernatural which is able to undergird a believer intellectually. Here is a decisive challenge to naturalism, to liberalism and to unbelief. If God could intervene in the order of natural law once, He can intervene now in a self-revelation in Jesus Christ to the soul of men. This has been vindicated in the redemptive experience of Christians from Paul to us today.

4 The fourth basis of orthodox Christianity is *the knowledge of salvation*. Paul said, "By which also ye are saved, if ye keep in memory what I have preached unto you." Salvation depends on what happened long ago, but that event of long ago has effects which continue today and we can put to trial the meaning of those events and find them true today. Experience will confirm the truth of the gospel. That experience must depend upon and be connected with the historical events, but it will prove Christ to be the living Saviour today, able to deliver, to comfort, to strengthen, to give assurance of eternal life. Such assurance comes from our meeting the formula of repentance or change of mind, of conversion or turning to Christ, of confession or acknowledging our sin, and the committal or believing on the Lord Jesus Christ.

In response to this activity of men, God gives the witness of the Holy Spirit which is the assurance of our salvation. He that hath the Son hath the witness in Himself. His spirit beareth witness with our spirit that we are the children of God. That witness is the assurance wrought in the soul that my sins are forgiven and that I am saved.

Coming from all this is the Christian life. Tragic is it when Christians do not live the life, when they are not men of this way and are not following Jesus Christ. For the Christian Christ becomes Example, Teacher and Wayshower. The truly orthodox in doctrine are orthodox in life.

That liberalism and orthodoxy are entirely incompatible is recognized by the leaders of both camps.[6] Dr. Charles Clayton Morrison, editor of the liberal *Christian Century*, in an editorial entitled, *Fundamentalism and Modernism*: *Two Religions,* said that

> There is a clash here as grim as between Christianity and Confucianism. . . . The God of the fundamentalist[7] is one God; the God of the modernist is another. The Christ of the fundamentalist is one Christ; the Christ of the modernist is another. The Bible of the fundamentalist is one Bible; the Bible of the modernist is another. The church, the kingdom, the salvation, the consummation of all things—these are one thing to fundamentalists and another thing to the modernists . . . Which is the true religion? . . . . The future will tell.[8]

Every area of the thought life of America was rent with controversy.

6. Contemporary evangelical literature of the period: *The Fundamentals.* A well-organized compilation of views of evangelical leaders on issues under discussion (1910). *The Fundamental Doctrines of the Christian Faith* by R. A. Torrey (1918), *Contending for the Faith* by Leander S. Keyser (1920), *Orthodox Christianity versus Modernism* by William Jennings Bryan (1924), *Christianity at the Crossroads* by E. Y. Mullins (1924), *What Is Faith?* by J. Gresham Machen (1925), *Christianity and Liberalism* by J. Gresham Machen (1923) and *Fundamental Christianity* by F. L. Patton (1926).

7. "Fundamentalism" is often used by liberals as a comprehensive term including all evangelicals. Dr. Bernard F. Ramm gives a fairer definition: "Fundamentalism originally referred to the belief that there are certain great truths in Christianity which, if charged, would dissolve Christianity. Each Christian is allowed personal conviction in respect to a great number of doctrines and interpretations but that personal liberty is hedged about by key infallible and eternal doctrines. This is the term in its historic and good sense. The movement included such stalwarts as James Orr, J. Gresham Machen, Benjamin Warfield, W. H. Green, and the numerous contributors to the famous *Fundamentals* papers. In more recent years another movement has developed within historic fundamentalism that has given the word an odious connotation. Men with much zeal, enthusiasm and conviction, yet lacking frequently in education or cultural breadth, and many times highly individualistic, took to the stump to defend the faith. Many times they were dogmatic beyond evidence, or were intractable of disposition, or were obnoxiously anti-cultural, anti-scientific and anti-educational. Hence the term came to mean one who was bigoted, and obscurantist, a fideist, a fighter and an anti-intellectual. Many of these men are godly in life, in belief thoroughly Christian and therefore spiritual brothers of all who accept biblical Christianity but not representative of the evangelical movement at large. Another movement has developed within historic fundamentalism which is marked by pre-millennial and dispensational theology. Because this movement is only mildly Calvinistic and in some quarters is out and out Arminian, Reformed theologians have identified fundamentalism with pre-millennialism and dispensationalism . . ." *UEA*, October 15, 1951, p. 2.

8. *Christian Century*, Jan., 1924. Cf. *Christianity and Liberalism* by J. Gresham Machen (1923).

Theology had been committed to evangelical, biblical forms. At first the theologians saw their problem as a reconciliation of adequate Christian doctrine with the "assured results" of physical science and biblical criticism. There was a wide difference of opinion as to what was truly "assured" but most leaders of theological thought felt sure that some radical adjustments must be made on the question of biblical inspiration and authority. Soon there was widespread acceptance of the "authority of Christ" as opposed to the "authority of the Bible." Then came the elimination of the Old Testament prophecies of Christ, the negation of His virgin birth, essential deity, incarnation, substitutionary atonement, and bodily resurrection, and His rejection as the only Mediator between God and mankind. Commitment to a basic belief in an Immanent Divine Will practically revolutionized the theology of most leading seminaries. Those who held to the traditional, evangelical, biblical view were gradually eliminated from the faculties.[9]

Philosophy, under the impact of the new naturalism, veered away from idealism to materialism. Whatever affinity philosophy had for religion came from the idealistic school. Materialism employing only reason has always been the breeding ground of atheism, humanism, naturalism, and all forms of skepticism; employing experience it produces sensationalism, naturalism, empiricism, experimentalism, positivism and pragmatism. Released from evangelical thought patterns the philosophers in church schools boldly proclaimed Christianity as a philosophy. The idealists, repudiating the supremacy of matter, led their pupils into a plethora of Ideas, Ultimates, All-Wills and Absolutes. The materialists, emphasizing science and the scientific method with their evolutionary correlatives, produced a new generation of atheists, rationalists and pragmatists.[10]

Psychology veered from the purposive school to the mechanistic school. The turn to liberalism in church-related schools opened the gate to those who believed that man is an animal and that human conduct consists of mechanical

9. *Christianity and Modern Thought* by Ralph H. Gabriel (1924), *Present Tendencies in Religious Thought* by Albert C. Knudson (1924) and *Religious Thought in the Last Quarter Century*, edited by Gerald Birney Smith (1927).

10. *A History of Philosophy* by W. Windleband (1926), *Main Currents of Modern Thought* by Rudolph Eucken (1912) and *Types of Religious Philosophy* by Edwin A. Burtt (1939).

responses to nerve stimuli, that man's actions are the result
of natural impulses over which he can exert no psychic or
spiritual control. While many nominally Christian professors held to a modified form of naturalism, they still were
quite free in declaring that "mind is incapable of recognizing truth from error, is limited in its ability to make moral
choices" and that "the greatest good for the individual and
society is achieved through the establishment of desirable
nervous reflexes." Prayer, according to the naturalists, was
a universal habit of the human race growing out of the
common desires of the mind, which has a reflex influence
capable of conditioning conduct. Every moral and religious
practice was robbed of its spiritual reality.[11]

Education, taking its cues from the new philosophy and
psychology, discarded the Bible and the Christ of the Bible.
God-centered education was exchanged for a man-centered
process. God's will was no longer the basic norm. Man's
mind became the measure of all things. The absolute truth
of God's revelation to man was scrapped for relative truth.
Human social welfare became a matter of primary concern.
The goal of education was no longer to fit men to live in
harmony with the will of God. Education, in the new view,
is an instrument by which the developing and changing
person may continue in the quest for certainty. Genuine
values and tenable ends and ideals can be found only within
the movement of experience and not from authority, human
or supernatural.[12]

The virus of liberalism penetrated all the phases, functions and institutions of Christendom, resulting in a tremendous defection from the things which Christianity
through the centuries had most surely believed.

Within a generation the churches began to show a marked
decline in attendance and spiritual power. The pulpits came
to be occupied by liberal ministers who lacked conviction
and passion because they had abandoned the Gospel that is
the power of God unto salvation. Conversions were rare.

11. *Mind and Deity* by John Laird (1914), *Essays of a Biologist*
by Julian Huxley (1923), *Psychopathology of Everyday Life* by Sigmund Freud (. . . .), *The Future of an Illusion* by Sigmund Freud
(1929) and *The Psychology of Religious Experience* by Edward Scribner Ames (1910).
12. *Democracy and Education* by John Dewey (. . . .), *Education
and Certainty* by Robert L. Cooke (1940), *Source Book in the Philosophy of Education* by W. H. Kilpatrick (1923) and *Religious Education* by G. A. Coe (1916).

Young men were not volunteering for the ministry or the mission field. The man in the pew had his doubts that Christianity was the true religion. In the office and in the social realm he found a world dominated by pagan ideas. From without the churches were beset by the perils of atheism, humanism, communism and statism; from within by secularism, sectarianism, pharisaism and liberalism.

III

THE BATTLE OF THE CENTURY

American liberalism so profoundly affected every area of the culture of the twentieth century that orthodox Chrisianity was driven to devote much of its talents and energies to an all-out defense of the Faith. Institutional Christianity and the cause of Christ in general suffered greatly because of the conflicts which ensued. This was, indeed, the Battle of the Century.

Evangelicals were primarily interested in the advancement of the Kingdom of God along apostolic lines. They "continued stedfastly in the apostles' doctrine and in fellowship, and in the breaking of bread, and in prayers"[1] and devoted themselves assiduously to seeking and saving the lost. They were not good politicians. Ecclesiastical strategy was foreign to their nature, but not so with the liberals. American liberalism had a genius for ecclesiastical politics. Their strategy was so effective that evangelicals were outwitted at every turn and were soon fighting desperately for survival.

Liberals first attacked strategic chairs of religion in the universities, colleges and seminaries. Evangelical professors were discredited by a well-directed propaganda which made them appear to be naive, obscurantist, unscholarly and reactionary. In many instances liberals represented themselves to be evangelical, accepting under oath evangelical confessions of faith with "mental reservations," using orthodox words to convey liberal thought, and moving with caution until circumstances afforded safe opportunity to take an open stand for the new doctrines. Often they used the so-called "inclusivist" strategy — persuading evangelical institutions to admit liberals to their faculties on the ground that "academic freedom" required presentation of all viewpoints. When liberals attained majority status they set up new standards and by other devices eliminated all evangelical professors. Once firmly entrenched in the insti-

1. Acts 2:41-47.

32

tutions which trained the leadership of the churches, liberals were in position to exert their influence on the entire denominational machinery.

The Methodist Episcopal Church (now the Methodist Church) furnishes a classic example of the over-all strategy used in all denominations. A small group of liberals met in Boston early in the new century and agreed to work together for the liberalizing of the denomination.[2] A four-point program was accepted: (1) place a rationalist in every chair of English Bible in the various church colleges; (2) liberalize the Book Concern; (3) liberalize the church rituals; (4) liberalize the approved Course of Study for the training of the ministry. Strongly evangelical Bishop Thomas B. Neeley said of this program,

> There is an anti-Methodist school of thought working through a few aggressive individuals to compel the Church to accept its views and, at the present time, to accomplish this without constitutionally changing the Articles of Religion or other standards of doctrine. The method is not that of frontal or open attack but of the sapper and the miner.

This strategy was overwhelmingly successful. In a generation the denomination was firmly in the control of liberals. Every Methodist college and university was in their hands. The Sunday School board had eliminated all its old evangelical leadership and was sending its emissaries to every conference in the land spreading the new educational philosophy. Exerting its influence in the production of Sunday School literature in the Book Concern, liberalism was able to reach and mis-teach the more than 4,000,000 children and youth in Methodist Sunday Schools. Anti-Methodist doctrine soon began to appear in the books bearing the imprint of the official denominational publishing house. The Foreign Missions board was taken over and the evangelical missionary testimony of this great church was soon a thing of the past. Finally, through political manipulation, the Bishopric came under liberal domination and the whole episcopal framework of the Church down through the district superintendents began to operate to the embarrassment of every evangelical minister. This was made possible through handpicked Conference delegates chosen from graduates of liberal Methodist colleges. A large evangelical constituency remained in the denomination,

2. *Leaven of the Sadducees* by Ernest Gordon (1926); Files of *The Methodist Challenge*, Robert J. Shuler, Sr., editor.

especially among the rank-and-file of the membership, but they were the "unvoiced millions" helpless and hopeless when it came to the ecclesiastical machine.

The tragic situation confronting Methodist evangelicals led to wholesale desertions of the denomination to newer and smaller bodies such as the Church of the Nazarene, the Free Methodist Church, the Wesleyan Methodist Church and to other Holiness groups.

The Presbyterian Church in the USA was one of the citadels of the evangelical faith in the early days of the century. With such stalwart theologians as Robert Dick Wilson and B. B. Warfield, missionary leaders like Robert E. Speer, lay-leaders like William Jennings Bryan and John Wanamaker, and clergymen of the stature of Maitland Alexander and Clarence E. Macartney, it seemed that these descendants of John Calvin and John Knox might be impervious to the onslaughts of liberalism. The General Assembly frequently warned the Church to be on guard to preserve the Faith as set forth in the Westminster Confession of Faith and the Holy Scriptures. Then the Union Theological Seminary of New York became the spawning ground for liberalism. Despite the fact that the institution came under scathing attack from denominational leaders, its influence, by strangely devious means, infiltrated other Presbyterian institutions. Before denominational leaders were aware of it there was sufficient strength in Presbyterian liberalism to declare itself boldly in the notorious Auburn Affirmation (1923). This document,[3] signed by 1,292 ministers, said, in effect:

(1) We do not believe in the inerrancy of the Holy Scriptures or accept them as final authority in faith and practice; (2) we accept the Incarnation of Christ as a fact but deny the biblical doctrine of the Virgin Birth; (3) we deny that on the cross Christ "satisfied divine justice and reconciled mankind to God"; (4) we doubt that Christ rose from the dead "in the same body in which he suffered"; (5) we deny the supernatural element in Christ's miracles and (by inference) the supernatural element in his redemptive work.

The text of the Affirmation taken alone seems comparatively harmless. It can only be understood in its true meaning and purpose when it is compared with the doctri-

3. For full text of the Auburn Affirmation see *The Presbyterian Conflict* by Edwin H. Rian (1940), pp. 291-297.

nal statements in the Westminster Confession of Faith and the "Five Points of Christian Doctrine"[4] adopted by the Presbyterian USA General Assembly in 1923.

There were still within the Presbyterian Church in the USA many individual churches that were veritable garrisons of orthodoxy, possibly a few presbyteries, and a whole host of ministers and laymembers, but the Presbyterian ecclesiastical structure came definitely to be controlled by liberals.[5] *The Presbyterian, The Presbyterian Banner,* and all her orthodox journals have disappeared. Her church-controlled colleges, with a few exceptions, are in the liberal camp.

The story of apostasy in the Northern Baptist churches[6] began with John D. Rockefeller's munificent gift of the University of Chicago. The Divinity School of the University was placed under Baptist control and soon became a hotbed of liberalism. In 1913 the Northern Baptist Theological Seminary was formed as a protest against this liberalism; later came Eastern Baptist Theological Seminary and other institutions that pledged themselves to remain faithful to the evangelical faith. Dr. Augustus H. Strong, honored president of Rochester Theological Seminary (later to succumb to liberal control), said in 1917 that the conflict centered around the person and nature of Jesus Christ —

> We need a supernatural Christ; not simply the man of Nazareth, but the Lord of Glory; not the Christ of the Synoptics alone, but also the Christ of John's Gospel; not merely a human example and leader, but one who "was declared to be the Son of God with power by the resurrection from the dead"; not simply Jesus according to the flesh, but "the Word who was with God and was God" in eternity past; not simply God manifest in human life nineteen centuries ago, but the God who is "the same yesterday and today, and forever"; not simply the humbled, but also the glorified Saviour, who sits now upon the throne of the universe, all power in heaven and earth being given into His hand. When we believe in an ascended Lord at God's right hand, the God of Creation, of Providence, and of Redemption, we have a faith that can conquer the world.

Soon the mission boards were under fire because of their compromises with liberalism. When evangelical churches

4. *Ibid.,* pp. 31-36.
5. Files of *The Presbyterian, The Presbyterian Banner; Tests for Church Fellowship* (1944); *Twentieth Century Reformation* by Carl McIntire (1944).
6. *Background and History of the General Association of Regular Baptist Churches* by Joseph M. Stowell (1949), *The Foreign Missions Controversy of the Northern Baptist Convention* by Chester A. Tulga (1950); Files of the *Watchman-Examiner.*

refused to support liberal missionaries, John D. Rockefeller, Jr., an ardent liberal, came forward with millions of dollars to make up the mission board deficits. In 1919 the Missouri Convention withdrew its 600 churches and joined the Southern Baptists. The following year the evangelicals, or "fundamentalists," of the Northern Convention called a pre-convention conference in Buffalo to restate "the fundamentals of the Baptist faith." Among them were such noble names as J. C. Massee, Curtis Lee Laws, John Roach Stratton, A. C. Dixon, W. B. Hinson, W. B. Riley and Cortland Myers. This proved to be a turning point in the history of the Convention. From this time forward there were wholesale desertions to the Southern Convention. Minnesota, Oregon and Arizona Conventions withdrew to become independent. The General Association of Regular Baptist Churches and at a later date the Conservative Baptist Association came into being (now numbering some 1,000 churches each). New missionary societies, Bible colleges, and service agencies were organized. Virtually barred from the official ecclesiastical machinery of the old denomination hundreds of thousands of Bible-believing Baptists felt that their only hope lay in building again on tried and true foundations.

The Disciples of Christ, the oldest and largest communion with American origins, which for a century had prided themselves as taking "the Bible and the Bible alone as its rule of faith and practice", became the veritable mother of aggressive liberalism.[7] *The Christian Century*, at first a Disciple magazine, edited by Dr. Charles Clayton Morrison, became the spearhead for liberal propaganda. A brilliant example of progressive religious journalism, its influence extended throughout Christendom. Associated with Dr. Morrison were other Disciple leaders such as Edward Scribner Ames, Herbert L. Willett, and W. E. Garrison. Almost simultaneously liberalism penetrated the Foreign Christian Missionary Society and such educational institutions as Transylvania University, the College of the Bible, Hiram College, and Eureka College. The International Convention was rent with controversy over "open membership" and other similar issues stemming from the over-all battle which was on full tilt throughout Christendom. A merger

7. *Fifty Years of Digression and Disturbance* by Edwin V. Hayden (1955) ; Files of the *Christian Standard*, the *Restoration Herald*, and the *Spotlight*.

of all missionary agencies into the United Christian Missionary Society delivered virtually all the missionary work of the communion into the hand of the liberals. Then followed, one by one, almost all the older educational institutions. The *Christian Standard,* advocate of the old faith, rendered yeoman service to the evangelical cause with the result that more than fifty per cent of the 2,000,000 constituency remained true. This body, strongly congregational in polity and jealous of the independence of the local church, sheltered many an evangelical minister, driven from his own liberal-controlled denomination because of ecclesiastical pressures.

The Disciples furnish a splendid example of the strategy of evangelicals in many denominations driven from the older educational and missionary institutions. Bible-believing educators set up some twenty new schools and seminaries training most of the men studying for the ministry. While the United Christian Missionary Society was forced to retrench its program of expanding missionary effort, the "independent" missionary program entered thirty lands, sent out some 400 missionaries and began to report thousands of baptisms. Unfortunately these moves were attended by bitter controversies provoking more nationwide unrest and more local church disunity than ever before in the history of the communion.

The battle of the century projected itself into the ranks of inter-church cooperation in America. Dr. John A. Hutchison in his history of inter-church cooperation in America[8] said that the credo of the Evangelical Alliance was a "theological strait jacket" and responsible for its disappearance from the American scene. He continued,

> One of the clues to the failure of the Evangelical Alliance was the theological rigidity which prevented it from adjusting itself to one of the major transitions in the history of the American church. . . . Educated people began to demand that religion put off the crudities of an earlier day, and put on the garments of refinement and culture.

Again Mr. Hutchison comments that

> The nineteenth century liberal revolt in New England brought into American Christianity currents of humane and ethical thought which before the end of the century had influenced even the most orthodox denominations. Nineteenth century scientific thought, with its concepts of evolution and progress, likewise made its mark on the churches. . . .

8. *We Are Not Divided* (1941).

The American Alliance, suffering from reactionary policies and overseas domination, no longer claimed the wholehearted allegiance of all the churches. Liberals had organized the National Federation of Churches and Christian Workers and had visions of translating something broadly-inclusive of all American Protestantism and making it a channel for their politico-social ambitions.

Accordingly, an invitation was sent out early in 1905 by a committee of the National Federation of Churches and Christian Workers calling for a conference of official representatives of all denominations. It was proposed that a new organization be set up "to express the visible unity of the Christian churches, to record their agreement on issues where they do agree and to cooperate in common tasks." Official delegates representing thirty denominations gathered in Carnegie Hall, New York, during the week of November 15-21, labored and brought forth the Federal Council of Churches of Christ in America.[9]

The Plan proposed in 1905 was ratified in Philadelphia in 1908. It is as follows:

PREAMBLE

WHEREAS, In the providence of God the time has come when it seems fitting more fully to manifest the essential oneness of the Christian Churches of America in Jesus Christ as their divine Lord and Savior, and to promote the spirit of fellowship, service and cooperation among them, the delegates to the Interchurch Conference on Federation, assembled in New York City, do hereby recommend the following Plan of Federation to the Christian bodies represented in this conference for their approval.

PLAN OF FEDERATION

For the prosecution of work that can better be done in union than in separation, a Council is hereby established whose name shall be the Federal Council of Churches of Christ in America.

Then follows a list of thirty-two churches deemed eligible for membership, after which the plan continues:

The object of this Federal Council of Churches shall be:

1. To express the fellowship and catholic unity of the Christian Church.

9. *Origin and History of the Federal Council of Churches of Christ in America* by E. B. Sanford (1916).

2. To bring the Christian bodies of America into united service for Christ and the world.

3. To encourage devotional fellowship and mutual counsel concerning the spiritual life and religious activities of the churches.

4. To secure a larger combined influence for the churches of Christ in all matters affecting the moral and social condition of the people, so as to promote the application of the law of Christ in every relation of human life.

5. To assist in the organization of local branches of the Federal Council to promote its aims in their communities.

Then followed the limitations that:

This Federal Council shall have no authority over the constituent bodies adhering to it; but its province shall be limited to the expression of its counsel and the recommending of a course of action in matters of common interest to the churches, local councils and individual Christians. It has no authority to draw up a common creed or form of government or worship or in any way limit the full autonomy of the Christian bodies adhering to it.

Liberals rejoiced that the "theological strait-jacket" of the old Alliance had been discarded and that they were now free to peddle their theological nostrums without let or hindrance. The nearest semblance to a confession of faith was contained in the Preamble in which Jesus Christ was acknowledge as "divine Lord and Savior." The word "divine" was not in the original draft, but Dr. Samuel J. Nicholls (Presbyterian), of Saint Louis, Mo., demanded its insertion to assure the evangelical character of the organization. After considerable discussion it was unanimously voted. At that early day evangelicals were scarcely aware that the word held a double meaning. Historically it carried all the connotations of deity, but the rationalists had now interpreted it to mean that Christ was divine as men may be divine, that His divinity may differ from man's only in degree. Trysting evangelicals did not realize that they had left open the gate to membership for Bible-baiters and disbelievers, but they were later to realize that their victory was only an empty one.

In the early days of the Council the cleavage between evangelicals and liberals was evident. Dr. William H.

Roberts, a self-styled "old-fashioned Presbyterian," constantly championed "fundamental Christian doctrine" while Dr. William Hayes Ward spearheaded for liberalism. Hon. John Wanamaker stood for Bible-centered education against the pleadings of Dr. George Richards for a "more intelligent and progressive type of education with less reference to emotional evangelism." Dean George Hodges of the Yale Divinity School "pled for an honest reception of new truth in both science and religion as a mode of God's progressive revelation of himself to man," while David H. Bauslin declared that the present age needed salvation from "rationalism, Voltaire and Tom Paine." Dr. Herbert L. Willett, accepting the findings of the "higher critics" of the Bible and covering his attacks on its infallibility with beautiful weasel words of tribute, was confronted by Dr. F. D. Power who believed it "from cover to cover." Dr. Frank Mason North made eloquent appeals for church action in industrial situations based upon a claim for Christ's sovereignty over social as well as individual life, while Dr. Henry Van Dyke held that "removal of ignorance," "better character" and the "improvement of human nature" and not "legal enactment" would produce a better society. Whenever the Council met there was debate but both parties were determined not to permit their differences to wreck this new attempt at Christian cooperation.

Naive evangelicals hoped that liberalism was only a passing fad soon to be absorbed in the approach of a new millennium, while liberals, biding their time, traded concessions in theology for concessions in ethics and negotiated a stranglehold on the Council's commissions and administrative machinery.

Beginning with thirty-two denominations in its official family the Federal Council was during two decades somewhat of a reflection of the church life of America. It vaguely exalted Christ and the Church and committed few flagrant sins against evangelicalism. While majoring in social programs it did not neglect evangelism. It gradually extended its activities in such fields as temperance, Lord's Day observance, social justice, international goodwill, labor and industry, health, marriage and the home, research and education, worship, war and peace, relief and reconstruction. In fact, it busied itself with every phase of life in organized society.

The Council formed advantageous alliances, some open, some *sub rosa*, with important functional cooperative agencies. It established state and local federations and councils of churches. Its influence — religious, social and political — was felt north, south, east and west in the Americas and across the seas.

As the years passed the line between "liberalism" and true Christianity in the FCCCA became more and more distinct.[10] While the Council maintained an "inclusive policy" with regard to membership it tended to practice an "exclusive policy" with regard to leadership. Dr. Harry Emerson Fosdick, acknowledged liberal leader, said in his *Adventurous Religion* (1926) that "the liberals are gaining, and if not stopped now, will soon be in control." Since that time they very definitely came into control of Council leadership, policy and program.

When the full realization of this tragedy broke in upon evangelical Protestantism the Federal Council of Churches of Christ in America lost its grip on the religious life of the nation. In 1940 the Council had become unacceptable to 176 Protestant communions out of the 200 in existence. Some communions (such as the Reformed Church in America, the United Presbyterian Church, the Presbyterian Church in the US) remained in its fellowship knowing that large numbers of their constituencies strongly opposed the relationship. Others, notably the Disciples of Christ and the Northern Baptists, were unable because of their policy to speak officially for the majority of their members. Still others spoke officially while millions of their members silently but resentfully disagreed.

The blight of liberalism was evident in almost every phase of the Council's activities. Evangelicals regretfully agreed that the FCCCA could no longer qualify as the representative of American Protestantism or of historic Protestant principles and essential Christian doctrine.

While vigorously opposing the political and ecclesiastical pretensions of Roman Catholicism the Council became a sort of neo-Catholic church "embodying the best in Protestantism."

10. *How Modern Is the Federal Council?* by J. Elwin Wright (1943), *Death in the Pot* by J. Elwin Wright (1944), *The Case Against the Federal Council of Churches* by Chester E. Tulga (1948), and *Ecclesiastical Octopus* by Ernest Gordon (1945).

In FCCCA's Cleveland convention in 1942 evangelicals were shocked when Metropolitan Antony Bashir of the Syrian Antiochian Archdiocese of New York and North America led a worship service in which he invoked the intercessions of "our all-immaculate Theotokos and ever Virgin Mary" and the great ecumenical teachers, hierarchs and saints of the Greek Catholic Church. In a resolution passed at the same convention the Roman Catholic Church was referred to as a "sister communion."

While its leaders protested that the Council was "evangelical" in doctrine, its bylaws specifically forbade any creedal test in the matter of membership and the liberal views of its leadership were a matter of abundant record.

Dr. Harry Emerson Fosdick, in a letter to a Sunday-school teacher said:[11] "Of course I do not believe in the Virgin Birth or in that old-fashioned substitutionary doctrine of the Atonement; and do not know any intelligent Christian minister who does."

One-time President Francis J. McConnell said concerning the deity of Christ:

> Critics point out to us that in the early days of the church it was quite common even for popular thought to deify a man. On that memorable occasion in Paul's missionary journey through south Galatia when multitudes called Barnabus Zeus and Paul Mercury, they were acting true to that idea of their time which conceived of gods as capable of appearing in human form and found it easy to believe that man could become a god. Is not this tendency to deify Jesus more heathen than Christian? Are we not most truly Christian when we cut loose from a heathen propensity and take Jesus simply for the character he was and for the ideal he is?[12]

Dr. Henry Sloane Coffin's writings were filled with denials of the historic Christian faith. He rejected the Bible as the infallible Word of God. In his volume, *What to Preach,* he called the Virgin Birth of Christ an "unscriptural exaggeration."

Dr. G. Bromley Oxnam, another Federal Council president, shocked evangelicals by this paragraph from his book, *Preaching in a Revolutionary Age:*

> Hugh Walpole, in *Wintersmoon,* tells of a father and son at church. The aged rector read from the Old Testament, and the boy learned of the terrible God who sent plagues upon the people and created fiery serpents to assault them. That night, when the father passed the boy's bedroom, the boy called him, put his arms around

11. *The Federal Council of Churches and the Reformed Faith* (1946).
12. *The Christlike God,* p. 15.

his father's neck, and drawing him close, said, "Father, you hate
Jehovah. So do I. I loathe him, dirty bully!" We have long since
rejected a conception of reconciliation associated historically with
an ideal of Deity that is loathsome. God, for us, cannot be thought
of as an angry, awful, avenging Being who because of Adam's sin
must have his Shylockian pound of flesh. No wonder the honest boy
in justifiable repugnance could say, "Dirty bully."

While those pronouncements were not officially representative of the Council itself, the Council shared responsibility for them in the sense that it habitually and almost
exclusively chose such liberal thinkers for its positions of
trust.

Evangelicals came to realize that the approach of the
Federal Council to social problems was essentially humanistic. In its special post-war meeting in Columbus, Ohio
(1946) the Council expressly stated that the common basis
of social reason and action is "the progressive realization
of the dignity and worth of man in every area of life."
President Truman in an address at the same gathering
made "the worth and dignity of man" *the one basic principle* upon which both religion and democracy are founded.

Dr. John A. Hutchison, Federal Council historian,
quoted[13] from Dr. F. Earnest Johnson to show that Council
sociologists were correct in making *"the essential divinity
of man a first principle, not a derivative"* for "when human
beings are seen by one another as embodiments of the divine
all their relationships will be shot through with creative
goodwill." Dr. Hutchison stated that the Council's social
program was a protest and a criticism[14] of the orthodox
position regarding man and that "the concept of sin has
received important qualifications at the hands of evolutionary and scientific thought."[15]

While the worth and dignity of man is, in its proper relation to the doctrine of the lordship of Christ, a Christian
principle, evangelicals believe it is not the basic principle
for social reasoning and action. When made basic it often
leads to humanistic and unchristian conclusions.

In the Council's "Social Creed," adopted in 1908 and
revised in 1932, two drastic positions were taken. Article 1
condemned the profit motive and Article 8 endorsed coop-
eratives. Some who were responsible for such pronounce-

13. *We Are Not Divided*, p. 303.
14. *Ibid.*, p. 340.
15. *Ibid.*, p. 301.

ments were frankly and openly socialistic, if not near-communistic, in their convictions.

Evangelicals felt that the Council would substitute political action for the ameliorating influence of the gospel and many red-blooded Americans hold that the Federal Council stopped "just short of proclaiming the allegiance of the church to a socialized economic system for America instead of the democracy of free enterprise."[16]

An increasing tendency of the FCCCA to trust in political pressure to further its social objectives was disconcerting to evangelicals. When President Oxnam, boasting of a Council accomplishment, said, "Washington politicians knew they were not dealing with a paper organization" he tacitly admitted that the Council had become a political pressure group. Another Council leader felt that the churches must develop "new techniques to impress the politicians." Still another that "the central international problem of the postwar world will be that of the responsible use of monopolized power" and that the churches "are in danger of failing to see the possibilities for order which exist, and of concentrating their attention so exclusively on the injustices which are present that their efforts may be irrelevant to the main issue." It is a well-known fact that the Council had a staff of politico-religious lobbyists in Washington and intended to increase its pressure tactics upon the Congress and the President.

Evangelical Christians sought a better world and sympathized with the desires of those who were working in that direction. They desired to see the principles of Christianity made the basis of the social order and translated into the legal codes of the land. Evangelicals contributed much toward the development of Christian civilization. They helped to build a Christian culture which functions as a means of social control and an agency of social progress. They did not believe in a merely personal, subjective and pietistic form of Christianity which isolates the individual Christian from the social issues of the times. Neither did they believe it possible to bring in the Kingdom of God by force or to impose the Christian ethic successfully upon an unregenerate society by the use of power politics. They looked upon the whole idea as the very antithesis of the Christian way of life.

16. Muskegon (Mich.) *Chronicle*, editorial February 8, 1945.

So far afield had the Council ventured in its social program that in 1935 the U. S. Naval Intelligence cited "The Federal Council of Churches of Christ in America" as "a large radical, pacifist organization." "It probably represents 20,000,000 Protestants in the United States," said Naval Intelligence. "However, its leadership consists of a small radical group which dictate its policies." Quite a sensation was caused when this report was read into the *Congressional Record*[17] for August 17, 1935, and when President Roosevelt came to the rescue of the Council's rapidly dwindling popular prestige.

When *Newsweek*[18] spoke of the Federal Council as "a virtual monopoly" in American Protestantism it expressed a common belief among evangelicals. Many held that it not only restrained the freedom of non-cooperating denominations but often promoted liberalism at the expense of Bible-believing, Christ-honoring Protestants.

In hundreds of cases the Council used its supposed status to speak as "the voice of American Protestantism," to prohibit the building of denominational and independent churches in government housing and other areas, to keep evangelical preachers out of army and navy chaplaincies, to cast aspersion on projects in mass evangelism and in many other ways to obstruct non-Council activities.

Finally came a dangerous monopolistic move of the Council in the proposing of a merger of the seven leading inter-denominational functional cooperative agencies of American Protestantism with the FCCCA to form a huge super-church.

This ecumenical church, as it was called, was described by Dr. Charles Clayton Morrison in the *Christian Century*[19] as an organization which receives new members; educates, selects and appoints a ministry; promotes missionary expansion; inculcates in its people the ideals, concepts, and lore of the ecumenical faith; determines the general substance and forms of worship; administers the Lord's Supper; and determines "the minimum but central belief" required for membership.

It was Dr. Morrison's opinion that "the concept of an ecumenical Protestantism can become a living reality only

17. *Congressional Record*, Vol. 79, No. 180, p. 15271.
18. *Newsweek*, September 29, 1941.
19. *Christian Century*, June 19 (p. 779) and June 26 (p. 802), 1946.

by the surrender of the functions of churchly sovereignty now exercised by its denominations . . ."

Pointing out that some of these functions were already implicit in the Federal Council, he then indicated that "the Federal Council and the two missions conferences and the council on religious education, having already established so well the principle of cooperation, [were] in a providential position, by uniting in one agency, to enlist the denominations in an ecumenical administration of these two functions and to awaken the first gleams of an ecumenical consciousness throughout Protestantism."

In other words, Christian unity and ecumenicity were goals which might be attained by organizational regimentation and by the compromise of fundamental Christian doctrine and traditional Protestant freedoms.

By 1940 most evangelicals had come to the conclusion that the FCCCA was no longer a fit vehicle for evangelical cooperation at the national level. The following "bill of particulars" probably represented their view of the Council's inadequacy:

1. Setting itself up as a Council of churches it nevertheless refused to adopt as a basis of fellowship the absolute minimum of fundamental evangelical Christian doctrine necessary to such a body. It committed itself to the institutional concept of Christian unity and showed itself willing to accept any generally approved human scheme or device which would achieve united action.

2. It admitted into its membership a host of "liberals" who were committed to a theology and philosophy which are definitely anti-Christian in the biblical sense. Still others in its ranks were avowed enemies of Protestantism and many of the basic principles for which it stands.

3. It created an organization which to all intents and purposes was under the rule of an "oligarchy." Real control lay in the hands of a few men who were definitely "liberal" in their viewpoint. Through clever unofficial devices they had virtual control of every arm of the organization.

4. The ramifications of the Council were such that it was already beginning to function as a "Super-Church," bringing pressures or exerting authority over both member and non-member churches. Evangelicals were being forced to take protective measures to insure unfettered liberty in preaching the Gospel and carrying on their church programs.

5. Its concept of the nature of the church, the character of Christ and of essential doctrine was inadequate. It at no time unequivocally stated its belief in the Bible as the inspired, the only infallible authoritative Word of God; in the deity of our Lord Jesus, in His virgin birth, in His sinless life, in His miracles, in His vicarious and atoning death through His shed blood, in His bodily resurrection, in His ascension to the right hand of the Father, and His personal return in power and glory; in regeneration by the Holy Spirit as essential to the salvation of lost and sinful man; in the present ministry of the Holy Spirit by whose indwelling the Christian is enabled to live a godly life; in the resurrection of both the saved and the lost — they that are saved unto the resurrection of life and they that are lost unto the resurrection of damnation.

6. It indicated both in pronouncements and practice that it considered man's need and not God's grace as the impelling motive to Christian action and that the amelioration of the social order is of primary concern to the Church. In this connection it attacked capitalism, condoned communism and lent its influence toward the creation of a new social order.

7. Its relation with Greek Orthodox churches and its general attitude toward the Roman Catholic church threatened to weaken if not eventually destroy the distinctive testimony of Protestantism.

8. It deliberately omitted or shamefully neglected to include provisions for the preservation and perpetuation of all the values and liberties inherent in historic Protestantism.

Under the circumstances there was no other alternative left to evangelicals but to perfect their own organization for cooperation and action at the national level.

IV

DISCOVERING A FORMULA FOR UNITED EVANGELICAL ACTION

After more than a decade of dissatisfaction with the Federal Council of Churches of Christ, evangelicals began moving constructively outside its auspices to create vehicles for Christian cooperation and action.

There was an evident leading of the Holy Spirit in many people in many places, without preconceived human planning and with no overall pattern.

A cursory survey of the evangelical situation revealed a tremendous constituency accomplishing great things for the Lord but without cohesion, or means of united action when under fire from the well-organized hosts of "liberalism."

In the field of *education* hundreds of evangelical Bible institutes, colleges and seminaries had sprung up with little but the faith of their founders to assure their perpetuity. These institutions were rapidly growing to maturity with strengthened faculties, splendid buildings and large student bodies. Among the Churches of Christ (Disciples) nearly twenty new schools had been established, training the majority of the students in the communion who were preparing for full-time Christian service. Many of the older denominations — notably the Southern Baptists, the Missouri Synod Lutherans, the Free Methodists, the Wesleyan Methodists and the smaller Presbyterian and Reformed bodies — had largely preserved their older institutions from contamination. In the undenominational field such schools as Wheaton College, Moody Bible Institute, and Los Angeles Bible Institute had grown to wide influence and power.

In foreign *missions* the blight of "liberalism" in many of the older societies and boards had compelled Bible-believing Christ-honoring missionaries, who hold the blood of Christ to be the only redemptive power for heathenism, to set up hundreds of faith missions across the globe. These, together with the denominational agencies that were still true to the Book, composed the chief hope of the winning of the world to Christ. Despite "liberal" efforts to bar the doors of foreign lands against evangelicals God kept them open and marvelous victories were being won through the power of the gospel. Forward-looking evangelicals had built great missionary radio stations such as HCJB in Ecuador; trained pilots to fly missionary planes into untouched areas; utilized recording devices, motion pictures, and every other helpful modern invention to spread the ancient gospel to the ends of the earth.

In *evangelism* thousands of Pentecostal flames had been lighted where "liberalism" had seemingly succeeded in smothering the desire for souls. Individual ministers and laymen in all the denominations were leading millions to Christ. In the union field Bob Jones, Sr., John R. Rice, Hyman Appelman, and others were carrying the torch long held aloft by Moody, Alexander, Sunday, and Biederwolf. Millions were gathering under tents and in municipal auditoriums to hear the gospel. On the radio Charles E. Fuller, Walter A. Maier, and hundreds like them reached other millions weekly. One shudders to think how crippled and emaciated Protestantism would be today without the courageous ministry of these heroes of the faith.

In the *publication* field besides such stalwart houses as the Broadman Press, the Concordia Press, the Herald Press, and the Light and Life Press in the denominational area, there were scores of independent publishers like Union Gospel Press, Scripture Press, Sunday School Times, Eerdmans, Moody, and Standard, who had refused to "bow the knee to Baal." From their presses millions of copies of evangelical literature flowed each working day of every week and were distributed to every nook and cranny of the nation.

With American *youth* engulfed in the most sinister tide of delinquency and crime in the history of the nation a new evangelical Youth for Christ movement was beginning to challenge them with the saving power of the gospel. On Saturday night (of all nights!) millions of young people were thronging the greatest auditoriums of the nation to hear and see Christ lifted up. State university and other secular college campuses were being invaded by Inter-Varsity Fellowships reaching the rising generation of "intellectuals."

American *business men* were being pointed "to the Lamb of God who taketh away the sin of the world" in thousands of Gideon camps, Christian Business Men's Committee meetings, and Breakfast Club gatherings. War veterans were being served spiritually in evangelical Service Centers and by chapters of the Christian War Veterans of America. *Labor* was being contacted for Christ by the developing industrial chaplaincy. Summer *vacationers* were finding spiritual uplift in thousands of conferences and camps patterned after the famous Winona Lake institutions.

Through the years something else had been happening — at once encouraging and unfortunate — the development of thousands of independent tabernacles, undenominational churches and new denominations. Almost without an exception these evangelical movements had been occasioned by the coldness, formalism, liberalism, and worldliness of the older churches. This development was unfortunate in that old fellowships had been severed and the fragmentization of Protestantism had apparently been multiplied. It was encouraging in that the shackles which hindered the free preaching and practice of the old-time religion had been broken and millions had been reached by the gospel who might otherwise have been lost. There were some contemnable people and events mixed up in this eversion within the ranks of Protestantism but no unbiased student of it can fail to see that the overall results were beneficial. Certainly many of the resultant elements as they now exist are productive of great good for the Kingdom of God.

In this tremendous upheaval history was being made. The headlines in the newspapers and in the denominational journals of the times were filled with news about the Councils of Churches and the "official doings of Protestantism," but very little was being said publicly about the spontaneous spiritual movement which might well bulk far larger in the ultimate history of Christendom. Out of all this began to emerge significant attempts at evangelical Christian cooperation.

Evangelical Christianity in America, like the true Church of Christ, is not synonymous with or entirely comprised within the ranks of any one denomination, movement, or organization. It consists "of all those in every place that profess faith in Christ as the Son of God and obedience to

Him according to the Scriptures and that manifest the same by their tempers and conduct."[1]

These people within denominations in and out of the Federal Council and within independent and undenominational movements and organizations felt a divine compulsion to join hands and hearts in a great forward movement. They were convinced that the forces of evangelical Protestantism should present a united front and move forward according to an integrated strategy. They were convinced that cooperation within the framework of the Federal Council or the projected National Council of Churches could only perpetuate an irreconcilable conflict between liberals and evangelicals and serve to obstruct the work evangelicals felt called of God to do.

It began to be a matter of prayer among men of this persuasion across the nation as to how this desire might be implemented. They were determined to break with apostasy but they wanted no dog-in-the-manger, reactionary, negative, or destructive type of organization. They were determined to shun all forms of bigotry, intolerance, misrepresentation, hate, jealousy, false judgment, and hypocrisy. They hoped to launch out on a constructive, wide-visioned program which would seek to accomplish the will of God for their time and demonstrate anew the validity of His promises.

The first organized effort along these lines to attract national attention was the New England Fellowship. Dr. J. Elwin Wright was the inspired leader of the movement.

The NEF organization was formed in 1929, as a united front for evangelicals and as a means of cooperation among them in various spiritual objectives. It was rather a free fellowship of all those who were of like precious faith. From the very beginning campaigns and Bible conferences were held throughout all the area. At Rumney, New Hampshire, a summer Bible conference drew hundreds. At Rumney, also, there were developed camps for boys and for girls, special conferences for young people, for pastors, women, business men, and general conferences for the entire family.

NEF expanded, soon after its organization, into the field of radio and began broadcasting programs on most of the

1. *Declaration and Address* by Thomas Campbell (1809).

stations in New England as opportunity afforded. Daily programs over WMEX and a Sunday program over WBZ, Boston, were vital links in the Fellowship's ministry. Local and state committees were set up throughout the area. Special attention was given to work in rural areas. Churches closed a long time were opened and supplied with pastors who were willing to work sacrificially to lay the foundations of a new spiritual work in towns that had been without the gospel. An extensive Christian education ministry was carried on in the public schools of Maine and Vermont by full-time teachers. NEF workers taught as many as 10,000 boys and girls regularly through the school year and nearly 10,000 more in daily vacation Bible schools during the summer months. Bookstores were established for the sale of evangelical Christian literature and supplies in Boston and Worcester, Mass., and Portland and Bangor, Maine. The New England Fellowship became a major religious force in New England where unitarianism, liberalism, and Roman Catholicism had become so firmly entrenched.[2]

Evangelicals in many sections of the nation looked with envious eyes on New England. New England lifted up her eyes to the possibilities of evangelical cooperation at the national level. The NEF conferences in 1939, 1940 and 1941 adopted resolutions calling for the organization of a national fellowship.

In the winter of 1940-41 a letter was sent out to a considerable number of Christian leaders by the Rev. Ralph T. Davis for the purpose of discovering the extent of their interest in attempting greater cohesion among evangelicals, especially in missionary effort.[3] There were many responses of an encouraging nature. NEF's Dr. Wright followed this by a tour of thirty-one states in 1941, interviewing personally many of these leaders. On October 27 and 28 of that year several men[4] who had manifested an unusual interest met in Moody Bible Institute, Chicago, for a round-table discussion and a season of prayer.

2. From data furnished the author by Dr. J. Elwin Wright.
3. *Evangelical Action*, a report of the organization of the National Association of Evangelicals for United Action (1942).
4. Dr. Will H. Houghton, Dr. William Ward Ayer, Dr. T. J. Bach, Mr. H. C. Crowell, Rev. Ralph T. Davis, Mr. Horace F. Dean, Dr. V. R. Edman, Dr. Charles E. Fuller, Dr. Harry Ironside, Dr. Stephen W. Paine, Dr. Charles A. Porter, Dr. Ernest M. Wadsworth and Dr. J. Elwin Wright.

In September of the same year the organization of the American Council of Christian Churches[5] was suddenly announced. It included two very small denominations, the Bible Presbyterian Church and the Bible Protestant Church. When the men planning the Chicago meeting learned of this development they immediately gave the ACCC leaders a special invitation to attend. The ACCC purpose, organization, and program were presented but it was the feeling of the larger group that it did not properly express and implement the constructive ideals which they had in mind.

At the Chicago meeting it was unanimously decided that the next step should be a call for a national conference of evangelicals, including leaders of the various denominations, mission boards, colleges, seminaries, institutes, the religious press, and interdenominational organizations at which all suggestions and plans might be received and considered, including those of the ACCC.

A committee for organization, designated as the Temporary Committee for United Action among Evangelicals, was created with Dr. J. Elwin Wright as chairman and the Rev. Ralph T. Davis as secretary. The other members of the Committee were: Dr. William Ward Ayer, Dr. John W. Bradbury, Bishop William Culbertson, Dr. Richard Ellsworth Day, Dr. Stephen W. Paine, the Rev. Clarence S. Roddy, the Rev. Alex Sauerwein, Mr. Horace F. Dean, Mr. Howard W. Ferrin, Dr. Harold J. Ockenga, Mr. Jacob Stam and Mr. Thomas E. Whiteman. Offices were opened at Brooklyn, N. Y., and correspondence was immediately be-

5. The American Council of Christian Churches numbers in its membership several small denominations. The only denomination of considerable size is the General Association of Regular Baptist Churches. An International Council of Religious Education release to its national and state officials entitled, *Movement Toward Cooperation Among Conservative Christian Groups* (1945), gives the following estimate of the ACCC: "Probably we can dismiss the American Council of Churches with the evaluation that it is not likely to become very strong nor significant. It is a movement now dedicated to bitterly attacking the Federal Council. It has recently turned on the National Association of Evangelicals with like bitterness. It will accept into membership only those who will separate themselves from any relationship with the Federal Council. It is divisive, within its own ranks, and probably built upon too negative a basis to gain much strength." The release continues: "The National Association of Evangelicals is quite different. Although it is highly critical of the cooperative agencies established by the denominations, its best leadership does not wish to waste time in destructive criticism. It has a positive program and is going ahead vigorously. . ."

gun looking toward a meeting in the Coronado Hotel, St. Louis, Mo., April 7-9, 1942.

The wording of the official call for the St. Louis conference, signed by 147 evangelical leaders,[6] was as follows:[7]

There is a widespread desire to bring together the various evangelical groups within the United States into a voluntary fellowship for purposes common to all. In response to this desire, we, the undersigned, feel that the time is ripe for frank discussion and exploration of the possibility of such an organization. As a tentative basis, we suggest the following principles:

1. The Association shall be purely voluntary and operated democratically.

6. J. D. Adams, W. J. Alexander, Archer E. Anderson, William Ward Ayer, T. J. Bach, James A. Baillie, J. A. Bandy, Irving F. Barnes, Robert J. Bateman, Romaine F. Bateman, R. S. Beal, Charles R. Beittel, L. Nelson Bell, William C. Bond, Arthur J. Bowen, John W. Bradbury, E. J. Braulick, Wm. W. Breckbill, Roy L. Brown, C. Gordon Brownville, Vincent Brushwyler, T. W. Callaway, Lewis Sperry Chafer, Lloyd C. Clark, George Alden Cole, Percy B. Crawford, William Culbertson, Robert B. Cunningham, Arthur F. Davies, Joseph A. Davies, Ralph T. Davis, Richard E. Day, Horace F. Dean, W. E. Duvall, H. E. Eavey, V. R. Edman, J. D. Eggleston, Richard A. Elvee, E. Schuyler English, Horace L. Fenton, Jr., Howard W. Ferrin, B. L. Fisher, G. Allen Fleece, J. Roswell Flower, R. A. Forrest, Charles E. Fuller, David Otis Fuller, Frank E. Gaebelein, Frank S. Gardner, Hobart S. Geer, O. H. Gerstenkorn, Graham Gilmer, J. W. Goodwin, R. C. Grier, Boyd W. Hargraves, Will H. Houghton, George B. Huebert, John A. Huff, Marion McH. Hull, H. A. Ironside, Daniel Iverson, Maurice E. Jacques, Harry J. Jaeger, Paul S. James, Albert Sidney Johnson, Edwin S. Johnson, Thomas H. Johnson, Bob Jones, Sr., C. Warren Jones, Russel Bradley Jones, William P. Jones, Peter R. Joshua, Alfred A. Kunz, Arthur C. Lambourne, William Sanford La Sor, Harry C. Leach, Robert G. Lee, A. E. Lewis, Oscar Raymond Lowry, Herbert M. Lyon, William McCarrell, Alva J. McClain, J. Renwick McCullough, Robert C. McQuilkin, Clarence E. Macartney, Clarence E. Mason, Jr., V. I. Masters, E. E. Masterson, John C. Medd, Thomas Moseley, Robert B. Munger, J. Palmer Muntz, J. E. Nelson, Wm. G. Nyman, Harold John Ockenga, Edwin J. Omark, J. Alvin Orr, Joseph S. Otteson, Stephen W. Paine, George A. Palmer, G. G. Parkinson, James S. Pemberton, S. Thomas Percival, Jr., Noel Perkin, Morris Peterson, William L. Pettingill, T. Roland Philips, Delavan L. Pierson, W. E. Pietsch, James P. Pressly, Edwin J. Pudney, F. Russell Purdy, Paul Stromberg Rees, J. Irving Reese, Edwin H. Rian, Harry Rimmer, Clarence S. Roddy, Allen L. Rogers, Paul W. Rood, Alexander H. Sauerwein, H. H. Savage, A. A. Schroeter, H. M. Shuman, John Bunyan Smith, H. A. Somerville, Jacob Stam, Tommy Steele, S. M. Stikeleather, Robert Lee Stuart, S. M. Sunden, W. L. Surbrook, R. E. Suther, E. C. Swanson, H. J. Taylor, J. H. Viser, Ernest M. Wadsworth, J. H. Walker, George R. Warner, Stewart S. Wells, C. Davis Weyerhaeuser, E. Leslie Whitaker, Thomas E. Whiteman, Nathan R. Wood, Charles J. Woodbridge, J. Elwin Wright, Grant Yerbury, Samuel M. Zwemer.
7. *Evangelical Action*, pp. 8, 9, 10.

2. It shall in no wise conflict with nor interfere with the rights and prerogatives of member bodies.

3. Membership will be on a basis of the traditionally accepted evangelical position.

4. It shall be an association consisting of member bodies — churches or groups of churches, evangelical organizations, denominations, with provision for conditional membership as may appear advisable.

5. A basis of representation shall be established.

6. Representatives shall not represent themselves but the organization designating each of them and in this sense will be bearers of the views of their organization.

7. Fields of cooperative endeavor shall be designed among which are the following needed at the present time:

(1) Relations with government.
(2) National use of radio.
(3) Public relations.
(4) Evangelism.
(5) Preservation of the principle of separation of church and state.
(6) Freedom for home and foreign missions.
(7) United efforts of evangelical churches within local communities.
(8) Christian education.

These suggestions indicate the lines along which we have been thinking. It is our belief that something of this nature can become a basis for an effective cooperation among evangelicals by which our mutual interests may be conserved and aided. There are millions of evangelical Christians in this country who feel that at present they have no corporate means of making their wishes known in matters common to all. We believe the time has come to render God this service.

We, therefore, the undersigned, issue a call to you to meet with others at the Hotel Coronado, St. Louis, Missouri, April 7-9, 1942. That we may inform you as to the time and place of meeting, will you please reply to the Rev. Ralph T. Davis, 373 Carlton Avenue, Brooklyn, New York.

The night of April 7 was spent in prayer. Like the apostles who tarried in Jerusalem until they were endued with power from on high for the undertaking of Pentecost A.D. 30, evangelical leaders waited on the Lord in earnest, agonizing prayer and in faith believing that He would guide them by the Holy Spirit to the discovery of the formula for evangelical fellowship and action.

High up on the agenda were periods of discussion but there were inspirational addresses as well. Dr. Harold John Ockenga, pastor of historic Park Street Church, Boston, Mass., spoke on "The Unvoiced Multitudes"; Dr. William Ward Ayer, pastor of Calvary Baptist Church, New York City, on "Evangelical Christianity"; Dr. Stephen W. Paine, president of Houghton College, on "The Possibility for United Action"; and Dr. Robert G. Lee, pastor of Bellevue Baptist Church, Memphis, Tenn., on "Jesus of Nazareth."

Dr. Lee made clear that Christ must be central and supreme in any movement for the unity of Christians and that the Holy Scriptures are the source and authority of Christian doctrine.

Dr. Paine searched the Scriptures to discover the nature of unity. He showed it to be primarily spiritual. He insisted that federative action must have a protected orthodox doctrinal basis without intrusion of criteria not really essential to the evangelical position and must avoid negative motives. The motives for abiding and effective cooperation, said Dr. Paine, are "love for one another and for God and His Son, Jesus Christ, and a desire to serve others." Only such motives are cohesive, magnetic and enduring.

Dr. Ayer deplored the fragmentized condition of evangelicals and showed that it endangered the evangelical testimony to the world. He pled for a common voice and a common meeting-ground which would enable them to exercise under God an influence that would advance the Kingdom and keep America free.

Dr. Ockenga gave a ringing challenge to evangelicals to abandon their rugged independency which was responsible for failures, divisions and controversies. He made it clear that there must be no compromise of basic Christian doctrine in any move for united action. Surveying the situation he showed that there were millions of evangelicals with a superb nucleus of leaders waiting for a feasible and effective technique of cooperation. Compared with the material and numerical resources of liberalism they were but a remnant, yet God can use the remnant as He did in the time of Elijah, Daniel and the Lord Jesus Christ. In a closing appeal that stirred the representative audience, Dr. Ockenga prayed:

God help us to humble ourselves; God help us to be sane; God help us to do His will. God bless you, my brethren in the Lord. We stand together under the shadow of the cross and cleansed by the blood of the Lamb. There let us unite to His glory!

The first formal business session of the conference opened at 9:30 A.M. with Dr. J. Elwin Wright presiding. Dr. Wright recalled the historical events leading up to the St. Louis meeting and outlined in a broad pattern some of the objectives before the delegates. A Nominating Committee and a Committee on Agenda were chosen which reported at the afternoon session.

Dr. R. J. Bateman, chairman of the Committee on Nominations, reported on the selection of names for temporary officers to serve for the period of the conference.[8] Thereupon the following were elected: Chairman, Dr. Robert G. Lee, pastor of Bellevue Baptist Church, Memphis, Tenn. Vice Chairman, Dr. Harold J. Ockenga, pastor of Park Street Church, Boston, Mass. Treasurer, Mr. Seward S. Wells, of Buffalo, N. Y. Record Secretary, Mr. W. B. Musselman, of Cleveland, Ohio.

Dr. Lee then assumed the chairmanship of the meeting.

Dr. John W. Bradbury, chairman of the Committee on Agenda, brought in the report of the committee. He stated that inasmuch as they had no precedent to follow they advised that the plan for the conference be progressively evolved as the meeting proceeded. He called attention to the fact that the afternoon session was to be of an executive nature and that only registered delegates were to be permitted to attend. The committee felt that it was desirable that the greatest discretion be exercised by all in attendance and that no reports be disseminated without the approval of the committee. Rules of procedure were recommended as follows:

1. That no delegate speak for more than five minutes and no more than twice on the same motion, except by a two-thirds vote of the delegates.

2. That representatives of the organizations existing for similar purposes who wished to be heard be asked to make their desires known to the Committee on Agenda. Time would be arranged, as far as possible, for them to be heard.

Provision having been made for hearing reports and suggestions of similar organizations, the American Council of

8. *Ibid.*, pp. 63-66.

Christian Churches, represented by its president and founder, Rev. Carl McIntire, of Collingswood, N. J., was granted opportunity on two occasions to present the work of that group. After listening to Mr. McIntire's statement, the Conference voted to proceed to the consideration of such an organization as would be in keeping with the purposes and policies embodied in the Call sent out by the Temporary Committee.

The meeting then proceeded to the task of creating the necessary committees to accomplish the purposes for which the Conference had been called.

A Committee of Fifteen, divided into three sections, was thereupon appointed. The first section was charged with the duty of drafting a Constitution and By-Laws. This committee was composed of the following members: Dr. J. Alvin Orr, of Due West, S. C.; Dr. Daniel Iverson, of Miami, Fla.; Dr. C. Gordon Brownville, of Boston, Mass.; Dr. O. W. Taylor, of Nashville, Tenn.; Dr. W. L. Surbrook, of Indianapolis, Ind. The second section was requested to prepare a Doctrinal Statement. This committee included in its members Dr. Albert Sydney Johnson, of Memphis, Tenn.; Dr. William Ward Ayer, of New York, N. Y.; Dr. John W. Bradbury, of New York; the Rev. R. H. Harvey, of St. Louis, Mo., and the Rev. John A. Huffman, of Cambridge, Mass. The third section was designated as the Policy Committee and included the following: Dr. Stephen W. Paine, of Houghton, N. Y.; the Rev. Noel Perkin, of Springfield, Mo.; Dr. David Otis Fuller, of Grand Rapids, Mich.; Mr. Frank E. Cheney, of Boston, Mass.; Dr. R. J. Bateman, of Memphis, Tenn.

There was remarkable unanimity of opinion in the discussions and, for the most part, a warm-hearted expression of the spirit of Christ. Despite the fact that some forty denominations were represented there was little difficulty in arriving at basic doctrinal agreement. There was universal conviction that the time had come for setting up an organization for united action at the national level.

Division of opinion was evident only on three matters:

(1) The necessity for immediate and complete separation from denominations and corporations in which apostasy existed;

(2) The wisdom of creating an official council of churches as against a fellowship of evangelicals for united action, and

(3) The wisdom of a constructive program as against one with a polemical and negative approach.[9]

When the two days of prayer, study, discussion and planning were over there emerged a clear pattern for future action. Only a small fringe group found it impossible to endorse wholeheartedly the findings of the Committee on Constitution and Doctrinal Statement and the Policy Committee. With fervor and joy the conference went on record as follows:[10]

Whereas: it is the desire of those assembled at the Hotel Coronado, St. Louis, Missouri, April 7-9, 1942 to make the largest possible contribution to the spread of the Gospel of Christ: and

Whereas: there is no existing organization which adequately represents or acts for a very large proportion of our evangelical Protestant constituency: and

Whereas: we realize that in many areas of Christian endeavor the organizations which now purport to be the representatives of Protestant Christianity have departed from the faith of Jesus Christ, we do now reaffirm our unqualified loyalty to this Gospel as herein set forth, declaring our unwillingness to be represented by organizations which do not have such loyalty to the Gospel of Christ; and we express our unqualified opposition to all such apostasy. And in this loyalty to the evangelical Christian faith and opposition to all apostasy, we do hereby unite our testimony.

We propose, therefore, to organize an Association which shall give articulation and united voice to our faith and purposes in Christ Jesus, while not considering ourselves as an executive or legislative body in any wise controlling constituent members, nor proposing to initiate new movements and institutions.

The tentative Constitution stated that the proposed "National Association of Evangelicals for United Action" was

9. These three issues were the ground for disagreement between the American Council of Christian Churches and the National Association of Evangelicals. The NAEUA favored a constructive program, opposed the formation of a council of churches and in certain cases opposed immediate withdrawal from denominations and corporations in which apostasy existed.
10. *Evangelical Action,* pp. 101, 102.

to be purely voluntary and operated democratically, its purpose at no time being to conflict with the function, rights or prerogatives of its members. Constituent members were to be denominations, organizations, churches or groups of churches which could subscribe wholeheartedly to the doctrinal basis of the Association and were evangelical in spirit and purpose. It should operate in such fields as (1) evangelism, (2) government relations, (3) national and local use of radio, (4) public relations, (5) preservation of separation of church and state, (6) Christian education and (7) the guarantee of freedom for home and foreign missionary endeavor.

It was evident that the delegates to the St. Louis conference were not legally capable of ratifying the constitution as representatives of their respective organizations. There was a strong feeling that the adherence of entire denominations and evangelical organizations would be essential to recognition as a vital factor in the religious life of the nation. Such adherence, it was agreed, would depend largely on whether such organizations would have opportunity of some official voice as to the form of the constitution. It was therefore agreed that the temporary constitution and the organization under it be continued for one year, during which time every effort would be made to publicize and promote the organization and secure provisional membership. It was also agreed that a Temporary Executive Committee should arrange for a Constitutional Convention a year hence in Chicago at which time duly qualified delegates could ratify a permanent constitution and by-laws. The general promotional program blueprinted at St. Louis was to be carried on purely on a temporary and exploratory basis in keeping with the newness of the project and with the understanding that a new Committee on Policy might review it and make whatever changes or emendations might be wise in the light of experience.

The last session[11] was convened by Dr. Harold J. Ockenga. The Nominating Committee submitted names for officers and members of the Executive Committee, as well as for an Advisory Committee of Twenty-five. The final choices were: Dr. Harold J. Ockenga, Boston, Mass., President; Dr. R. J. Bateman, Memphis, Tenn., First Vice President; Bishop Leslie R. Marston, Greenville, Ill., Second Vice

11. *Ibid.*, pp. 69, 70.

President; the Rev. Ralph T. Davis, Brooklyn, N. Y., Secretary; Mr. H. J. Taylor, Chicago, Ill., Treasurer. Members-at-Large: the Rev. H. M. Shuman, New York, N. Y.; Dr. T. Roland Philips, Baltimore, Md.; Dr. John W. Bradbury, New York, N. Y.; Dr. J. Alvin Orr, Due West, S. C. Committee of Twenty-five: Dr. William Ward Ayer, New York, N. Y.; Mr. Rasmus Berntsen, Chicago, Ill.; Dr. C. Gordon Brownville, Boston, Mass.; Bishop William Culbertson, Philadelphia, Pa.; the Rev. Horace F. Dean, Philadelphia, Pa.; the Rev. R. L. Decker, Fort Collins, Colo.; Mr. Howard W. Ferrin, Providence, R. I.; Dr. Dan Gilbert, San Diego, Calif.; Mr. R. H. Harvey, St. Louis, Mo.; the Rev. George B. Huebert, Reedley, Calif.; the Rev. John A. Huffman, Cambridge, Mass.; Dr. Daniel Iverson, Miami, Fla.; Dr. Albert S. Johnson, Memphis, Tenn.; Judge John McCall, Memphis, Tenn.; Dr. Clarence E. Macartney, Pittsburgh, Pa.; Dr. Stephen W. Paine, Houghton, N. Y.; the Rev. Noel Perkin, Springfield, Mo.; the Rev. Ivar Sellevaag, Portsmouth, N. H.; W. L. Surbrook, Indianapolis, Ind.; Dr. Nathan R. Wood, Boston, Mass.

Immediately after the St. Louis conference a temporary office was established at Zero Park Street, Boston, Mass., with Dr. J. Elwin Wright in charge. A busy year ensued in which many regional conferences were held in all parts of the nation. Everywhere there was enthusiastic response to the new venture. Gospel broadcasting on radio, an issue about which there was much heated controversy, occupied much of the attention of the new organization. Evangelism and the separation of church and state came in for their share of public interest. In a number of instances the value of evangelical cooperation was demonstrated. Evangelicals were convinced that the time had come for the development of such an agency, more powerful numerically and spiritually than any single denomination, for united evangelical action.

V

THE NATIONAL ASSOCIATION OF EVANGELICALS

The year which followed the convention at St. Louis was a crucial one. The temporary organization was on trial in the minds of many evangelicals and was viewed as a menace to Protestant unity by leaders in the Federal Council. Its warm supporters were clear as to their over-all objectives but somewhat in doubt as to the type of organization which would best serve their constituency and accomplish results.

Regional conferences and mass meetings were held in all parts of the nation. Here the new leaders of the National Association of Evangelicals for United Action had opportunity to present their tentative program and to evaluate the reactions of local and area evangelicals.

One thing became clear. Thousands had come to the conclusion that they could no longer cooperate with the Federal Council of Churches. These Christians were not interested in drawing up indictments and in spending their time in war-like strategy to reform or to destroy the Council. They believed that too much time and energy, money and talent had already been lost in such endeavors. They desired a constructive, aggressive, dynamic, and unified program of evangelical action in the fields of evangelism, missions, Christian education and every other sphere of Christian faith. They wanted a sound doctrinal basis for such action. They sought leadership in these realms. They believed that the time had come to demonstrate the validity of their faith and the ability of evangelicals to work together and build together in a great constructive program.

Everywhere there was an atmosphere of faith and hope. American evangelicals did not underestimate the strength and the dangers of liberalism. They realized that many denominations and institutions were spiritually sick because of this infectious disease. But they remembered that materialism, humanism, deism, worldliness, and many other maladies had swept through the church in other times and that through prayer God had raised up men of faith who brought a new day. Had His arm been shortened in this generation? Was He no longer able to bring in the tides of faith and revival? The answer was obvious to evangelicals.

The Temporary Executive Committee and Dr. J. Elwin Wright, promotional director, busied themselves at their task. Many conferences were held with evangelical denominational leaders and with key laymen and Christian workers. Memberships began to pour in. The temporary office in the Park Street Church, Boston, soon became too small to handle the affairs of the Association and a suite of offices in a downtown office building was obtained.

In radio, missions, education, government chaplaincies, and other areas of national concern a "strange new organization" presented its claims on the ground that Protestantism was divided into irreconcilable sections in which there were fundamental differences of belief and methods of action. The NAEUA representatives were friendly and courteous but firm in their position. They asked for consideration and got it, but the need for a strong, representative inter-church organization to back them up became more and more evident.

During this interim period the NAEUA leadership steadfastly refused to enter into any kind of controversy with those who attacked them. Such attacks occurred again and again. Some misunderstandings resulted on the part of honest and earnest evangelicals. To many united constructive cooperation was a new adventure and they had not yet learned its techniques.

As the time approached for the Constitutional Convention a call was addressed to all concerned in which it was made clear that the views of everyone would be given careful consideration at Chicago. Work-study groups were set up in seven different fields of activity. One was to consist of those interested in radio broadcasting; another of those interested in evangelism; others dealing with separation of church and state, missions, education, chaplains and war services, and public relations. Looking toward agreement on permanent organization, committees on Constitution, Statement of Faith, Membership and Representation, Publications, Finance, Location of Offices and Public Relations were to arrive at final conclusions.

Simultaneously evangelicals throughout the nation were summoned to united prayer. Said the call:[1]

> One thing of greatest importance has not been overlooked and must not be in these next weeks. That one thing needful is earnest, intercessory prayer for a new infilling of the Spirit upon every delegate. Without this, everything that has been done will fall to the ground.
> The most significant moments of our country-wide conference have been those when the pastors have knelt in prayer together. Those precious seasons will not be forgotten for God has manifested Himself. The rain has fallen upon our hearts as we bowed in His presence. Prejudices have melted away and mutual love and understanding have been greatly increased.
> We trust that arrangements may be made for special Pullman cars to Chicago from a number of points so that the delegates may have the joy of fellowship in prayer en route.
> Possibly the most important of all the sessions at Chicago will be the pre-convention evening of prayer on the night of May 3. Many delegates will plan to arrive on the afternoon of that day so that they may spend the evening together in intercession for the convention. There is no reason to expect that we may succeed in launching a movement which will really bring Christians together in united action unless the melting and fusing power of the Holy Spirit shall work in our hearts.

Churches were asked to observe a special day of prayer on May 2 and to enlist members to pray daily during the Convention for the guidance of the Holy Spirit in its deliberations.

On May 3 a thousand evangelical Protestants began to converge upon Chicago's Hotel LaSalle for the history-making gathering. They represented in one way or another some fifty denominations (with a potential constituency of 15,-000,000).

There was an atmosphere akin to Pentecost. The preliminary session was a prayer meeting. Over two hundred men were on their knees for an hour asking for the infilling of the Spirit and divine guidance. The presence of God was evident to every heart. There were frequent prayer periods throughout the Convention. At the closing session Dr. J. Alvin Orr called on the whole assembly to get down on their knees in a climactic moment before the throne of grace.

Dr. Harold J. Ockenga brought the keynote address[2] giving in broad outline the task before the Convention. The chairman of the Temporary Executive Committee linked liberalism with the destructive forces then threatening the world and showed that they all sprang from the same satan-

1. *United Evangelical Action*, April 1943, pp. 1, 2.
2. "Christ for America," *UEA*, May 4, 1943, pp. 3, 4, 6.

ic source. He challenged all those who were still on the Lord's side to drop their separatism and prejudice and join hands for united action. Time after time during the address "Amens" chorused through the auditorium and applause frequently forced the speaker to pause. Local newspapers, *Time*, and the American press in general carried excerpts from the challenging message.

The great need of America, said Dr. Ockenga, is a new life in Christ. He alone can bring hope, but who can bring Him to the nation? This, he made clear, was in a unique sense the task of evangelicals.

Constitution building in Chicago was done in a careful, statesmanlike manner. The work-study groups, committees and sub-committees studied all phases of the problem and made their recommendations to the whole convention. After free discussion these reports were referred to the Committee on Fields of Endeavor and Policy. There was a sincere desire to make the findings representative of all participating groups. Finally, the Committee on Fields of Endeavor and Policy reported back to the general assembly whose open decisions formed the basis for the final draft of the Constitution.

Central to all planning and discussion was the Statement of Faith. The representatives of some forty denominations were of varied theological beliefs, yet were one in their acceptance of the deity of Christ and the Bible as the Word of God. They were concerned that the "least common denominator" of Christian faith basic to cooperation should be explicit as to the issue which had divided Protestantism. They wanted cooperation, but not cooperation which would permit compromise of the evangelical Christian testimony. Some pessimists declared that the Convention would never be able to agree unitedly to any statement that might be devised. But there was a strange moving of the Spirit of God which brought agreement with a minimum of discussion. Without dissent the Convention adopted the following statement:

1. We believe the Bible to be the inspired, the only infallible, authoritative word of God.

2. We believe that there is one God, eternally existent in three persons, Father, Son and Holy Ghost.

3. We believe in the deity of our Lord Jesus Christ, in His virgin birth, in His sinless life, in His miracles, in

His vicarious and atoning death through His shed blood, in His bodily resurrection, in His ascension to the right hand of the Father, and in His personal return in power and glory.

4.   We believe that for the salvation of lost and sinful man regeneration by the Holy Spirit is absolutely essential.

5.   We believe in the present ministry of the Holy Spirit by whose indwelling the Christian is enabled to live a godly life.

6.   We believe in the resurrection of both the saved and the lost; they that are saved unto the resurrection of life and they that are lost unto the resurrection of damnation.

7.   We believe in the spiritual unity of believers in our Lord Jesus Christ.

Not only were members required to sign this Statement of Faith when they joined the Association, but annually when they renewed their membership, and their duly appointed representatives were required to sign it personally before being admitted as voting members in the annual convention.

Of great importance was the safeguard in the expressed Purpose of the organization:[3]

> To provide a medium for voluntary united action among the several groups of Evangelical Christians of America, without, however, exercise of executive or legislative control over the constituent members. The fields of endeavor shall be Evangelism, Foreign Missions, Home Missions, Education, War Service, Public Relations, Moral Welfare, Radio, and such other fields of endeavor as the governing board may from time to time deem appropriate.

The new "National Association of Evangelicals" was to be composed of several classes of members: (1) Denominations, (2) independent religious organizations, (3) local churches and (4) groups of churches. The rights and privileges of each participating body were zealously guarded. The smaller denominations were permitted one delegate to every 5,000 members or fraction thereof; denominations of 200,000 members or more, after forty delegates, were permitted one delegate to every 15,000 members. Organizations and institutions were permitted one delegate each. Local churches and groups of churches not having denomi-

---

3. Original draft of the Constitution, as adopted at Chicago in 1943, appears in *UEA*, June 1, 1943, p. 7.

national connections were given one delegate each. No one religious body could ever have more than ten per cent voting representation in the Convention.

An impressive feature of the Convention was the spirit of fairness shown in the wording of the Constitution, in the debates, and in the consideration given the smaller denominations in the selection of Association leadership.

The Constitution provided that the business of the Association should be conducted by a Board of Administration to consist of its elected officers together with not fewer than twenty nor more than forty members at large properly representative of the membership both geographically and organizationally. They were to be elected for a term of one year. This Board was to establish an Executive Committee to consist of the officers of the Association and six other members of the Board and delegate to the Committee such powers and authority as might be deemed necessary to the proper functioning of the Association.[4]

Other proper provisions were made to assure a thoroughly representative and effective body.

The Committee on Policy and Fields of Endeavor, under the handicaps of all pioneers in an unmarked land, set the stakes for united evangelical action. They recognized the unwillingness of evangelicals to be represented by organizations and agencies unfaithful to the Gospel of Christ and

4. The personnel of the NAE in the first year of its official constitutional existence was as follows:

Officers: President, Dr. Harold J. Ockenga; First Vice President, Bishop Leslie R. Marston; Second Vice President, Judge John W. McCall; Secretary, Mr. J. Willison Smith, Jr.; Treasurer, Mr. H. J. Taylor; Field Secretary, Dr. J. Elwin Wright.

Executive Committee (in addition to officers): Dr. John W. Bradbury, the Rev. J. Roswell Flower, Dr. Harry J. Hager, Mr. Kenneth S. Keyes, Dr. Stephen W. Paine, Dr. T. Roland Philips.

Board of Administration (in addition to above named): Dr. Clarence Bouma, Rev. D. Shelby Corlett, Dr. Howard W. Ferrin, Mr. Carl Gundersen, Dr. George B. Huebert, Dr. T. Christie Innes, Dr. Albert Sidney Johnson, Dr. John E. Marion, the Rev. Robert B. Munger, the Rev. William R. Nicholl, Dr. J. Alvin Orr, Dr. Paul S. Rees, Dr. Robert P. Shuler, Sr., Dr. W. L. Surbrook, Dr. Carey S. Thomas, the Rev. J. H. Walker, Dr. C. Hoyt Watson.

National Advisory Committee: Dr. Archer E. Anderson, Mrs. Phillip Armour III, Dr. Lee E. Baker, Dr. R. S. Beal, Mr. Philip A. Benson, Dr. R. Berntsen, Dr. John E. Brown, Dr. C. Gordon Brownville, the Rev. Richard H. Harvey, the Rev. John A. Huffman, Dr. James Henry Hutchins, Dr. Harry A. Ironside, Dr. Floyd B. Johnson, Dr. J. P. McCallie, Dr. J. Renwick McCullough, Dr. J. Irvin Overholtzer, the Rev. Earle V. Pierce, Mr. George Quam, the Rev. Ivar Sellevaag, the Rev. John Bunyan Smith, Mr. Claude A. Watson, Mr. C. Davis Weyerhauser, Dr. Nathan R. Wood.

expressed the view that in time new functioning units in all fields of inter-church cooperation would have to be formed. They appreciated the fact that their proposals to the Chicago convention[5] were largely tentative and would be modified or enlarged as time and experience and the leadership of the Spirit would determine. Their proposals included:

1. A central promotional headquarters with regional offices covering the nation and functioning under the Board of Administration.

2. A Committee on Evangelism with an executive secretary to formulate plans for the promotion of such evangelistic efforts as might meet the approval of the participating members of the Association.

3. A Missionary Department which would

> a. Seek to promote prayer for the salvation of souls through intensive and extensive evangelism.
>
> b. During this year study ways and means to encourage and assist home missionary enterprise and rescue missions.
>
> c. Encourage the observation of the generally recognized rules of mission comity, in order to speed the evangelization of the unreached and to stimulate unity and harmony both at home and abroad, and
>
> d. As desired, represent evangelical missionary organizations before the government on matters concerning permits and passports, cooperate with the missionary societies in securing transportation of missionaries to the field, and assist in the transmission of funds to foreign countries.

4. A Committee on Education which would encourage the planning of conferences, in connection with existing youth organizations, for students in the higher brackets of college and seminary life, give special encouragement to seminaries committed to the evangelical faith, undertake a survey of Bible institutes and Bible colleges which would ascertain the types of instruction and training being provided, looking toward greater cooperation and the solution of common problems.

In this connection a rather extensive proposal was made with regard to Christian education in the local church, including a special study of such problems as curriculum, teacher training, Sunday school conventions, a sub-committee being charged with making a report at the next NAE Convention.

Furthermore, the need for week-day Christian education and Christian Day Schools was recognized and

5. *UEA*, July 1, 1943, p. 5.

exploratory studies suggested in the broad field of elementary and secondary Christian education.

5. The Executive Committee was charged with the task of conferring with governmental and denominational leaders looking toward the setting up of certain "War Services." World War II was still on and such problems as governmental chaplaincies, war relief, and evangelization of the armed services bulked large in the thinking of the convention.

6. In the field of Moral Welfare and Social Service the Committee said:

> We feel the necessity of a strong Christian testimony on the part of all believers with regard to moral questions.
> We feel that all Christians should abstain from fleshly lusts that war against the soul, and that they should "be not conformed to this world," inasmuch as God has said, "Be ye holy, for I am holy." We recommend that in practice and teaching all members strive to promote holiness in character and conduct, "avoiding even the appearance of evil."

7. Separation of Church and State was a particularly live issue since President Franklin D. Roosevelt had only recently appointed a "personal envoy" to the Vatican. Said the Committee:

> Since God has ordained that there shall be human government, and since Jesus Christ is head of the church it is obvious that both state and church alike have their origin in the counsels of God and are designed to serve His purposes on earth.
> However, being different in nature, each has its distinctive functions and may be expected to employ the appropriate means by which to exercise these functions. The functions of the state are political and moral, and it may employ material means in their operation. The functions of the church are spiritual and moral and the means to be employed in their exercise are spiritual.
> The principle of the separation of church and state does not mean that they have no common interests or concerns. Both should work for the general welfare, each cooperating with the other to this end.
> The separation of church and state does mean that neither shall at any time intrude upon the domain of the other in the exercise of its proper functions. By the same token neither shall hinder nor obstruct the other in the exercise of its legitimate functions.
> In the observance of this rule the church as such shall not dictate the laws nor determine the elections of the officers of the body politic, although its members may function as citizens of the state with the full exercise of their Christian consciences.
> On the other hand the state should never sanction nor support any legislation which looks toward the establishment of any form of religion or the abridgement of the free exercise of any that may be established. Likewise it should not use any public funds for the benefit of any sectarian institution. The state should have no voice in the doctrines that are taught by the

church, neither should the state concern itself with the forms of worship that are observed by the church, nor with the personnel of the officiary of the church.

8. And finally, the Committee attacked one of the most crucial problems confronting evangelicals. The future of evangelical radio broadcasting was in jeopardy. It therefore proposed that a Committee on Radio be set up to present a united front in dealing with the radio industry, to provide a clinic for the improvement of the quality and effectiveness of evangelical broadcasting, and to prepare a code of ethics mutually acceptable to the industry and evangelical broadcasters.

Liberals immediately criticized the Association as "giving sectarianism a new lease on life" and as encouraging "the reactionary and dissident wings of the great Protestant denominations" in the Federal Council.[6] What they failed to see was that at least a remnant of American Protestantism (always strongly evangelical in character), had declared its freedom from the shackles which liberal leadership had forged. The Chicago meeting was a practical expression of the inherent characteristics of Protestantism. Here was no effort to build another organic ecclesiasticism. This was a thing of the Spirit and grew out of a common faith "once for all delivered to the saints." Chicago said again that American Protestantism is essentially democratic and free. It believed in a religious freedom that will not go along on any road that leads to Rome. It despised totalitarianism in any form and feared councils of churches which assumed to speak for the churches and carried within them the seeds of a coming super-church.

Liberals needed to mark well the events of Chicago. They were witnessing the beginning of an open, organized rift in American Protestantism which was bound to affect every Protestant denomination and institution in the land. If liberalism insisted on controlling the machinery of these bodies it would no longer find supine submission on the part of evangelicals. Those who believed in the basic truths of the Christian faith were through trying to cooperate with those who had branded themselves as apostate. Evangelicals were saying, "As for me and my house, we will serve the Lord." They were not content to continue as suppressed minorities or in inarticulate and misrepresented

6. "Sectarianism Receives a New Lease on Life," *Christian Century*, May 19, 1943.

majorities in the traditional organizational patterns. They were eager to burst their bonds and launch out in a great evangelical revival that would bring new light, life, and growth to the true body of Christ. Possibly several decades might elapse before their courageous action at Chicago should bear full fruitage but they were completely committed and had great confidence that they had chosen the high road and that all they had done was to the greater glory of God.

In the chapters which follow we shall see how the National Association of Evangelicals met the needs of its constituency. Beyond the broad pattern of service proposed at Chicago in 1943 there was a minimum of central administrative planning. The national leaders, in the true evangelical spirit, met specific problems and issues as they arose, with prayer to God for guidance and in the "multitude of counsel."

There was an unmistakable spiritual and doctrinal unity underlying the whole movement. This was evident whenever its leaders came together. There was also an utter lack of ambition to develop an ecclesiastical machine. In situations requiring the development of a new program of united evangelical action they generally sought tried and true leadership outside their immediate company and accorded these men the utmost freedom of action.

At first, these new developments came so fast and in so many areas that little attention was given to proper integration with the central organization; but, after ten years of expansion, adjustments were made which vastly increased the efficiency and effectiveness of the Association and enabled it to make a united impact in its undertakings.

In considering the development of NAE's service arms — radio-television, Christian education, foreign missions, evangelism and church extension, Sunday School, religious liberty, human welfare, social action, publications and international relations — the reader should bear in mind that all of these agencies are definitely interrelated phases of the growing service program of the National Association of Evangelicals.[7] They have one faith, one objective and move forward as one body in Christ.

7. Chapter XV gives a unified chronological survey of the Association's development in terms of its annual conventions and its administrative leadership.

VI

THE RESCUE OF EVANGELICAL BROADCASTING

Evangelicals were in the forefront of the forces of religion which recognized radio broadcasting as an effective means of propaganda. Their forebears had so recognized the printing press and had used it to disseminate the Gospel to the "four corners of the earth." Radio reached out everywhere; it carried its messages at a speed of 186,000 miles a second; it leaped over boundaries, penetrated walls and touched people never before accessible to the Gospel.

Such aggressive exponents of Bible truth as Dr. John Roach Straton of Calvary Baptist Church, New York City; Dr. Robert P. Shuler of Trinity Methodist Church, Los Angeles, Calif., and Dr. Clinton H. Churchill of Churchill Gospel Tabernacle, Buffalo, N. Y., secured licenses and built their own radio broadcasting stations. Other evangelicals began to develop programs which were broadcast over a network of stations across the nation. Notable among these were Dr. Charles E. Fuller and the "Old-fashioned Revival Hour," Dr. Walter A. Maier and "The Lutheran Hour."

It was not long until evangelicals were receiving a hearing across the nation that was mounting into the millions. They credited this wide acceptance to the drawing power of the evangelical faith. Thousands who had been denied Bible preaching by liberal ministers in their own churches rejoiced at the opportunity once again to hear the old Gospel.

Then complications began to set in. Religious racketeers began to use radio preaching as a medium of exploitation. Liberals were quick to identify these men as "fundamentalists." In the *Christian Century* a St. Louis clergyman took issue with "fundamentalist broadcasts" in language like this: "These programs and others of the same stripe have long been distasteful to liberal church leaders, to much of the listening public and to network officials." He went on to declare that the Mutual Broadcasting Company had "tolerated" programs like The Lutheran Hour because of the revenue which they brought into the Mutual treasury. He referred to these programs as "the network religious program racket, capitalized by independent superfundamentalist revivalists." In loose and easy fashion he appealed for "the elimination of paid religious programs" and called upon Mutual in particular to "go the whole way and ban paid religious programs altogether, as the other networks have done." The writer claimed that "the public gets a distorted and one-sided picture of current religious thinking, because most of these programs follow the ultra-conservative fundamentalist pattern." He concluded his smear with the assertion, "Perhaps the only way such programs can be eliminated is by a rule of the Federal Communications Commission against the sale of time for religious broadcasting."

This letter was a straw in the wind that indicated what was going on behind the scenes. Pressures were being brought to bear by the Federal Council of Churches to eliminate evangelical broadcasting. The great networks were advised that only such programs as were approved by the Council were acceptable to Protestantism. This offered a simple solution to the difficulties confronting the networks. The National Broadcasting Company, for example, allocated three blocks of time to the Roman Catholics, Protestants and Jews. The Protestant time was almost completely preempted by the Federal Council. Since the spokesmen of the Council were, to a great degree, men who denied the inerrancy and inspiration of the Holy Scriptures as well as the cardinal doctrine of salvation by grace through faith in Christ, FCCC domination meant that almost all conservative Protestantism received no representation of any kind on this great network. Pressures continued until it was finally announced[1] in 1943 that Mutual would follow the lead of its competing networks, sell no time for religious broadcasting, and turn Protestant broadcasting over to the Council on a "sustaining basis."

The Federal Council of Churches had early recognized the importance of this means of disseminating religion. At a conference in Atlantic City March 19 and 20, 1929 Dr.

1. "Gospel Programs to Go Off the Air," *UEA*, December, 1943.

Charles C. MacFarland, then FCCCA secretary, made this widely publicized statement:[2]

> Our ultimate plan will probably be for the local federations of churches to endorse and local stations to present national programs provided on Sunday by the Federal Council whereby all will have their choice of hearing . . . a few selected preachers who have received the full endorsement of the Federal Council. . . . The Federal Council is now surveying the entire field throughout the country and is signing up all available stations to carry its programs.

Mr. Frank R. Goodman, later head of the FCCC's Department of National Religious Radio, made this survey and signed up fifty or more stations "with ironclad contracts obliging them to use the Federal Council religious programs and none other."

At the Atlantic City conference a reporter asked, "Did you mean, Dr. MacFarland, that it is the expectation of the Federal Council to control all religious broadcasting, making it impossible for denominational conventions to get on the air and for pastors to broadcast sermons without Federal Council sanction?" Dr. MacFarland replied, "Precisely. The Council feels this to be a wise policy." Thus was laid down the policy which continually dogged the efforts of evangelicals to get their fair share of radio time.

In a land of boasted freedom of speech and freedom of religion it was difficult for the Federal Council to achieve its purpose openly by contractual relations. A much more subtle approach became necessary. It opposed the *sale* of broadcasting time to any religious organization. It favored *free,* or *sustaining,* religious programs which might be controlled, according to Dr. MacFarland's "ultimate plan," through "local federations of churches."

With Mutual's action it appeared that the Council had finally achieved its original purpose.

However, in 1942 the National Association of Evangelicals had begun to study ways and means of succoring evangelical broadcasting.[3] Dr. Harold Lundquist and Dr. J. Elwin Wright were sent to Columbus, Ohio (May 3-6) where a Religious Work-Study Group of the Institute for Education by Radio was about to draft a recommendation

2. Author's correspondence with Dr. Eugene R. Bertermann and Dr. Walter A. Maier of The Lutheran Hour, accompanied by photostatic copies of press releases of the Religious Publicity Conference at the Hotel Chalfonte, Atlantic City, N. J., March 19 and 20, 1929.
    3. Report of NAEUA Promotional Director at NAE Constitutional Convention, Chicago, May 3-6, 1943, *UEA,* May 4, 1943, p. 5.

to the radio industry that would forever bar the sale of radio time for religious broadcasting. Their gentlemanly but firm stand was able to secure modifications of the proposals. They served notice that evangelical broadcasters were uniting for the preservation of their rights under the Constitution and the Bill of Rights.

The NAE laid its course to protect the rights of evangelical broadcasters in three areas: (1) The preaching of doctrinal sermons over the air. (2) The purchase of time for Gospel broadcasting over both National networks and local stations. (3) The right of representative evangelical inter-church organizations to their share of the sustaining time allotted to Protestantism.

Mutual's action late in 1943 touched off nation-wide resentment. Outside the NAE there were evangelicals who held mass meetings and employed high-powered publicity through the press to castigate the FCC and the radio industry. Many of these impetuous evangelicals counseled legal action and bitter attack. The NAE leadership, on the other hand, felt that God was in His heaven and that those in positions of authority in both government and the radio industry were fairminded, public spirited and most certainly not enemies of religion. They felt that once these leaders were acquainted with the facts of the situation they would listen to reason and deal justly with the demands of evangelicals. NAE's representatives were sane, judicious, constructive, consecrated, yet positive and insistent, with the result that the radio industry and the government agencies began to develop an increasing respect for them and their cause.

Upon the invitation of the NAE approximately 150 evangelical radio broadcasters gathered April 12, 1944 for a conference in connection with the second annual convention of the NAE in Columbus, Ohio.[4] Dr. William Ward Ayer of New York was elected temporary chairman and the Rev. Dale Crowley of Washington, D. C., secretary pro tem. The purpose of the gathering was brought forward by Dr. Vincent Brushwyler of Muscatine, Iowa, in the form of a motion that "we form a national association of Gospel broadcasters, to be affiliated with the National Association of Evangelicals." The motion was seconded by Dr.

4. Official brochure National Religious Broadcasters, Inc., issued May, 1945, p. 3.

C. Gordon Brownville of Boston, Mass., and after discussion was carried unanimously.

At this Columbus Conference it was resolved that "the general officers of the body, including William Ward Ayer, Dale Crowley, David J. Fant, Clinton H. Churchill, and C. Gordon Brownville, constitute the Executive Committee."

A special committee appointed to draft a Constitution and By-Laws met in the Deshler-Wallick Hotel in Columbus on April 14, and it was decided that the Constitution and By-Laws recommended by this Committee be recognized as the "tentative governing body" until the time of the regular Constitutional Convention.

The Executive Committee met in New York, May 2, 1944, and on motion of Dr. Clinton H. Churchill voted to engage counsel to advise on Constitution and By-Laws and on Code of Ethics, and also with regard to legal steps to complete the organization. Dr. Ayer, Dr. Churchill, and Mr. Crowley were authorized to engage counsel, and they retained Attorney Louis G. Caldwell of Washington, D. C.

On May 10, the Committee met in Mr. Caldwell's office and consulted with him on legal phases of the proposed organization.

On September 21, 1944, the Religious Broadcasters held a Constitutional Convention in the Moody Memorial Church in Chicago at which it was decided to incorporate, the following officers and directors being elected.[5] (The officers are ex-officio members of the Board of Directors) :

President, Dr. William Ward Ayer, New York City; Vice-President, Dr. Clinton H. Churchill, Buffalo, N. Y.; Secretary, the Rev. Dale Crowley, Washington, D. C., and Treasurer, the Rev. David J. Fant, New York City.

Directors to serve until April, 1945: Dr. Eugene R. Bertermann, St. Louis, Mo.; Dr. Myron F. Boyd, Seattle, Wash.; the Rev. Walter J. Feely, Billings, Mont.; Dr. Howard W. Ferrin, Providence, R. I.; the Revs. Leroy M. Kopp, Los Angeles, Calif.; Lance B. Latham, Chicago, Ill.; Charles M. Leaming, Waterloo, Iowa; Dr. Glenn V. Tingley, Birmingham, Ala.; the Revs. J. H. Walker, Sevier, Tenn., and Vernon S. Wilson, Carthage, Ill.

5. Presidents of the NRB in order of succession: Dr. William Ward Ayer (1944-45), Dr. Clinton H. Churchill (1945-47), Dr. Theodore H. Elsner (1947-50), Dr. Myron H. Boyd (1950-52), Dr. Eugene R. Bertermann (1952-54), the Rev. Thomas F. Zimmerman (1954-56), Dr. James DeForest Murch (1956-   ).

Directors to serve until April, 1946: the Revs. C. F. Clifton, Apollo, Pa.; B. H. Gaddis, Winona Lake, Ind.; Jesse Hendley, Atlanta, Ga.; O. F. Johnson, Brownsville, Texas; Torrey M. Johnson, Chicago, Ill.; Dr. Byon Jones, Portsmouth, Va.; the Revs. Paul Myers, Los Angeles, Calif.; Frank W. Smith, Des Moines, Iowa; O. W. Webb, Tulsa, Okla., and Thomas F. Zimmerman, Springfield, Mo.

Directors to serve until April, 1947: Dr. C. Gordon Brownville, Boston, Mass.; Dr. M. R. DeHaan, Detroit, Mich.; the Rev. Theodore H. Epp, Lincoln, Neb.; Dr. Don Householder, Los Angeles, Calif.; Dr. Bob Jones, Sr., Cleveland, Tenn.; Dr. Walter A. Maier, St. Louis, Mo.; Dr. James DeForest Murch, Cincinnati, Ohio, and Dr. John E. Zoller, Detroit, Mich.

On the advice of counsel the Board of Directors decided to incorporate the Broadcasters in the State of Delaware and to establish an office in Washington, D. C. Dr. Howard W. Ferrin, Dr. Glenn V. Tingley, the Rev. Thomas F. Zimmerman, Dr. James DeForest Murch, the Rev. Charles M. Leaming, and Dr. John E. Zoller were appointed to serve with the Officers as the Executive Committee.

A Code of Ethics[6] was adopted for evangelical broadcasters which immediately branded the NRB constituency as favoring the highest and best in the field of religious broadcasting. It read:

Recognizing the vital and increasingly important role played by radio broadcasting as an agency of mass communication, vastly extending the potential audiences of the church and the classroom, the National Religious Broadcasters believe that the propagation of the Gospel by radio is essential to the religious inspiration, guidance, and education of the public, to the enrichment of the national life, and to the full use of this blessing of modern civilization in the public interest. In furtherance of this belief and of its purposes to foster and encourage the broadcasting of religious programs, and "to establish and maintain high standards with respect to content, method of presentation, speakers' qualifications, and ethical practices to the end that such programs may be constantly developed and improved and that their public interest and usefulness may be enhanced," the Association has adopted, and each of its members has subscribed to, the following Code of Ethics:

6. Official brochure NRB, issued May, 1945, pp. 22, 23.

I

Sponsorship of all programs broadcast by or in the name of the Association or any of its members shall be solely by a non-profit organization whose aim and purpose is the propagation of the Gospel.

II

The message disseminated in such programs shall be positive, concise and constructive.

III

The content, production, and presentation of such programs, including both music and continuity, shall be consistent with the program standards of the station or the network over which they are broadcast, and with the requirements of all Federal and State laws and of all regulations of the Federal Communications Commission.

IV

Persons engaging in the broadcasting of such programs shall, by prompt appearance, scrupulous conformity with the limitations imposed by physical, technical, and economic characteristics of radio, Christian courtesy, and otherwise, cooperate with the station or network management.

V

Appeals shall be of a bona fide character for legitimate religious purposes, and shall be presented in a dignified Christian manner. All donors shall be promptly furnished with receipts, and an accounting thereof shall be furnished to the Board of Directors on request of the Board.

This Code became a veritable "Declaration of Independence" from radio racketeers on the one hand and ecclesiastical boycotters on the other.

Copies of the Code were later sent to every radio network and to every local radio station manager in the industry, along with the Constitution and By-Laws of the National Religious Broadcasters, Inc., and a copy of the following resolution[7] adopted at Minneapolis in 1946. It read in part —

Inasmuch as there exists among the Federal Communications Commission, radio network executives and man-

7. *UEA*, March 1, 1949, p. 19.

agers of local radio stations an understandable misconception as to the situation within modern American Protestantism and its proper representation on the radio, we feel that it is incumbent upon the National Religious Broadcasters, Inc., an affiliate of the National Association of Evangelicals, to clarify the situation.

We believe that once radio broadcasting understands the issues involved it will be entirely fair to all parties concerned.

One misconception is that American Protestantism is one unified religious group, whereas in fact there are two distinct kinds of Protestants in America today. Each adheres to a particular form of teaching — the one the antithesis of the other.

One group believes the Bible to be the infallible rule for belief and conduct whereas the other does not.

We believe it could be demonstrated that the majority of American Protestants belong to the former group. Yet this group is not given time or representation on the radio, either by the networks or by individual radio stations, in proportion to their numerical strength. . . .

National Religious Broadcasters, Inc., became essential when it was evident that existing interdenominational organizations, while claiming to be representatives of all Protestantism, were in reality representative of the point of view heretofore described — namely, that which rejects the infallibility and absolute authority of the Bible.

We stand ready to cooperate with the Federal Communications Commission and the radio industry in every possible way to ameliorate the present situation.

After many months of correspondence and conference, understandings were reached which fully protected the rights of all accredited religious broadcasters at national and local levels. The distinctively evangelical testimony was assured of a voice on the air. Means had been provided whereby the airlanes would be kept perpetually available for the preaching of the Gospel. The National Association of Evangelicals was given its proportionate share of sustaining time on all the national networks and evangelicals were recognized as having a valid claim to consideration at the local levels.

The exact place of the NRB in relationship to the NAE was worked out in later conventions. While separately incorporated, the National Religious Broadcasters works in complete conjunction and cooperation with the NAE on all broadcasting matters. A majority of the members of the executive committee of the NRB must be composed of members of the NAE in good standing. In turn, the NRB Executive Committee constitutes the Commission on Radio of the NAE. All matters pertaining to broadcasting and telecasting must be cleared through this joint committee. The chief concern of the NRB lies in the field of "commercial religious" time and that of the NAE in "sustaining time." This mutual understanding has formed the basis for a most cordial relationship through the years.

The problem of proper representation of evangelicals in local radio religious programming is being solved slowly. Complete national coverage at the local level waits upon the development of grassroots associations of evangelicals. Because of agreements with the industry and the government agencies nationally the way is paved for satisfactory negotiations. The city of Cincinnati, Ohio, may serve as an example. The Greater Cincinnati Association of Evangelicals, after becoming well established, approached the managers of local radio stations requesting a share of sustaining religious broadcasting time. Presented in each instance was a brochure setting forth: (1) The story of the NAE and its working agreement with the radio industry, (2) the local organization, its purposes, personnel, and program, (3) a listing of some 150 churches whose pastors expressed a preference to clear their radio time through the GCAE instead of the Council of Churches, (4) examples of other cities in which evangelicals were receiving sustaining time from radio stations, etc. Little or no difficulty was experienced in concluding arrangements. Now the city is constantly made aware of the existence of the evangelical testimony and the GCAE is becoming an increasing power for good in the area.

The NRB continues to foster, protect and encourage evangelical religious broadcasting, creating and maintaining high program standards, promoting good public and industry relations, and seeking to make worthwhile contributions to the welfare of the church and nation.

Today the NRB numbers in its membership the major nationwide "religious commercial" (paid-time) broadcasts in America, such as The Lutheran Hour and Billy Graham's Hour of Decision. It is estimated that NRB members pay over $10,000,000 each year to the radio industry for the broadcasting of the Gospel.

The miracle of electronics and its import for the guidance of human beings becomes more significant with the passing of the years. With the advent of television evangelicals were quick to avail themselves of this medium in the dissemination of the Gospel. It is believed that the first televised service of worship in history was broadcast by a member of the NRB — The Lutheran Hour, over KSD-TV, St. Louis, Mo., January 1, 1948. Dr. Eugene R. Bertermann, as director of radio for The Lutheran Hour, was responsible for this progressive step. Despite the high cost of televised programming a number of evangelicals have launched out in this field with encouraging results. They are asking for their share of sustaining time. They are perfecting television techniques and every method will be employed which is consistent with the Christian ethic.

Machinery for the effective utilization of radio and television for the proclamation of the Gospel and the support of the churches is now available to evangelicals everywhere, thanks to the foresight of the early leaders of the NAE. Without that vision it is altogether likely that evangelicals would today be without the means of challenging America with their radio TV message.

VII

A NEW DAY IN EVANGELICAL CHRISTIAN EDUCATION

From the very beginning of the National Association of Evangelicals Christian education has been a matter of chief concern. Some of the factors which motivated the formation of the Association's educational policies and program of action need to be considered.

Evangelicals believe that distinctly Christian education is committed to a philosophy entirely different from that which is basic to secular education or to "liberal" religious education.

The evangelical educator views the pupil in the light of the Bible teaching concerning man. He holds that the New Testament fails to support the liberal view that man is inherently good and that all the pupil needs to attain his highest capabilities is to fan the divine spark. Evangelicals believe that man was created by God in the divine image but that image was ruined by sin. As man turns from his sin and believes Christ his sins are forgiven and he enters the family of the redeemed as a new creature. This belief requires that Christian education have as its first aim the salvation of the soul and, secondly, Christian nurture.

Christian education must be God-centered, say evangelicals, rather than pupil-centered. It rests on a world view that recognizes the universe as the product, the property and the purposive instrument of God. Pupil and teacher are accountable to Him. The one true God is known to them through Jesus Christ, His Son. It is their educational task to demonstrate the relation of every subject, every policy and every practice of Christian education to Christ who is Lord of all.

Christian education must enrich the capacity of the pupil to know God and to live in accord with God's will. It involves the commitment of the whole being — body, spirit, mind — intellect, emotions, will.

Christian education derives its knowledge from personal contact with Christ through the Holy Spirit; the natural world all about us; and through God's revelation of Himself and His will in the Holy Scriptures. When it comes to eternal moral and spiritual principles the Bible speaks with ultimate authority. Christian education has room for the books of men but it classifies them as secondary to the Holy Scriptures.

The goals of Christian education are realized in the life of the pupil when he has come to know Christ as Saviour, when his life is motivated by the love of Christ, nurtured by the Holy Scriptures, when he is constant in prayer, his body a temple of the Holy Spirit, his soul regnant over the flesh, his thinking grounded in "the acknowledgment of God in Christ" and his whole being obedient to the will of God. These goals may not all be achieved but once fixed in the heart many of them will be realized in ever-growing actuality during the span of a lifetime.

Dr. Frank E. Gaebelein well states the six criteria which evangelicals believe to be essential to a Christian educational institution:[1]

> (1) It must be built on a thoroughgoing Christian philosophy of education. (2) It must have a faculty thoroughly committed to its distinctive philosophy. (3) The entire curriculum must be Christ-centered. (4) It must have a student body that will actively support its philosophy and its aims. (5) It must recognize the two aspects of Christian education—the required and the voluntary. (6) It must actually do the truth through applying the Christian ethic in all its relationships.

Higher education in America had, until the advent of liberalism, been molded in the evangelical Christian pattern. Yale, Harvard, Princeton and all the great eastern universities which continue to have such a tremendous influence in the educational affairs of church and nation were either church sponsored or headed by presidents, faculties, and trustees who were leaders in the Christian thought and life of the land. Many great colleges and universities, particularly after the advent of Unitarianism in America, had protective clauses written in their charters which were designed to keep them true to the fundamental evangelical Christian doctrines of the traditional creeds of Christendom.

1. *Christian Education in a Democracy*, Frank E. Gaebelein, ed. (1951), p. 43.

When modern liberalism began to infiltrate the colleges, universities, and seminaries the mind of man was exalted above the will of God as revealed in the Scriptures. Modern naturalistic science committed to the basic evolutionary theory came to dominate the American educational process in both secular and religious realms. In the secular field educators came to believe that the individual recapitulated the evolutionary history of the race and should be allowed to express his resident desires freely with a minimum of guidance. They held that truth was only relative and that which was expedient. Its validity was dependent upon the pupil's ability to assimilate, corroborate and verify. Education, in the view of this new generation of educational leaders, was an instrument by which the developing and changing person might be conditioned for the quest of security and certainty. Religion became for them merely an escape mechanism. They condemned all authority, human or supernatural or from any transcendent source, and held to the view that "genuine values and tenable ends and ideals are to be found within the movement of experience." In the distinctly religious field most educators followed meekly in the secular frame of reference. Liberals in theology undermined faith in the Bible and raised grave questions concerning the character and the claims of Christ. God-centered education was exchanged for man-centered. God's will was no longer the norm, for who could know it with any certainty. Man's mind became the measure of all things. The absolute truth of God's revealed will according to the Holy Scriptures was scrapped for relative truth. Human social concerns, the task of bringing in the kingdom of God by moral legislation and legal enforcement supplanted the evangelical Christian educational goal of fitting men to live in harmony with the will of God in all of life's relationships. It is impossible to put into a paragraph all the elements involved in this educational revolution which swept America's schools and colleges. Suffice to say — the very foundations of evangelical education were shaken. The educational institutions and the vast endowments built up by evangelicals through two centuries of faithful service were taken from their rightful heirs and put to purposes entirely foreign to those for which they were originally chartered.

The classic example of the liberal method of capturing colleges and seminaries was the looting of Andover Theological Seminary.[2] Andover was founded especially to combat the Unitarian doctrines which had made such inroads on the orthodox Congregationalism of New England. In the charter of the Associate Foundation were written such passages as:

> Every professor . . . shall be . . . an ordained minister of the Congregational or Presbyterian denomination . . . an orthodox Calvinist . . . He shall on the day of his inauguration publicly make and subscribe a solemn declaration of his faith in divine revelation and in the fundamental and distinguishing doctrines of the Gospel as expressed in the following creed.

Then followed eight clauses which would seem, even in our day, to guarantee the orthodoxy of the institution forever. Evangelicals had faith in Andover and gave it many rich bequests through the nineteenth century until it became a plum ripe for picking. The story of jockeying which finally delivered the institution to the liberals is too long to tell here. Many high-minded liberal professors, such as Dr. J. Henry Thayer, when confronted with the necessity of conforming to the "Andover creed," withdrew for conscience' sake. But there came a time when Prof. E. C. Smith and four other faculty members conspired to take the oath "with mental reservations," set up a liberal cell within the school and collaborated with unfaithful members of the Board to achieve their purposes. Evangelicals were deceived into believing that the school was still orthodox until the famous case of the "Visitors of the Theological Institution at Andover vs. Trustees of Andover Theological Seminary" was tried in the courts of Massachusetts. The liberals won by specious devices which will ever be a blot on the escutcheon of Christianity. An interesting footnote to the story was written by an Institute of Unitarian ministers which after "the rape of Andover" met in the halls long sacred to orthodox faith. In the assignment of rooms in the dormitories cards were used with such jocose names as Tophet, Canaan, Babylon and the Dead Sea. A mock trial was staged in which "Albertus Carolus Dieffenbachus" was finally acquitted of the charge of "Fundamentalism." The loss of Andover shocked evangelicals from one end of the nation to the other. It was to prove but the beginning of scores of similar episodes in which almost all of the leading seminaries, colleges and universities of American

2. "The Looting of Andover," *The Leaven of the Sadducees* by Ernest Gordon (1926).

Protestantism were taken over by liberalism, in most instances without resort to the courts and with the consent of denominational and interdenominational authorities. Only a few conservative denominations were able to keep their educational institutions true to the evangelical faith.

Then began the voluntary evangelical movement to set up new schools and colleges. Dr. J. Gresham Machen, one of its distinguished leaders, reasoned,[3] "Christianity is indeed a way of life, but it is a way of life founded upon a system of truth. That system of truth is of the most comprehensive kind; it clashes with the opposing systems at a thousand points. The Christian life cannot be lived on the basis of anti-Christian thought. Hence the necessity of Christian schools." He and others like him could not agree with either the liberals who completely abandoned the supernatural or the moderates who held that natural reason, plus supernatural revelation, constitutes a synthetic base of knowledge. They believed that the starting point in Christian education is a thorough knowledge of God as revealed in the Holy Scriptures. Soon there were new evangelical schools and colleges springing up all over the land. It was the leaders of this movement together with the handful of educators heading institutions still true to the faith who came to the National Association of Evangelicals' Chicago convention in 1943 for fellowship, encouragement and aid.

The Committee on Policy and Fields of Endeavor[4] placed education high on the list of objectives approved by the Convention. Their recommendations included: (1) Planning conferences in cooperation with existing agencies to provide an evangelical ministry to students in liberal colleges and universities, (2) a Committee on Education which might give special encouragement to seminaries which are committed to the evangelical faith and eventually provide a seminary program within the evangelical movement, (3) a survey of the Bible institutes and Bible colleges to ascertain types of instruction and training being provided, which might be made the basis of a report to the next convention and of a program to advance the interests of these schools, (4) a Sub-Committee to deal with the problems of Christian education at the local church level,

3. *What Is Christianity?* by J. Gresham Machen (1951).
4. Report to the NAE Constitutional Convention, Chicago, May 4-7, 1943, *UEA*, July 1, 1943, p. 5.

(5) a declaration of faith in "the liberal arts college as essential to the fabric of our American system of higher education" and the expression of an intention to "preserve its continuance of freedom" within a "God-centered and evangelical philosophy of education," (6) the employment of a field secretary of education as soon as funds might be available.

Those who voted for this recommendation little realized the problems that lay ahead in the implementation of their vision. The could scarcely understand the significance of their adventure which has since meant so much to the cause of Christian education in America.

Under the leadership of Dr. Stephen W. Paine the machinery of NAE's educational program began to take shape.[5] He was ably assisted by representatives of every sphere of evangelical educational activity.[6] There is now a Commission on Educational Institutions operating in four areas: (1) Liberal Arts Colleges, (2) Theological Seminaries, (3) Bible Institutes and Bible Colleges, (4) Secondary Schools and the related area of (5) Christian day schools. The Commission is divided into sub-committees to consider the interests of the various educational levels and to take such action as may be necessary for the welfare of these interests.

The original proposal for a sub-committee to deal with education at the local church level has grown into the National Sunday School Association. (See Chapter X, p. 124.)

Probably the most significant contribution the NAE has made to the cause of evangelical Christian education is the report of its Commission on a Christian Philosophy of Education which was set up in 1946. A group of Preparatory School conferees recommended to the Commission on Educational Institutions at the Minneapolis Convention that a study of the philosophy and practice of Christian education be undertaken and that a comprehensive report of the findings be published. The recommendation was accepted and the following October the new Commission was set up. Its membership as finally constituted consisted of Dr. Frank E. Gaebelein, chairman,

5. NAE Convention Reports, 1944-50.
6. Chairmen of the NAE Commission on Education have been: Dr. Stephen W. Paine (1945-47); Dr. Enock C. Dyrness (1947-50); Dr. T. Leonard Lewis (1950-53); Dr. Merrill C. Tenney (1953-56); Dr. Charles E. Seidenspinner (1956-   ).

Headmaster The Stony Brook School; Dr. Robert L. Cooke, Chairman Department of Education, Wheaton (Illinois) College; Dr. Ruth E. Eckert, Professor of Higher Education, University of Minnesota; Mr. Mark Fakkema, Executive Secretary National Association of Christian Schools; Dr. Carl F. H. Henry, Professor of Theology and Philosophy of Religion, Fuller Theological Seminary; Dr. Harold B. Kuhn, Professor of Philosophy of Religion, Asbury Theological Seminary; Dr. Leslie R. Marston, Bishop of the Free Methodist Church, former president of Greenville College; Dr. Stephen W. Paine, president Houghton College; Dr. Safara A. Witmer, president Fort Wayne Bible Institute; Dr. Enock C. Dyrness, chairman Commission on Education of the National Association of Evangelicals.

At the 1951 NAE convention in Chicago the Commission presented its final report in the form of a book entitled, *Christian Education in a Democracy*, published by the Oxford University Press. It did for evangelical Christian education what the famed Harvard Report, *General Education in a Free Society* (1945), did for secular education. The fact that the work bore the imprint of the Oxford Press gave it a prestige which compelled the attention of all educators. It marked a turning point in Christian education as carried on in evangelical institutions. Not only did the Report present basic educational philosophy from the Christian viewpoint but it spoke boldly of areas of improvement in the evangelical educational program. It is today serving as a blueprint by which evangelical education is building for the new day.

The contents reveal the scope of this timely book: (1) Preface to Christian Education — its relevance and need in an age of crisis; (2) Upon What Foundations? — the biblical and evangelical basis of Christian education; (3) the Idea of a Christian School — the essential criteria for a Christian educational institution; (4) Christian Education looks at the public school — a candid survey of religion and public education; (5) Christian Education and the Independent School — Christian day and boarding schools, other "private" religious schools, their philosophy and achievement; (6) The Strategic Place of the Christian College — Christian education at the college level, its aims, opportunities, and needs; (7) A New Form of American Education — an evaluation of the Bible institute and the Bible college; (8) With What Teachers? — the Christian

teacher, his recruitment, training and opportunity; (9)
The Church As Educator — the Sunday school, the daily
vacation Bible school, and similar church-centered agencies;
(10) Christian Education and the Home — the inescap-
able educational responsibility of the parents; (11) This
Then Is Christian Youth — the end product of Christian
education, a presentation of the goal in terms of individual life; (12) The Unfinished Business of Christian Education — areas to be developed, needs to be met, purposes
to be realized.

The standardization and accrediting of Bible institutes
and Bible colleges was a problem early faced by the NAE
Commission. The survey that was proposed by the 1943
convention revealed a complicated situation with problems
not easily solved.

At their inception, Bible institutes represented almost
a grassroots evangelical movement to provide once again
for the Church training centers true to the Word of God
and with a deep spiritual emphasis. These developed quite
independently of one another in standards, inter-relation-
ships, or work. The last few years have marked, however,
a definite spirit of cooperation in the field of Bible institute and Bible college leadership. Parallel with the
development of the National Association of Evangelicals
is the development of its affiliate, The North American
Association of Bible Institutes and Bible Colleges.

This organization came into being in 1944 to provide
a vortex of fellowship and work for Bible institute and
Bible college leaders. Originally it also included the thought
of providing a system of accreditation for schools in this
field. However, in order to provide for a larger area of
cooperation than would be permitted through an affiliate
of the National Association of Evangelicals, this phase of
the North American Association was willingly surrendered
to a second organization (American Association of Bible
Institutes and Bible Colleges) whose distinct field of work
would be that of accreditation.

From that time the North American Association has
continued to function in providing helpful stimulus and
leadership to Bible school faculties and administrators.
Regional Conferences for faculties and staffs are held in
centers across the country, under the leadership of the
North American group. The NAABIBC also provides a
Summer Institute for faculty members. Here regular work

may be secured in a College on a Graduate level. In addition, during Institute sessions conducted by the leadership of the North American Association, a careful study is made of the history of Christian Higher Education, and of a working philosophy of education in the Bible Institute and Bible College field.

The Accrediting Association of Bible Institutes and Bible Colleges[7] was organized in 1947 at Winona Lake, Indiana, following a call by Dean Samuel H. Sutherland of the Bible Institute of Los Angeles and other interested persons who believed that such an organization should be independent of inter-church control. The majority of the educators represented were active in the work of the National Association of Evangelicals and had participated in the establishment of the Commission on Education.

Today the AABIBC is completely independent of the National Association of Evangelicals or any similar body. It has a large number of schools accredited in its Collegiate Division and in its Intermediate Division.

Periodic surveys keep the standards of the AABIBC ever before the member institutions. The first step in the accrediting process is to ask each school to evaluate itself in the light of the Association's forty-page document explaining the criteria for Collegiate Division Bible Schools. These self-evaluative studies stimulate academic and spiritual leadership within each school and many excellent reports are produced. A set of detailed questionnaires is then filled out by each institution and these along with the self-evaluative report are placed in the hands of the examiners in order that they may compare the school's description of itself with their own findings after a two or three day visit to each campus.

On the basis of these written materials and the findings of their visit to the campus, the examiners prepare a fifteen to twenty-page report for each school and a list of fifty to one hundred specific recommendations. The examiners' report and their recommendations are used by the Executive Committee to determine whether the school's accreditation should be continued or whether it was to be placed on probation. In general it may be said that these surveys have provided tremendous stimulation to the member institutions.

7. From data furnished by Dr. Terrelle B. Crum.

All appropriate federal agencies, the National Educational Association, the American Council on Education, the New York State Department of Education, and other educational bodies too numerous to list here have now given formal recognition to the Accrediting Association of Bible Institutes and Bible Colleges. The entire segment of Christian education represented by the Bible institutes and Bible colleges in the United States and Canada has been greatly advanced by the progress of the Accrediting Association because many of its services have been offered without charge to non-member schools and to educators and officials generally.

The Christian day school cause has become an American movement which stems from American evangelical life at the local level. The movement is marked with a vitality which is self-impelling and self-sustaining.

In 1947 the National Association of Evangelicals sponsored the organization of the National Association of Christian Schools to promote the establishment of new Christian Day Schools throughout America and to provide a united front and voice for schools of all evangelical denominations and groups.[8] Dr. Mark Fakkema who has given distinguished leadership to the Reformed School system, was chosen educational director.

Christian day schools can be divided into two distinct groups: (1) Christian schools sponsored and controlled by the local church acting in the name of organized (institutionalized) religion; (2) Christian schools sponsored and controlled by individuals, organized on a locally acceptable doctrinal basis serve the children of the constituency of its membership and such other children as the school board may admit.

The *church* schools are called "parochial" schools. They are conveniently classified by the church sponsoring them: such as (1) Lutheran, (2) Seventh-Day Adventist.

The schools of *individual initiative* are designated — for want of a better name — as "non-parochial." These schools may be classified on the basis of their religious emphasis: (1) Reformed, (2) Mennonite, (3) other evangelical groups.

Whereas formerly the Christian school movement was confined to comparatively few denominations, of late the

8. From data furnished by Dr. Mark Fakkema.

movement finds supporters among an ever-increasing number of evangelical communions.

The NACS is committed more especially to the promotion of schools of the "individual initiative" type in which parents of a given community cooperate in forming and maintaining the school.

During its brief history the NACS has projected a seven-point program:

1. *The Printed Page.* The preparation of pamphlets and brochures dealing with Christian Day School principles and methods.

2. *Public Addresses.* Christian day school promotion addresses given by the Educational Director while in the field.

3. *Christian Textbook Activity.* Besides cooperating with Lutheran and Reformed groups in the matter of placing their textbooks, NACS is in a direct way placing at the disposal of its constituency other books of real Christian school merit.

4. *Christian School Survey.* Includes a listing of not only all the new schools recorded in the NACS office but also listing of Lutheran schools, Mennonite schools, and those of Reformed persuasion. The number of schools on the elementary and high school level that are in agreement now on basic evangelical doctrines totals over 2,000.

5. *NACS Teaching Program.* Two thirty-hour courses have been prepared: "The Philosophy of Moral Discipline" and "The Philosophy of Christian Teaching." These courses, either in full or in somewhat abbreviated form, have been given many times in various parts of the country, often in schools which award regular college credit.

6. *The Teacher Placement Bureau.* Serves to introduce the teacher-needing schools to school-seeking teachers and vice versa. Only schools that claim to be evangelical are served, and only teachers who have subscribed to the evangelical doctrinal statement are aided. The whole field is served, from the Christian kindergarten to the Christian university.

7. *Organizational Setup.* The National Association of Christian Schools is made up of a two-fold membership: Christian school organizations and individuals interested in the cause.

The evangelical educational picture would not be complete without reference to two other organizations which are not related in any way to the National Association of Evangelicals but in which many individual members of the NAE actively cooperate — the Evangelical Theological Society[9] and the Inter-Varsity Christian Fellowship.[10]

In Cincinnati, Ohio, on December 28, 1949 the Evangelical Theological Society was organized, with a plea for American scholarship to return to the great affirmation of historic Christian faith.

The idea of effecting a permanent organization composed of educators, ministers, and students to foster biblical research, whether in the exegetical, historical, or theological areas, was originally projected by the faculty of Gordon Divinity School in Boston. It was developed, however, through the endorsement and cooperation of representative schoolmen across the nation.

ETS standards of membership include not only subscription to the doctrinal pledge which affirms the inerrancy in its original autographs of Holy Scripture, but also advanced attainments in theological study. Members must hold a Th.M. degree or its equivalent or have made worthwhile contributions in the field of teaching or writing. The large majority of its present members are teachers in seminaries, Bible institutes, and Christian colleges and are thus in a position to influence the orthodox Christian students of the future.

The Society challenges the assumption and claims of liberalism that believing in the historic Christian faith and in the full truthfulness of the Scripture can only be done at the sacrifice of the intellect. Its members have faced the critical question and declare that the claims of the Book and of the orthodox Christian faith are valid against all attack. They believe that the Bible is capable of scholarly exposition and defense and that it has the only truly relevant message for the distress of our times. The Society exists not only to expose the fallacies of unbelief, but also to encourage a reverent and thorough study of the Bible and related subjects using all of our modern advances and discoveries.

The Society serves, as its Constitution says, as "a medium for the oral exchange and written expression of thought and research in the general field of the theological disci-

9. From data furnished by Dr. R. Laird Harris.
10. From data furnished by Dr. C. Stacey Woods.

plines as centered in the Scripture." Primary in the program of the Society is the annual meeting held during the Christmas vacation at which papers are read by various members expressing their views and reporting their research. Criticisms and suggestions are offered by the others present which are of help to the speaker in his further study.

The Society has set up a mechanism and provided funds for the publication of individual studies of scholarly subjects that may be of value and of general interest. The papers read at the annual meetings are also published.

To encourage the participation of students who are not yet qualified for membership, the Society has set up a category of Student Associates which allows students to join in its benefits. The Society also encourages liaison and inerchange of information with the American Scientific Affiliation.

Today on some 351 American college and university campuses an interdenominational organization that is uncompromisingly evangelical and true to God's Word is at work presenting "Christ according to the Scriptures" as the answer to materialistic unbelief. Spiritual reality is emphasized in daily prayer and Bible study; students are won to Christ and kept for His service. This organization is the Inter-Varsity Christian Fellowship."

The origins of Inter-Varsity are in Holy Trinity Church of Cambridge, England, where locked and empty pews were the futile protest of church wardens to the powerful evangelistic preachings of young Charles Simeon — but for ten years the aisles of that church were crowded with Cambridge University students. Simeon, despite the jeers and cat-calls that greeted him wherever he appeared in public, continued to preach faithfully to those eager students. From his ministry stems the Cambridge Inter-Collegiate Christian Union, best known for its first famous missionary seven who blazed a trail across heathendom, a group including such illustrious men as C. T. Studd, Bishop W. W. Cassels, and D. E. Hoste, the successor to Hudson Taylor of China Inland Mission. Hundreds of Inter-Varsity students have followed in their wake.

Cambridge students soon carried the message to Oxford. There the students crowded in to hear their Cambridge

11. Inter-Varsity Christian Fellowship outdates the NAE and is separately organized and operated.

rivals boldly tell what Jesus Christ meant to them — and a strong witness was born at Oxford.

The movement surged ahead rapidly at the end of World War I; chapters were established throughout Great Britain. Then it leaped across the seas. Inter-Varsity was established in Canada, New Zealand, Australia.

At the same time similar work began in India, Scandinavia, and other countries of Europe, and ten years later the movement caught fire in the United States.

Following Pauline missionary methods, IVCF encourages each chapter to function as an autonomous evangelical union of Christian students. Inter-Varsity staff members travel from campus to campus working in one place as long as necessary to encourage, to purify, to establish, and to guide the students in effective soul-winning.

Usually students on a campus meet to pray each day. There are weekly meetings for Bible study. They study missions, evangelism, apologetics. They are active with evangelistic meetings, personal work, conferences, tracts. Through these means students are led to Christ and to go out into worldwide service for Him.

Student officers, speakers, Inter-Varsity staff members, the Board of Directors, and the Council of Reference subscribe to these principles of faith:

1. The unique Divine inspiration, integrity, and authority of the Bible.

2. The Deity of our Lord Jesus Christ.

3. The necessity and efficacy of the substitutionary death of Jesus Christ for the redemption of the world, and the historical fact of His bodily resurrection.

4. The presence and power of the Holy Spirit in the work of regeneration.

5. The glorious appearing of the great God and our Saviour Jesus Christ.

A department of Inter-Varsity, the Student Foreign Missions Fellowship, works among students on the campuses of Christian colleges, seminaries and Bible schools. There are eighty-four established chapters and groups on as many campuses, but the publications of the Student Foreign Missions Fellowship are used on many more campuses. The missionary periodical *Mandate* with its comprehensive coverage of international news interpreted in the light of missionary activities and needs, is published monthly during the school year. About 14,000 copies of *Mandate* are printed at each issue, but a much larger number of students are reached by it.

The Nurses Christian Fellowship is another department of IVCF which works in hospitals and nurses training schools. There are at present 133 organized chapters and groups in addition to eighty-four unorganized contacts and groups. Subtracting this number from the 804 training schools open to Nurses Christian Fellowship, there are 587 unreached mission fields among nurses. The Nurses Christian Fellowship staff of six graduate nurses holds the same relationship to the student nurses as do Inter-Varsity staff members to students in universities. Nurses Christian Fellowship publishes a bi-monthly magazine, *The Lamp*, which carries articles of particular interest and spiritual help to the nursing profession.

Summer training camps, established and maintained by Inter-Varsity, provide intensive student leadership training during two month-long sessions of specialized instruction in campus witness for Christian students. These camps are located in Ontario, Canada (Campus in the Woods), and off the coast of southern California on Catalina Island (Campus by the Sea). A year-round camp is also maintained in the Rocky Mountains at Bear Trap Ranch near Colorado Springs. Both month-long and week-long student conferences are held here throughout the year. In addition to the camp program Inter-Varsity provides a year-round schedule of week-end and week-long conferences throughout the country for college and university students and student nurses to encourage spiritual development among them.

The United States Inter-Varsity Christian Fellowship has a general secretary, more than fifty workers and several specialized staff members, such as a missionary secretary and office members. Its journal, *His*, is highly commended by leading educators throughout the nation. The ultimate objective of IVCF is an aggressive testimony for Christ in every one of America's more than 1,638 institutions of higher education and among the 804 nurses training schools.

VIII

UNITED ACTION IN EVANGELICAL FOREIGN MISSIONS

Evangelicals are by nature missionary. The largest per capita giving in Protestantism for foreign missions is in strictly evangelical denominations.[1] For some years now the largest number of new foreign missionaries have been sent out by evangelical boards. In fact, if it were not for the newly-developing strength of these boards there would be a tragic loss of zeal and accomplishment in the total picture of Protestant Christian missions.

It is unfortunate that the once-universal Protestant fellowship in the task of world evangelization has been broken. There was a time when the missionary leadership of the world was united in its belief that Jesus Christ, God and Saviour, is the only hope of a world lost in sin and shame. Today humanistic activism and an intellectual and religious syncretism have been projected into world missions to the destruction of this unity and evangelicals have been forced to build again the foundations.

The only authentic Christianity that ever was or ever will be is the Christianity that is both Jesus, the historic Son of Man and Son of God, and the Eternal Christ, the risen and ever-living Master and Lord. This Christianity is not a search of man for God. It is God's offer of Himself to men in Christ, who was not a "fellow seeker with us after God," but "the fullness of the Godhead bodily." This Christianity does not admit that mankind is capable in itself of constant progress and improvement and of advancing toward perfection, but holds that motive and power are in Christ to those who are born again through the Gospel.

Evangelicals are, therefore, convinced that the preaching of the Gospel is the essential task of missions and must always remain so. They do not object to programs for

1. Report of the Department of Stewardship NCC.

the solution of agricultural, social, political and industrial problems, but they believe that each country, race and generation must solve its own problems in the light of God's Word through the native churches. Their chief aim is the personal conversion of men to a new life in Christ, to complete surrender to God's will as revealed in His Word and to new relations of love to their fellowman.

Evangelicals refuse to identify Christianity with non-Christian religions. They believe that Christianity is not a religion in the sense that it is a search for God. They refuse to compromise with heathenism. They believe Christianity should perceive and hold fast the truth of its own uniqueness. It should be proclaimed in a simple positive message by words and deeds transfused with love. It should anticipate the absolute triumph of Christ as acknowledged Lord and Saviour. To this end evangelicals shall not be satisfied until all men everywhere have heard the Gospel and have had an opportunity to accept it.

So much for the basic principles of evangelical missions. Evangelicals seek always to build constructively upon these foundations. But they are also realistically face to face with "liberalism" in foreign missions. Liberalism came into the missionary picture as a parasite, living on the boards, institutions, and missions built up by evangelicals, and undermining the fundamental beliefs and practices that have made Christian missions a vital force in the world. Liberals deny that men are lost without Christ, in the full New Testament sense. They look upon the authentic historical facts of the New Testament as "symbolic and imaginative expressions" of Christianity. They consider non-Christians as brothers in a common quest for ultimate truth. They link the name of Jesus with Buddha and Mohammed as one of the great founders and teachers of religion. Rejecting the deity of Christ, the doctrine of redemption through His shed blood, the justification of the sinner by faith, the work of the Holy Spirit in conversion, and the eternal punishment of the wicked, liberal missionaries are not interested in converting the world to Christ. They preach a social gospel and seek rather to build a "Kingdom of God on earth" with their non-Christian "brothers in the common quest."

This liberal doctrine infiltrated many educational institutions and missionary boards and eventually found expression on the mission fields. In 1930-32 it made a well-calculated assault on the denominational missionary programs through the Laymen's Foreign Missions inquiry.[2] The Inquiry was financed by John D. Rockefeller, Jr., and headed by Dr. W. E. Hocking of Harvard. Its theological findings originated in the minds of highly-placed liberals in mission boards who, daring not to make known their revolutionary views to their own denominations, took advantage of lay anonymity to spread their poison. But the Protestant world was not ready for an atomic explosion. Such great missionary leaders as Dr. Robert E. Speer of the Presbyterian Board of Foreign Missions took the field against the Inquiry's report. Dr. Speer stumped the nation for the preservation of evangelical Christian missions, appearing in practically every city where Dr. Hocking went. The liberals "lost the battle," but they "won the war" insofar as the old boards and inter-church agencies were concerned.

At the time the NAE was in process of organization Protestant missionary cooperation was being channeled through the Foreign Missions Conference of North America. The FMC was an association of missionary societies, instead of churches or denominations, established in 1893. It served 102 Protestant bodies, probably the largest number ever to be associated in American inter-church activity.

For many years the leadership of the FMC was, by and large, theologically conservative. The Southern Baptists, with a membership of some 8,000,000, and the Lutheran denominations usually cast the weight of their influence with other conservative bodies in keeping policies and programs on the side of evangelicalism.

In later years, however, liberal influence was greatly strengthened by leadership turn-overs in numerous denominational boards and societies.[3] FMC reports began to show a decline in the number of new missionaries sent out. The number of ordained ministers and evangelistic personnel on the missionary rolls fell by hundreds, while those registered in the fields of teaching and technical specialization increased by more than fifty per cent. These figures

2. "Rethinking Missions," Report of the Laymen's Foreign Missions Inquiry (1932); *"Rethinking Missions" Examined* by Robert E. Speer (1933).
3. *The Growing Super-Church* by James DeForest Murch (1952), Chapter 8.

were indicative of liberal trends in policy and program within the denominations themselves.

Then came the merger idea. Propaganda began to fly. Missionary ecumenicists told the FMC that the old idea of a voluntary association was *passe;* there must be a closer knit organization which would be more under control of the church and bring missions "into the mainstream of church life." The blueprints were ready for merger. But the plan met a cool reception. In Buck Hill Falls in 1949 the merger was rejected by a vote of 63-51 (twelve abstaining). A two-thirds majority of the voting delegates was required for approval.

But this did not deter the liberals and ecumenicists. They raised a great hue and cry about isolationism, conservatism, fundamentalism, and reactionism and set up a campaign to discredit the evangelical leadership in the Conference. Then they devised plans for setting up a Division of Foreign Missions within the newly-planned National Council of Churches which would begin to operate regardless of the continued existence of the FMC. With these persuasive devices they proceeded to threaten an open break in the hitherto solid front of Christian missions. At this point the Southern Baptist Foreign Mission Board voted unanimously to withdraw from the FMC "and thus leave the conference to make such changes in its structure and functions as a majority of its members may deem suitable to their needs." At about the same time a number of other conservative Boards withdrew. Having accomplished their purposes, merger advocates called a special meeting of the Conference in Philadelphia, April 25, 1950 where the merger was approved, by a vote of 76-7 (three abstaining).

It may be well to look back for a moment at the wreckage of the American Christian missionary enterprise, caused by the infiltration of liberalism.

The Northern Baptists (American Baptist Convention) were rent by the issue as far back as 1923. After a succession of cases in which liberal missionaries were upheld by the Foreign Mission Society, the Conservative Baptist Foreign Mission Society was established in 1943. The CBFMS soon had over 200 missionaries in the field and an annual income of around one million dollars.

The Disciples of Christ experienced the same debacle. The United Christian Missionary Society lost the support

I 2 8 34

of thousands of churches because of its liberalism. Conservatives began sending out "direct-support missionaries" and today have over 400 workers on the field with an annual income of over a million dollars.

At about the same time there developed a veritable tidal wave of new missionary organizations — "faith," "independent" and "direct-support" missions — created to take the place of the older societies. Many, such as The Evangelical Alliance Mission, and The China Inland Mission, had incomes in excess of a million. Numerous denominational boards representing the Holiness and Pentecostal movements had developed extensive foreign mission operations in mission fields around the world.

When the National Association of Evangelicals was organized in 1943 it set up a "Department of Home and Foreign Missions" to serve those denominations and missionary organizations outside the aegis of the FMC.[4] There was still the hope in the hearts of many evangelicals that the FMC might somehow be transformed into a great evangelical force and kept as an independent agency representative of all Protestantism in America.

For a brief time this NAE department (later set up as a Commission) sought to promote prayer for missions, encourage the observation of comity, represent evangelical missions before the government in securing permits and passports, and arrange transportation of missionaries and transmission of funds to foreign lands.

The Association opened an Office of Affairs in the nation's capital in 1944 with Dr. Clyde W. Taylor in charge. This former missionary of the Christian and Missionary Alliance in Latin America proved to be of inestimable aid in representing the evangelical cause in national and international situations. Missions executives found in Dr. Taylor an understanding heart and a remarkable ability to aid and advise them in missions strategy. It soon became evident that a full-scale evangelical missionary organization must be created to meet the needs of evangelicals.

Accordingly a call was issued by the Commission to seventy-five mission boards and agencies asking them to send representatives to a conference in Chicago May 1, 1945. The meetings were held in the Stevens (Conrad

4. *UEA*, July 1, 1943, p. 5. LINCOLN BIBLE INSTITUTE

Hilton) Hotel with Dr. R. L. Decker of the Commission on Missions presiding.[5]

Many of the missions executives responding were unknown to each other, with little or no previous cooperation existing between them. After a time of discussion and fellowship it was suggested that they organize an Association of evangelical missions. Dr. A. C. Snead was elected temporary chairman of the proposed Association and a committee was appointed to draw up the Constitution and By-Laws. A report of this action was sent to the NAE Convention then in session in Chicago and was approved.

The Evangelical Foreign Missions Association adopted its Constitution on September 19, 1945 and became a legal entity by incorporating in Delaware, December 29, 1945. The first meeting of the Board of Directors took place on March 30, 1946 in Philadelphia, and the first annual convention of the Association met in Minneapolis, Minnesota on April 25 of the same year. Fifteen mission boards were received as members of the Association at this first convention.

The Evangelical Foreign Missions Association,[6] in order to promote evangelical Christianity effectively, was formed to "provide a medium of voluntary united action among evangelical foreign missionary agencies, without, however, exercising executive or legislative control over the constituent members." It is affiliated with the NAE by contract, and its Constitution and By-Laws were so drafted as to be in accordance with the policy of the NAE. Its Statement of Faith includes belief in the infallible inspiration of the Bible as the Word of God, the Trinity, the Deity of the Lord Jesus Christ, His death, burial and resurrection, the regeneration by the Holy Spirit in the believer, the resurrection of the saved and the lost, and the unity of believers in the Lord Jesus Christ.

To be eligible for membership an evangelical foreign mission agency must accept and comply with the Statement of Faith, be properly organized with a responsible board of at least five directors, operate as a sending agency having not less than ten active foreign missionaries (excep-

5. *Progress*, Report 1945 NAE Convention, pp. 12-15.
6. Data furnished by Mr. Bryant K. Schlutow, of EFMA's Washington office. (See articles, "Foreign Missions Service Arm of the NAE," *UEA*, February 15, 1953, pp. 11, 12; "EFMA at a Glance," *UEA*, July 1, 1955, pp. 11, 12.)

tions being made for those having less than ten), publish annually a properly audited financial report, and be of good repute, subscribing to and abiding by the standards of comity.

Christian comity implies a sympathetic interest in and a spirit of consideration toward other Christian bodies of like nature. Observance of this Christian courtesy and comity provides frictionless, positive action and cooperation, the lack of which hinders the spreading of the Gospel. Unless harmony exists, the task of preaching the Gospel to every creature cannot be realized.

The Evangelical Foreign Missions Association requires that its members subscribe to the following rules of comity:

1. The missionary message must be recognized as evangelical if it is in accord with the Statement of Faith. From the fundamental doctrine set forth in the Statement of Faith there can be no retreat, but all must recognize the right of constituent bodies to have their own additional doctrinal emphasis.

2. The guiding principle in territory is the reaching of the greatest number of people with the message of salvation. Difficult matters such as geography, language grouping, methods, and standards of work, are settled by consulting all groups interested in certain areas and working out an advantageous plan by mutual agreement. Any mission contemplating a new area or field should first make a survey, and not enter upon activities until interested evangelical missions have been consulted.

3. The right of an individual missionary to resign from one missionary board to seek the employment of another is fully recognized, but the practice of inducing or provoking changes from one mission to another is decried.

4. In presentation of the Gospel, wrong impressions are sometimes given by an over-statement of the facts. A dangerous practice to be avoided is the use of pictures or stories representing the work of another organization without giving credit where it should be given.

The EFMA endeavors to cooperate in promoting better field fellowship among evangelicals around the world. The practice has been to cooperate with all worthy evangelical boards regardless of their cooperation with the EFMA.

The Association[7] now has a membership of some fifty mission agencies,[8] over thirty more than the original number. There are more than 4,000 missionaries serving under these boards, and more than 15,000 full-time national workers. These missions and their staffs are serving in over 100 foreign countries. In view of the fact that there are 108 recognized mission fields in the world, it is easily seen what a wide coverage EFMA has.

EFMA is unique in evangelical circles. Its standards of ethics, policy, and evangelical doctrine are as high as any in America, and mission agencies are closely checked before being granted membership.

7. Presidents of the EFMA and chairmen of the NAE Commission on Foreign Missions have served as follows: Dr. George R. Warner (1945-48); Dr. Vincent Brushwyler (1948-50); Dr. Frank R. Birch (1950-53); Dr. Vincent Brushwyler (1953-55); Dr. Albert C. Snead (1955-57).

8. Boards composing the membership of the EFMA (1955): American Advent Mission Society, Boston, Mass.; American Leprosy Mission, Inc., New York, N. Y.; Assemblies of God, Springfield, Mo.; Baptist General Conference of America, Chicago, Ill.; Bethel Mission of China, Pasadena, Calif.; Bible Meditation League, Columbus, Ohio; International Child Evangelism Fellowship, Pacific Palisades, Calif.; Christian and Missionary Alliance, New York, N. Y.; Christian Reformed Board of Missions, Grand Rapids, Mich.; Church of God Foreign Missions, Cleveland, Tenn.; Church of the Nazarene, Kansas City, Mo.; Conservative Baptist Foreign Mission Society, Chicago, Ill.; Domestic, Frontier, and Foreign Mission Society, Huntington, Ind.; Eastern European Mission, Pasadena, Calif.; Evangelical Free Church of America, Minneapolis, Minn.; Evangelical Mennonite Church, Woodburn, Ind.; Far East Broadcasting Company, Whittier Calif.; Far Eastern Gospel Crusade, Minneapolis, Minn.; Free Methodist Church of North America, Winona Lake, Ind.; Free Will Baptist Foreign Mission Board, Nashville, Tenn.; Friends Foreign Missionary Society (Ohio), Damascus, Ohio; Greater Europe Mission, Chicago, Ill.; International Church of the Foursquare Gospel, Los Angeles, Calif.; Inter-Varsity Christian Fellowship, Chicago, Ill.; Krimmer Mennonite Brethren Church, Inman, Kans.; Mennonite Brethren Church of North America, Hillsboro, Kans.; Missionary Bands of the World, Indianapolis, Ind.; Missionary Church Association, Fort Wayne, Ind.; Missions Visualized, Inc., Hollywood, Calif.; Open Bible Standard Missions, Des Moines, Iowa; Oregon Yearly Meeting of Friends Church, Boise, Idaho; Orient Crusades, Los Angeles, Calif.; Oriental Missionary Society, Los Angeles, Calif.; Pentecostal Holiness Church, Roanoke, Va.; Primitive Methodist Foreign Mission Board, Wilkes-Barre, Pa.; United Missionary Society, Elkhart, Ind.; United World Mission, Dayton, Ohio; Wesleyan Methodist Missionary Society, Syracuse, N. Y.; Woman's Home and Foreign Mission Society, Boston, Mass.; Woman's Missionary Association, U. B., Huntington, Ind.; World Gospel Mission, Marion, Ind.; World Radio Missionary Fellowship, Talcottville, Conn.; World Vision, Inc., Los Angeles, Calif.; Worldwide Evangelization Crusade, Ft. Washington, Pa.; Youth for Christ International, Wheaton, Ill.

It is the only evangelical agency established in America that receives as members and serves both denominational and non-denominational boards. Of its total membership, sixteen agencies are non-denominational or "faith" boards. In addition to this unique characteristic, the Association differs from all other evangelical agencies in that it is both a service organization and the official representative of its missions before foreign governments, colonial offices, and the many departments of the U. S. government.

In order to serve effectively both its members and other evangelical groups, the Association maintains three offices: The Washington Office, handling all diplomatic matters; the Purchasing Office in New York City, buying missionary equipment at wholesale to the extent of about half a million dollars annually; and the Universal Travel Service in Chicago, official agency of the EFMA, serving most of its member missions to the amount of half a million dollars last year. As part of the services rendered in the Washington office, there is a daily contact maintained with the Passport Division, obtaining approximately 275 passports during each of the fiscal years for member and cooperating missions. In addition, the office secures over 200 visas from those foreign governments maintaining visa services in the nation's capitol. Many countries not granting visas in Washington usually have consular service in New York or Chicago where EFMA offices there assist in obtaining these visas.

The activities of EFMA include all functions that the Association can perform for the mission agencies without duplicating their efforts. Excellent relations are maintained with the government in Washington so that whenever it becomes necessary the Association can intercede for member missions. Thus far it has sponsored five annual retreats for missionary executives that have been greatly appreciated for the helpful suggestions received from the various boards represented and for the valuable information given on the activities performed by mission stations all around the world. In cooperation with as wide a constituency as possible, the Association has made a complete survey of all evangelical Spanish literature (having perhaps the most complete library of evangelical Spanish literature in the Western hemisphere in its Washington office), has printed a catalog that was widely distributed in Central and South America, and has concluded a second survey of Spanish literature.

EFMA enjoys a unique privilege in that as an Association of mission agencies it can lean back on the NAE constituency whenever such a constituency is needed as a basis of authority in dealing with United States or foreign government. Through the Washington office the NAE officially serves evangelical missions in their problems with selective service, immigration, and the State Department. The tremendous effort on behalf of religious liberty for evangelical missionaries and national Christians where intolerance or violence has caused intense suffering is always made in the name of the NAE and not by the mission boards. This strategy gives the Association greater influence with governments and the Congress, and also keeps the names of evangelical mission boards out of unfortunate controversies.

In addition to all of these activities the EFMA endeavors to keep its missions informed regarding the many changes that occur in missionary mechanics; that is, requirements for visas, permits, travel, laws, etc. In all of these matters, the EFMA offices are used by approximately one hundred mission agencies, a majority of which are not members.

Evangelicals are facing a new era in Christian missions.

The under-privileged peoples of the world are on the march. They are crying for bread, for relief from poverty and disease, and a thousand physical ills. They are tired of being the pawns of self-seeking nations and economic imperialisms. Atheistic Communism is on the march with a spirit of daring, of boldness, and of sacrifice promising these discontented peoples "the world with a fence around it" and branding Christianity as the enemy of their highest hopes. Country after country is being closed to Christian missions.

The crisis of the hour is intensified with the growing political tensions between the East and the West and the threat of destruction implicit in a possible worldwide atomic war.

Thus a new urgency and compulsion confronts the whole missionary enterprise. Is the Christian message adequate in the face of world upheaval? Are the missionary methods of yesterday effectual now? Are the missionaries themselves competent to meet the crisis? Is the Church aware of the necessity for a new dedication of her resources to the missionary task?

Evangelicals have not the slightest doubt that the only answer to the world's need today is the Christian answer. They are not ready, as are some sectors of Christianity, to sit down with non-Christians as brothers in a common quest to seek some new ultimate in religion.

But evangelicals have the conviction that the day has come for new missionary methods, new missionary strategy to meet the situation in which they find themselves. By this they do not mean that the time has come, or ever will come, to make the preaching of the Gospel and the personal conversion of men to a new life in Christ anything less than the prime and essential task of missions. What many evangelicals are beginning to realize is that they have largely departed from the New Testament methodology in spreading the Gospel. They have been depending too much on *foreign* missionaries who have had an *institutional* approach to their task. The time has come to restore the Pauline method of establishing small groups of believers in pagan lands, entrusting them with the Word of Life and encouraging them to evangelize their own people in their own way.

After all, it is the dynamic of the Gospel and the power of the Holy Spirit which always has been and always will be the secret of the conquest of the world for Christ. Christ is more than a match for atheistic Communism. Iron curtains cannot keep the Gospel out of the hearts of men. Dictators cannot purge nations of a Church which is made up of "living stones" and whose Shekinah glory glows within men's souls. Marxist error cannot destroy the Truth of God, which crushed to earth will rise again. The eternal years of God belong to a triumphant Christianity!

The call of the hour is for a new daring and a new heroism in Christian missions. Evangelicals have the heart of the Gospel. They have boldly stood against the humanisms and liberalisms and agnosticisms which have robbed much of Christendom of its will to spread the Gospel to the uttermost parts of the world. They need only to divest themselves of their *passe* traditionalisms and their outworn methodologies and get a new touch of God upon their souls through the cleansing and enduement of the Holy Spirit. It was Pentecost which gave meaning to the Great Commission and precipitated the great missionary advance of the Church in the first century. The first disciples were just ordinary men in social standing, erudition and political influence but they became extraordinary under the compulsion of the Holy Spirit, able to devise adequate strategies and miraculously achieve the impossible. The arm of the Lord is not shortened in this day and generation.

Evangelicals are convinced the word "finis" will not be written to the history of Christian missions by communism or paganism or humanism or secularism. The last word will be spoken by Him who is the Alpha and the Omega, the first and the last, is alive from the dead and is alive forevermore and holds within His hand the keys of death and hell. That word will be spoken when He has put all His enemies under His feet and every knee shall bow and every tongue confess that He is Lord to the glory of God the Father!

IX

THE REBIRTH OF AMERICAN EVANGELISM

The proclamation of the Gospel of Jesus Christ for the salvation of lost and sinful men is the hallmark of evangelical Christianity. It is quite natural, therefore, that the National Association of Evangelicals in its inception should manifest a special interest in evangelism in all its forms.

At that time there were 75,000,000 in the USA who had no connection with the churches and very little was being done to win them to a saving knowledge of the Son of God. "Liberalism," naturalism, and humanism had made such inroads within the churches that evangelism was pretty largely discounted and looked upon as a relic of a bygone age.

Liberalism laid emphasis upon education, social service and world betterment. It had abandoned belief in Christ as redeemer, in the sense that His shed blood is essential to man's salvation.

Dr. George A. Buttrick said of the atonement:

> Jesus was not a sinner. He had done nothing to incur God's wrath. And if God dealt with Him as if He were the greatest sinner, then we must say of God (as a cynical Frenchman did say of these penal theologies): "Your God is my devil."[1]

Dr. Edwin McNeil Poteat is reported as saying in an address before an Illinois Baptist Convention:

> We are often inclined to think of people as lost because they are bad. What is "bad"? Generally, a pattern of conduct not identical with your own . . . People may have followed their normal, natural instincts, not being particularly bad, but yet find themselves wandering alone. These are the people to whom the church must minister.[2]

Another liberal leader of the time speaking at a New York state convention of Disciples of Christ said:

> I received my own son into the fellowship of God's people recently. I did not have the heart to tell him he was a sinner and needed to repent of his sin and receive salvation of some kind or

1. *Great Themes of the Christian Faith.*
2. *Church News,* Peoria, Ill.

other. He is not and never was a sinner. He is finding joyous
fellowship in a newly-acquired sense of Christian community.

Having no sense of the lostness of sinful men and the
necessity of preaching for the salvation of souls the liberal
churches became cold, formal, lifeless and without any
passion for evangelism. Empty pews, loss of membership,
abandoned prayer meetings, retrenchment in all departments of activity characterized the trend of the times.

The two bright spots in the history of the church during the rise of liberalism were the evangelistic eras in
which Dwight L. Moody (1810 - 1890) and Billy Sunday
(1900 - 1930) and others like them — all ardent evangelicals, stirred the masses with the simple Gospel and led
thousands to accept Christ as Saviour. These men believed
that men without Christ were lost and that only as they
heard the Gospel, according to the Scriptures, and accepted
it, according to the Scriptures, could they be saved. Furthermore, they believed that the mere convincing of men
by the sheer logic of the Christian philosophy was not
enough; there must be the working of the Holy Spirit in
the heart to enlighten the dark mind and incline the way-
ward heart to the Saviour. They believed that the living
Christ is the only Saviour and that He must be received
into the heart by faith for a work of grace if conversion
is to be truly effective, changing the man of sin and transforming him into a new creature fit for the Master's use.

The evangelicals who gathered at St. Louis (1942) and
Chicago (1943) to launch the NAE were of this evangelistic
succession. They were hungry for a new day in which revival might sweep the churches, the nation, and the world.
Dr. Harold J. Ockenga in an appeal to his colleagues said:

> The desire for a widespread and sweeping revival of
> religion has been constantly expressed by Christian
> leaders for two decades, but as yet no great movement
> of spiritual quickening has been experienced.
>
> Now voices are heard telling that it is too late for
> revival, that the age of grace is almost over, that the
> Holy Spirit is being withdrawn, and that apostasy will
> grow worse and worse.
>
> The first were voices of hope; the second are voices
> of despair; both are within the Christian camp.
>
> Is there any sound Scriptural reason for expecting a
> revival? Ought we in the face of the prophetic hope to
> give ourselves in the latter days to the means to the

promotion of a revival? Will the Lord revive His work in the midst of these dreadful years?

May I remind you that the very prophetic word speaks of revivals throughout this entire age. Jesus began His ministry by quoting Isaiah 61:1, 2, "The Spirit of the Lord is upon me; because the Lord hath anointed me to preach good tidings unto the meek; he hath sent me to bind up the brokenhearted, to proclaim liberty to the captives, and the opening of the prison to them that are bound; to proclaim the acceptable year of the Lord." Here He ended, though the prophet added, "and the day of vengeance of our God." This is the gospel age, the age of God's favour when the profuse blessings of His grace are poured out. These will be the characteristics of the age till its end.

Confirming this are Peter's words spoken on Solomon's porch after the healing of the lame man at the gate Beautiful, "Repent ye therefore, and be converted, that your sins may be blotted out, *when times of refreshing shall come from the presence of the Lord;* and he shall send Jesus Christ . . . ." These times of refreshing will continue till God sends Jesus at the time of restitution.

There is reason to believe that God will send a great ingathering before the end of the age. When Peter at Pentecost said, "This is that which was spoken by the prophet Joel; and it shall come to pass in the *last days,* saith God, I will pour out of my Spirit upon all flesh . . . before that great and notable day of the Lord come," he referred to the greatest revival of all times, which the prophet Joel connected with the day of the Lord's coming.

Likewise Hosea makes a fervent plea in language which immediately applies only to Israel, whereas the principles may be taken as applicable for us today. "Come let us return unto the Lord; for he hath torn and he will heal us; he hath smitten, and he will bind us up. After two days (eras) he will revive us . . . Then shall we know if we follow on to know the Lord: His going forth is prepared as the morning; and He shall come unto us as the rain."

. . . God is ready and willing to move among us as the latter rain, but He has restricted His activity to conditions which the Church must meet. God's sovereignty does not mean arbitrary reviving or judging of men. It means the fulfillment of spiritual laws, as inexorable as natural laws.

The most hopeful factor in the National Association of Evangelicals for United Action is the revival spirit which has characterized its convention and rallies. In every place those present have been bowed down before the Spirit of God in prayer, confession and intercession. Why could not this be the vanguard in the movement of revival? With purity in Apostolic Christian doctrine, with unity of endeavor among evangelicals, and with a new anointing of Divine love, we believe that it will be such a leadership. Let us pray to that end.[3]

The St. Louis conference passed the following resolution:

Recognizing the urgent need for cooperation of orthodox evangelistic efforts in our day, we recommend the appointment by the Executive Committee of a Committee on Evangelism consisting of three members which shall, with the Executive Secretary, formulate plans for the promotion of such cooperative evangelistic efforts, putting said plans into operation as soon as possible.[4]

The Chicago Constitutional Convention reiterated the St. Louis statement[5] and called upon evangelicals to "give themselves to prayer in behalf of this committee and its work."

As soon as the Commission on Evangelism began to function great conferences on evangelism[6] were projected throughout the nation. These were significant meetings which drew church leaders from all sectors of Protestantism. They considered such themes as "God's Challenge to Evangelism," "Personal Evangelism," "Mass Evangelism," "Revival for Our Time," "The Evangelistic Church," etc. There were prayer meetings in which the whole conference would be upon its knees beseeching God to send revival. There were conferences and workshops on "The Program of Organized Modernism," "Opportunity for Radio Evangelism," "Evangelism Through Government and Industrial Chaplaincies," "Tract and Sign Evangelism," "The Evangelism of the Printed Page," "Lay Evangelism," "Visitation Evangelism," "United Evangelical Action in the Community," etc. The impact of these gatherings can never be measured, but it is a known fact that from this time there came a new interest in evangelism among the churches. Great revivals broke out simultaneously in many parts of the nation. A new generation of evangelists was called out. Voluntary organizations of laymen whose hearts were on

3. "The Hope of Revival," *UEA*, September 1, 1942, p. 1.
4. *Evangelical Action* (1942), p. 112.
5. *UEA*, July 1, 1943, p. 5.
6. *Ibid.*, January 1, 1945, p. 12 and many other issues.

fire for souls came into being in many places. Youth for Christ began to pack great auditoriums with young people on Saturday nights and reported hundreds won to Christ as Saviour.

Among the leaders in these conferences were such men as Paul W. Rood, Bob Jones, Sr., Harry Ironside, Howard Ferrin, Bob Shuler, Sr., John W. Bradbury, Clyde W. Taylor, Dan Iverson, Russell Bradley Jones, Harry Hager, Horace F. Dean, John R. Rice, and many others too numerous to mention.

In 1945 the NAE called the Rev. Melville G. Hatcher, a youthful Baptist minister who had distinguished himself in the field of evangelism, to become its first and its last full-time Secretary of Evangelism. This move represented a concept of the NAE's service in this field which called for employing evangelists to go out under its auspices to hold revivals and plan citywide campaigns. The authors of this policy little realized that they were encroaching upon one of the most cherished functions of the churches themselves and that they were proposing methods of procedure which were distasteful to some of the constituent members of the Association. The viewpoints of Pentecostals, Presbyterians, Methodists, and Reformed churchmen on the method of evangelism were widely divergent. These facts were discovered when local associations of evangelicals began to promote revival meetings. In some communities Presbyterian and Reformed pastors withdrew from these associations and controversy on NAE policy emerged at the national level.

After prolonged discussions at the Indianapolis convention in 1950 it was decided that the NAE should continue to promote evangelism with all the passion which had characterized its earlier efforts in this field but leave the actual functioning of evangelism to the churches themselves. The resolution passed, with a scattering of dissent, at Indianapolis read:

The National Association of Evangelicals taking note of the great interest shown in the present-day evangelistic campaigns conducted in various sections of our country, campaigns conducted with evident blessings—expresses its gratitude to God for crowning the effort of His servants with His indispensable favor and for the unmistakable evidence that in these days of darkness and unbelief the gospel of Christ is a power of God unto salvation to everyone that believes—urges its constituent churches, and all churches loving the only gospel which leads to God, to consider earnestly their calling and opportunity in such a time as this to call the people of our generation back to the triune God and His infallible Word and to do all in their power to lift up Jesus Christ as the Saviour of the world before the eyes of men and women now walking in the darkness of unbelief.

The National Association of Evangelicals, furthermore, urges the churches to devise such ways and means for promoting evangelism which are best suited to the needs of their particular communities. The NAE, according to its formulated policy, is a service organization called into being to serve all evangelical churches, offers its facilities for the promotion of true evangelism and declares its readiness to serve churches or groups of churches with advice and such other help it is able to give in inaugurating evangelistic campaigns. The NAE authorizes its commission on Evangelism to so serve the churches.[7]

Henceforth the Commission on Evangelism operated on a plan which encourages evangelism by: (1) regional conferences in which evening rallies present addresses dealing with the great evangelical issues of the day and an inspirational evangelistic message in which the churches are encouraged to fulfill their evangelistic task; (2) study groups in which churches are instructed how to launch united evangelistic campaigns in mass meetings, simultaneous meetings, and in individual church meetings; (3) providing an evangelistic literature which churches may obtain and use for instruction in the art of soul-winning.[8]

While still advocating mass evangelism, the NAE placed a new emphasis on such accepted principles as: (1) The Church of Jesus Christ is the divinely established agency to proclaim the Gospel of Christ; (2) All preaching should be evangelistic and have an evangelical undertone; (3) Christian parents are called of God to seek to influence their children for God and His Christ; (4) All members of the church have a responsibility toward the unsaved; (5) Churches should not be satisfied with sporadic evangelistic campaigns but both preachers and lay members should consider evangelism a constant and neverending duty; and (6)

7. *Ibid.*, May 1, 1950, p. 5.
8. *Ibid.*, May 1, 1951, pp. 25, 26.

Earnest prayer at all times is a condition to and a necessity for successful evangelism.

Thus there came a happy meeting of minds on the part of Calvinists and Arminians with most salutary results. The NAE continues to major in evangelism. Most of America's greatest evangelists are members of the NAE. Its conventions and conferences are marked by their evangelistic emphasis.

The work of Evangelist Billy Graham is probably the finest example of the undergirding influence of the NAE in the modern revival which is sweeping the world. Beginning to preach at the age of seventeen this North Carolinian of Southern Baptist background became associate pastor of the Gospel Tabernacle of Tampa, Florida, and later succeeded Dr. V. Raymond Edman as pastor of the Wheaton (Ill.) Tabernacle. Impelled to an evangelistic career he was first associated with Youth for Christ, drawing mammoth audiences wherever he went. Evangelicals associated with the NAE in Los Angeles, California were largely responsible for the preparations for the great revival in 1949 which gave Mr. Graham his first national recognition. Everywhere he went from there on he turned to NAE leaders for the nucleus of his Crusade organizations and the unfailing prayer and financial support which helped so much to assure success. It was the World Evangelical Alliance[9] in London which laid the groundwork for the great revival in Harringay Arena that startled Britain out of its ecclesiastical stagnation and paved the way for miraculous evangelistic victories in Scotland and the great cities of Continental Europe. While Dr. Graham has always insisted on the widest possible cooperation of all elements of Protestantism in a given situation, it has been the evangelicals who have helped to encourage him in the times of crisis, who have stayed through to the end and who have carried on the follow-up. Dr. Graham has been most appreciative of that support. He has been a loyal member of the NAE, contributing generously to its support and often speaking in its conventions.

In Dr. Graham's great London campaign he called on Dr. Paul S. Rees, then president of the NAE, to be his chief assistant. Taking time out from his busy schedule he sent a personal message to the Cleveland convention by trans-

9. *Evangelical Christendom,* September 1954.

Atlantic telephone. Said Dr. Graham to his fellow evangelicals:

Greetings to the annual convention of the National Association of Evangelicals. I well remember the spiritual times we had together in Cincinnati a year ago. And it is our constant prayer that this year you will have the greatest spiritual feast and harvest in the history of this great organization.

I want to take this opportunity to thank you for your prayers, your confidence, your fellowship, and especially for the ministry of Dr. Paul Rees. Dr. Paul Rees has been our right arm, spiritual counselor, and friend during these days of ministry here in the city of London. God has mightily used him in speaking to ministers and leadership groups across the city of London. There is no man in London today more loved than your own Dr. Rees. We thank God for the day that he came to fellowship with us in this ministry of the Gospel and presenting Christ to the city of London.

Also, we want to give all the glory and praise to God for what has been happening here. It is the Lord's doing and it is marvelous in our eyes. We have more confidence and faith in the prayers of God's people than ever before. Probably more people have prayed for this London campaign than for any single event of modern times. No wonder God has been moving. He has been doing it in answer to the prayers of His people. No glory and praise and honor can go to a man or to a group of men. It all goes to God who has been answering the prayers of millions of people around the world.

We want to give glory to God because once again He is honoring His Word. The sermons that we have been preaching have been messages that have been based upon the Word of God. I am more convinced than ever before that the Word of God when anointed by the Spirit of God can be used to win men to Jesus Christ. There is a hunger today for God's Word in Britain as probably no time in recent years.

We want to thank God for the power of the Holy Spirit. Sometimes we have stood almost detached, realizing that this is God's doing. It is God the Holy Spirit moving in these audiences night after night. I am convinced that the developments in the last few days in Indo-China, Geneva, Australia, Western Germany, and other parts of the world give indication that our time is short. The night is far-spent, the day is at hand and what we are to do for Christ, we must do quickly. I believe that our alternative is simple. If we, as a Western World, will turn to God at this hour, I believe God will spare us. But if we refuse, there is no other alternative for the world except the judgment hand of God.

I also believe that for the Christian there is hope in the coming again of the Lord Jesus Christ. I believe that all of these signs that we see on every hand point to the soon coming of our Lord and Saviour, Christ Jesus.

The Scripture says that we are to comfort one another with these words. But the Scripture also says that we are to occupy till He comes. And we are to make sure that we have oil in our lamps and that we are ready, "for at such an hour that ye think not, the Lord cometh." God bless all of you.[10]

What has been true of the ministry of Dr. Graham could be said of countless other evangelists such as Merv Rosell, John R. Rice, Hyman Appelman, Jack Shuler and Torrey M. Johnson.

In recent years NAE's Commission on Evangelism has been called upon at many times and in many ways to keep the channels open for the preaching of the Gospel.

Councils of Churches in many cities have adopted comity programs and policies which have effectively shut out evangelical denominations from developing churches in new subdivisions and government housing projects.[11] A director of "cooperative field research" goes into ripe areas "at the invitation of local councils of churches" to shape up the program. He confers with local Ecumenical Church leaders and helps prepare the master plan showing the proper location of churches "in relation to population and other considerations." They determine the location and relocation of churches so as to "eliminate overlapping of parishes" and "the unseemly competition that so often goes with this condition." Then these ecumenical overlords go to the City Planning Commission or to the developers and offer their "cooperation," thus establishing an important political liaison with government authorities for the enforcement of their decisions.

In many cities territories have been assigned certain denominations to the exclusion of all others. In the City of Cincinnati a home missionary organization of the Churches of Christ (Disciples) made a canvass of a suburban area

10. *UEA*, June 1, 1954, p. 11.
11. *The Growing Super-Church* by James DeForest Murch (1952).

to determine where a new church might be established. Forty families of the communion were discovered in the suburb who were being forced to travel many miles to attend the church of their choice, because the Council of Churches insisted that no church but a Presbyterian church could operate in this territory. The home missions body proceeded to buy a lot without permission of the Council and to organize a church. When the Council secretary heard of it, he immediately presented protests to the City Planning Commission who blocked the erection of a new church building on zoning technicalities. At the edge of the same city a new government housing project barred the same home missions organization from establishing a new church there, despite the fact that it was able to prove that a considerable number of the citizens were of its faith. The Council of Churches was then asked to establish an "Ecumenical Church" which it did under the leadership of a "liberal" minister. Thus it will be seen, that an unholy alliance between church and state is already in existence in some sections of the nation, to prevent strictly evangelical churches from being established.

In 1955 the problem became so crucial that it became necessary for the NAE to present evangelical claims to the American Institute of Planners and other non-religious but authoritative bodies. Dr. George L. Ford, speaking before the Chicago convention in that year, said:

> This year will largely determine whether the evangelical voice will be heard in matters of community planning, guaranteeing the religious liberty that is so much a part of American life or whether the liberal ecumenical movement will usurp the right of the churches. Let me assure you that this is no imaginary threat. I have seen their plan. It proposes in many cases the federation of churches, the purchase of property by a super-church organization for allocation later according to population developments, and downtown worship centers which would not only take the place of regular Protestant churches but would be headquarters for Catholics and Jews as well. Ecumenicity would replace evangelism: the right of propagation, which is so basic to religious liberty, would be traded for the doubtful advantages of a non-competitive church life: Bible-believing churches would be forced to a hands-off policy in many communities even though the only Protestant churches might deny every essential doctrine of Christ and the people be entirely

without a true Christian witness. We have the opportunity now to do something about this but unless we keep our light clear and distinct, both nationally and locally, the opportunity will soon pass.[12]

With the NAE now recognized in national planning organizations local evangelical churches are able to appeal to a national organization which is capable of defending their right to preach the Gospel anywhere without compromise.

In 1946 a Commission on Home Missions was established to provide a medium through which denominational leaders in this field might exchange ideas and work out cooperative understandings in the promotion of their work. Because the Commission duplicated in many particulars the program of the Commission on Evangelism the NAE Board of Administration authorized the merger of the two to form the Commission on Evangelism and Church Extension.

There was a merging of several Commissions including three important areas of responsibility: Evangelism, Church Extension, and Home Missions.[13] Under the reorganization the foundations have been laid, reorientating the work, defining the areas of responsibility, and outlining the plans of procedure. Committees under strong leadership have been named to represent each area of the Commission's responsibility.

The Executive Committee, which includes the officers and the chairmen of the three committees, has formulated the programs and outlined the work and procedures of the Commission. The responsibilities of the Commission break down into four important lines of endeavor: (1) *Information*, wherein the Commission is serving as a fact-finding agency; (2) *Representation*, for churches, organizations, and denominations at important meetings having to do with the three areas of its responsibility; (3) *Inspiration*, in terms of meetings, literature, and any aids possible to pro-

---

12. *UEA*, May 15, 1955, p. 6.
13. *UEA*, March 15, 1956, p. 16. Chairmen of the NAE Commission on Evangelism: Dr. Paul S. Rees (1945-46); Dr. Harold J. Ockenga (1946-47); Dr. H. H. Savage (1947-48); Dr. Howard W. Ferrin (1948-50); Dr. Paul P. Petticord (1950-52); Dr. Don R. Falkenberg (1952-54); the Rev. Hiram Van Cleve (1954-55). Commission on Home Missions: Dr. R. L. Decker (1946-47); the Rev. Fred Vogler (1947-48); Dr. J. Roswell Flower (1948-54); the Rev. Dean Gregory (1954-55). Commission on Evangelism and Church Extension: Rev. Jared F. Gerig (1955-).

mote these great fields of work; and (4) *Education,* or the cooperation with Bible Schools, Christian Colleges, and Seminaries in doing whatever is possible in adequately training leadership.

Looking toward the future evangelicals firmly believe that a world-sweeping revival is imminent. Their faith and their conviction is well stated by Dr. Ockenga in his Indianapolis (1950) address, "Is America's Revival Breaking?" Fresh from a great evangelistic crusade in Boston which saw hundreds converted, he restated his belief that revival would come when a thoroughly cleansed and dedicated church, aflame with zeal and power, would place itself so completely at God's disposal that He could use it to achieve His purpose. Then, he said, must come great preaching.

God ordained that by the foolishness of preaching people should be saved—spiritual preaching—preaching of the Word that is like a seed that will break rock; that is like a hammer that can break a stone; that is like a fire that can burn the chaff; yea, like a sword that can divide asunder between the thoughts and intents of the heart. If we will preach God's Word, God's Law, God's Gospel of the substitute Christ on Calvary people will turn to Jesus Christ. We see them turning to Jesus Christ! The Spirit of God rested on Jesus Christ! The Spirit of God rested on Jesus Christ when He said, "The Spirit is upon me, for He has anointed me to preach the Gospel . . ." Let a man preach anything but the Gospel, let him preach anything but the one Gospel that was written from Genesis to Revelation of the Lamb of God that was slain before the foundation of the world, the Lamb of God that taketh away the sins of the world, the Lamb of God who alone died for us, let him preach anything else but that and the Spirit of God will not be upon it. When it is preached the Spirit will be upon it and with conviction and righteousness and judgment. The Spirit will convict and declare unto men the truth and bring them unto the Saviour. He will do it today just as He has done it many other years in history. There is no question about it.[14]

14. *Ibid.,* July 1, 1950, p. 14.

X

REVITALIZING THE AMERICAN
SUNDAY SCHOOL

One of the most significant developments in the current evangelical movement is the organization and growth of the National Sunday School Association. It was inevitable that such an organization come into being once the evangelical philosophy of education was applied to the Sunday School field.

"Liberal" leadership in this field had definitely accepted the theories of William E. Channing, Theodore Parker, and Horace Bushnell regarding Christian nurture.[1] They believed that the natural state of the pupil was good; that if he were protected from baneful outside influences and given full freedom in the educational process, all the good, true, just, pure, and great elements within him would be released. They believed that righteousness and truth, religion and social order, are not in any sense fixed or absolute but that through the educational process changing values would be discovered, leading man ever onward and upward. They accepted the doctrine of the immanence of God and the historical Jesus and rejected the Bible as the source of infallible and ultimate truth.

Evangelical Sunday School leadership held to the view that man is a lost and sinful creature. They believed that the supreme task of the church is to save men and to fit them to live in harmony with the will of God. They looked upon the Sunday School as primarily religious in its purpose and in its educational process. They accepted the Bible as the central factor in curriculum. They recognized the limitations of the theory of gradual development as the solution of the problems of character and kept clearly in view the important place of crisis, conflict, and choice in the making of Christian character. While willing to accept all the best in the fields of educational philosophy, psychology,

1. *Faith and Nurture* by H. Shelton Smith (1941).

and pedagogy, evangelical Sunday School leaders were unalterably opposed to substituting them for growth in grace and in the knowledge of the Lord Jesus Christ which comes as the fruitage of a heart and life yielded to Him in obedience to the Word of God.[2]

The International Council of Religious Education (the legal successor of the great evangelical International Sunday School Association) favored the liberal view in its choice of national leadership and had been growingly committed to that view. Because of its representative ecclesiastical nature it compromised rather than repudiated the evangelical view. There were many evangelicals in its organizational structure (now the Commission on General Education of the National Council of Churches). But the evangelical view was definitely not the official view of the organization. In fact, this body in its own promotional program and in its liaison relationship with liberal denominational boards and educational institutions was slowly but surely destroying the last vestiges of evangelical Sunday School affirmation in its organization.[3]

From 1916 to 1940 there had been a steady decline in Sunday School enrollment in American churches. The Rev. Clarence H. Benson of Moody Bible Institute in a review of U. S. Government statistics released in 1942 showed that Sunday School enrollment had decreased 12.6 per cent in that period. The Northern (American) Baptist Convention schools had slipped from 1,052,794 in 1926 to 892,872 in 1936. The Disciples of Christ saw their Sunday School numbers fall from 1,000,416 to 761,257 and the Methodist Episcopal Church from 3,796,561 to 2,515,181. This retrograde movement was nationwide among denominations which were experiencing the blight of liberalism. Only the Lutherans, the Assemblies of God, the Church of the Nazarene and other strictly evangelical communions were reporting increases in Sunday School enrollment.

With the abandonment of the strictly evangelical policy of the International Sunday School Association in 1922 there began to develop among evangelicals a definite dis-

2. A more comprehensive study of the history and principles involved in the American religious education situation may be found in the author's textbook, *Christian Education and the Local Church* (1943; revised, 1957). See also, Chapter IX, "The Church As Educator," *Christian Education in a Democracy*, Gaebelein (1951).
3. "International Council Faces Disillusionment," James DeForest Murch, *UEA*, April, 1944, p. 1.

satisfaction with that organization. This dissatisfaction increased with the advent of the International Council of Religious Education, with its so-called "inclusive" policy.

Evangelicals unfortunately failed to express themselves in a united policy and program. Some hoped to reform the ICRE. Some launched independent splinter agencies. Some altogether lost their interest in the Sunday School. This fact, coupled with the loss of denominational and inter-denominational prestige and the lack of influential support, resulted in the dissipation of the forces of protest. The great Sunday School masses of America were unaware of what had happened at the top echelons of the movement. There was no medium through which they could be told.

It was not until 1939 that any united evangelical move worthy of note was taken to retrieve lost ground. In that year a group of so-called independent publishers called a conference to discuss the Uniform Lesson situation as it was related to the ICRE. All of them were conscious of a growing dissatisfaction with curriculum trends. The agitation was not in any sense confined to this group. Denominational publishers whose communions were definitely evangelical had long studied the ICRE lesson situation and sought a solution.

Evangelicals objected to the lesson outlines because—

1. They gave evidence in theme, structure, aim and editorial comment of the "modernist" theological and the "progressivist" educational approach.

2. "Social gospel" teachings were given undue emphasis, and topical outlines were given a definite "liberal" and "social gospel" slant.

3. Many lessons were chosen on a topical basis with little regard for Bible context, resulting in the use of unrelated sections of Scripture to teach ideas other than those intended by the Bible writers.

4. There was a failure to provide a comprehensive view of the Scriptures historically, textually or theologically.

5. Topics were inadequate for instruction in fundamental Christian doctrine.

6. Scriptures suggested for printed texts for Primary children were often too short to provide an adequate basis for instruction.

7. There was a tendency to introduce a lesson plan (different rather than uniform Scripture texts for the

various departments) which destroyed the strictly uniform lesson idea and made the lessons almost unusable in small schools.

8. Scriptures selected seldom dealt with evangelism or lent themselves to evangelistic emphasis.

9. The guiding principles in ICRE curriculum building were no longer clearly evangelical and Scriptural but basically humanistic in religious principle and naturalistic in application.

10. The Lesson Committee failed to establish any official consultative relationship with the evangelical editors and publishers who produced the majority of the Uniform Sunday School lesson literature of the nation.

In the fall of 1943 the National Association of Evangelicals, in the meeting of its Board of Administration in New York City, considered the possibility of the development of a new evangelical system of Uniform Sunday School Lessons. At the December meeting of the NAE executive committee Dr. Clarence H. Benson was announced as chairman of a new lesson committee.[4]

April 12-17, 1944, upon the call of the Church School Commission of the NAE, a meeting was held in the Deshler-Wallick Hotel, Columbus, Ohio, in which were represented in this project, without regard to organization or denomination, independent publishers, denominational publishers, editors and religious leaders of denominational and interdenominational and undenominational organizations. Dr. Harold John Ockenga presided at the sessions.[5]

All present were concerned about the apostasy of the International Council of Religious Education. It was here proposed that new Uniform Sunday School Lesson outlines should be produced and that *the task should be committed to a new national Sunday School association organized on strictly evangelical principles.* As an outgrowth of the Columbus meeting over 100 leaders in the field of Christian education gathered in the Stevens Hotel, Chicago, April 30-May 1, 1945, where a temporary organization of the National Sunday School Association was effected. The executive committee of the new organization called a meeting in the Central YMCA, Chicago, August 21 and 22 of the same

4. *UEA*, January 1944, p. 1.
5. *Ibid.*, May, 1944, "Report of the Field Secretary," p. 3.

year and set up a committee for the preparation of new Uniform Lesson outlines.[6]

Sunday School workers from thirty-five states and two provinces of Canada met in Chicago, October 2-6, 1946, in the first national (constitutional) convention of the National Sunday School Association.[7] Meetings were held in Moody Church with audiences ranging from 400 in the mornings and afternoons to 1,000 in the evenings and 4,000 on Saturday night.

The delegates were of one mind concerning the necessity for the setting up of a new national framework of organization for the revitalization of the Sunday School. A constitution was adopted for the NSSA; officers were elected; the new Uniform Bible Lesson project was approved, and a program of expansion planned.

The NAE Statement of Belief was adopted, assuring the doctrinal future of the Association.

Dr. Archer E. Anderson, pastor of First Presbyterian Church, Duluth, Minn., president of the temporary organization, opened the convention on Wednesday night with an address depicting the need for a new Sunday School association and giving a broad outline of the program it should undertake. Other outstanding addresses were delivered by Bishop Leslie R. Marston of the Free Methodist Church of North America; Dr. Harold C. Mason, professor of Christian Education in Northern Baptist Theological Seminary; Dr. Henry L. Smith of the Indiana State Board of Education and former president of the National Education Association; Dr. Robert C. McQuilkin, president of Columbia (S.C.) Bible College; Dr. Clarence H. Benson, general secretary of the Evangelical Teacher Training Association; Dr. Walter L. Wilson, president of Kansas City Bible College; Dr. H. H. Savage, pastor of First Baptist Church, Pontiac, Mich., and Dr. James DeForest Murch, former editorial secretary of the Standard Publishing Company who had just become editor of NAE's *United Evangelical Action* magazine.

Work-study groups and departmental conferences were held morning and afternoon and were largely attended. Sankey Hall was filled with exhibits of denominational and independent publishers of Sunday School literature.

6. Minutes of the Secretary, 1944-46.
7. *UEA*, October 15, 1946, p. 10.

The first Board of Directors, elected at Chicago, consisted of Dr. Archer E. Anderson (Presbyterian USA), president; Dr. Clarence H. Benson (Presbyterian US), vice-president; Dr. James DeForest Murch (Disciples of Christ), secretary; Mr. Robert C. Van Kampen (Northern Baptist), treasurer; the Rev. Jesse R. Hastings (Methodist) ; the Rev. A. L. Brown (Free Methodist) ; Dr. J. P. McCallie (Presbyterian US) ; the Rev. J. R. Mumaw (Mennonite) ; the Rev. Ralph M. Riggs (Assemblies of God) ; Dr. H. H. Savage (Northern Baptist) ; Dr. J. H. Walker (Church of God) ; the Rev. J. Clair Peters (United Brethren) ; Dr. W. L. Surbrook (Pilgrim Holiness) ; Mr. A. L. Stewart (Canadian Presbyterian) ; Dr. Roy S. Hollomon (Southern Baptist). Mr. C. V. Egemeier was re-elected executive secretary. The Association was incorporated under the laws of the State of Illinois and Chicago was made permanent national headquarters.

Official relationship with the National Association of Evangelicals was through its Sunday School (Church School) Commission composed of the members of the executive committee of the NSSA.

It is interesting to note in passing that the old International Sunday School Association had its origin in the solution of a problem similar to that now posed to evangelicals. The Sunday School leaders of America had agreed to unite in the production of Uniform Sunday School Lesson outlines to be used by all Protestant Sunday Schools. The implementation of their plan required some overall organization representative of the schools. Accordingly the ISSA was organized in Indianapolis, Ind., in 1872.

The chief concern of the newly-formed NSSA was its uniform lesson project.[8]

The Lesson Committee, which tackled the new job in 1946 consisted of Dr. Clarence H. Benson, chairman (Presbyterian) ; Dr. James DeForest Murch, secretary (Disciples of Christ) ; Bishop Leslie R. Marston (Free Methodist) ; Miss Henrietta Mears (Presbyterian) ; Dr. H. C. Mason (Free Methodist) ; Dr. Harry A. Ironside (Plymouth Brethren) ; Dr. H. H. Savage (Baptist) ; Dr. R. C. McQuilkin (Presbyterian) ; the Rev. Stanley H. Frodsham (Assemblies of God) and Dr. R. H. Fritsch (Lutheran).

8. *The New Uniform Bible Lessons*, official brochure NSSA (1953).

An Advisory Committee of One Hundred was also set up to work with the Lesson Committee. It consisted of educational leaders, pastors, local Sunday School teachers and leaders, editors, publishers, and lesson writers from practically every major Protestant body in America.

The Lesson Committee immediately adopted the Statement of Belief of the National Association of Evangelicals as the minimum basis of theological agreement.

A careful study of the history of the original Uniform Lessons since their inception in 1872 was then undertaken by the NSSA Committee. It gave much consideration to the work of the Uniform Lesson committees of the old International Sunday School Association under whose aegis these lessons reached their widest acceptance. They sought to discover and utilize the wisdom, experience and methods of these evangelical educational leaders of the "Golden Age" of the American Sunday School.

The Lesson Committee finally adopted the following policy as a guide for its work:

1. The name of the new lesson series shall be the "Uniform Bible Lesson Series."

2. The curriculum shall be Bible-centered in content. The text for study shall be related to and in harmony with the context both in letter and spirit.

3. The supreme purpose of the series shall be the winning of every pupil to the Lord Jesus Christ and the submission of his life to the will of God.

4. The lessons shall be directed to the teaching and training of the pupil for Christian character and service.

5. Recognizing the limitations of the theory of gradual development as the solution of problems of character, the curriculum will keep clearly in view the important place of crisis, conflict and choice in the making of Christian character.

6. Each cycle will be five years in length.

7. Cycle content will consist of selections of Scripture approximately 40 per cent from the New Testament, 40 per cent from the Old Testament, and 20 per cent from both Old and New Testaments in a related study. One quarter each year will consist of related lessons on Christian doctrine and life. Thus three quarters will be devoted primarily to instruction in a body of Bible truth with the other quarter devoted to further emphasis on application.

8. The selection of lessons shall be determined by the nature and capacities of childhood with necessary adjustment to adolescent and adult life.

9. Topical lessons shall be limited in number and always grounded in Scripture.

10. The schedule of lessons shall be geared to major observances of the church year.

When the Constitutional Convention of the National Sunday School Association met in Moody Memorial Church, Chicago, October 2-6, 1946, the Lesson Committee was ready with its report. When Dr. Murch, as secretary of the committee, presented the project it evoked such interest and discussion that the assembly decided to devote the entire morning to its consideration. When a final vote was taken the gathering expressed its unanimous and enthusiastic approval of the Uniform Lessons.

On Sunday, January 4, 1948, it was estimated that a million Sunday School pupils across the nation began the study of lessons based on the Uniform Bible Lesson Outlines prepared by the NSSA. It was a good beginning. Today some 4,000,000 pupils are using the new lessons provided by some fifteen publishers and the number is growing with every passing year.

There are three committees which are involved in the preparation of the lesson outlines: (1) The Central Committee, (2) The General Committee, and (3) The Advisory Committee of One Hundred. All members of all committees must subscribe to the official statement of faith of the NSSA.

The Central Committee consists of nine members chosen annually by the Board of Directors of the National Sunday School Association and a group of departmental experts appointed by the committee. It has two regular meetings — one in June and one in December — and as many special meetings as may be necessary. The Chairman presides at the meetings, expedites the work of the members and has general oversight of the task of lesson preparation. The Secretary keeps the minutes of all meetings, sends out notifications, and retains the files of all official papers. All members of the committee are divided into Initiators and Collaborators. Initiators, following basic decisions by the whole committee, make Initial Drafts of assigned sections of the cycle, four years in advance of current dates. After the whole committee has approved these Initial Drafts, the

Collaborators assist in completing supplementary data for the Final Draft.

The General Committee consists of the Central Committee and representatives of all the publishers who produce lesson materials based on the NSSA outlines. The Committee meets only once a year, prior to the submission of the work of the Central Committee to the Advisory Committee of One Hundred. The General Committee considers the lesson outlines in the light of the needs of their constituencies and the technical problems involved. They make recommendations both as to the character of the lessons and the policies under which they are produced.

The Advisory Committee of One Hundred critically examines the work of the Central Committee in Final Draft and makes further recommendations concerning changes and emendations. This Committee is set up with extreme care in order that it may be representative of a cross-section of evangelical Protestantism in America. Its members represent denominations, publishers, pastors, educators, Sunday School teachers and leaders, and are chosen with reference to regional and geographical location.

Following a careful review of all comments and recommendations on the Final Draft, a revision is made by the Central Committee and the official Final Draft goes to the Board of Directors of the NSSA for its approval and official permission for release to publishers, editors, and writers.

The NSSA now provides Uniform Lessons that have a special appeal to the evangelical Sunday Schools of America—

They are sponsored by a doctrinally orthodox organization controlled by evangelicals.

Their preparation is strictly in the hands of trustworthy evangelicals.

Their basic principles are evangelical and biblical.

The outlines give evidence in theme, structure, aim, and editorial comment of evangelical theological and Christian educational approach.

Biblical doctrine, evangelism, and soul winning receive emphasis; proper application is made to life's problems.

The lessons are Bible centered and true to context.

They provide a comprehensive view of Scripture historically, textually, and theologically within limits of the uniform system.

Topics are adequate for instruction in fundamental Christian doctrine.

The lesson plan adheres strictly to the uniform lesson idea.

The use of the lessons will serve to advance the evangelical cause.

The interest of the NSSA in the Uniform Lesson system is in no way indicative of a preference for this curricular method. Graded Lesson systems are provided by evangelical publishers and promoted with equal zeal by NSSA leaders.

Soon after the Chicago convention it became evident that the outstanding role of the NSSA was not to be lesson building but rather providing leadership for a great Sunday School revival in America.[9] The Association adopted as its slogan: "Revitalize the American Sunday School," and "Revival Now Through the Sunday School."

National Sunday School conventions[10] have been held annually in Cincinnati, Ohio; Denver, Colorado; Oakland, California; Philadelphia, Pennsylvania; Detroit, Michigan; Portland, Oregon; Minneapolis, Minnesota; Indianapolis, Indiana; Providence, Rhode Island; Spokane, Washington; Chicago, Illinois, and other great American cities. Oakland marked a spiritual high point in the progress of the NSSA. Philadelphia, with the adoption of a revised constitution, gave new promise of permanency and efficiency. Minneapolis was overwhelming evidence that a tidal wave of Sunday School revival was on.

The NSSA has spearheaded the organization of new Sunday School associations in many metropolitan areas. It has set up new state associations. It has inspired hundreds of local groups to initiate old-fashioned Sunday School conventions. But this is only a beginning of the vast task ahead. NSSA leaders believe that only as all areas of America are enlisted and every Sunday School leader in the

---

9. Presidents of the National Sunday School Association and chairmen of the Church School Commission of the NAE have served as follows: Dr. Archer E. Anderson (1946-48); Dr. H. H. Savage (1948-49); Dr. James DeForest Murch (1949-51); the Rev. A. L. Brown (1951-53); Dr. Harold W. Erickson (1953-56). General Secretaries: the Revs. C. V. Egemeier (1946-47), and William E. Kirschke (1947-50); Mr. Russell T. Hitt (1950-52); Dr. Clate A. Risley (1952-). Miss Winona Walworth served as Associate General Secretary 1950-1956.

10. Annual Sunday School Convention numbers of *UEA*.

nation put to work "revitalizing the American Sunday School" will NSSA's goals be achieved.

A free consulting service is maintained at national headquarters. Problems are ironed out by Sunday School experts. A monthly bulletin of plans for superintendents is mailed to all member schools. So great has been the growing demand for this clinical aid that the Association has set up new Commissions dealing with every phase of Sunday School work. They produce helps which will express in methodology the basic doctrinal position of the Association and act as consultants with evangelical Sunday School leadership at local, regional and national levels.

Three basic emphases characterize the work of the NSSA: (1) the Bible, (2) evangelism, and (3) spiritual power. All these had been lost in the infiltration of "liberalism" into the Sunday School, beginning with the early 1900's. Largely through the work of the Association the following has been effected:

The Bible has been restored to its rightful position as the textbook of the Sunday School. It is not only central in curriculum, but its teachings determine the principles and methods used in the educational and promotional process. Teachers are no longer ashamed to say, "We teach *the Bible!*" despite the sophistries of "progressive" educators about teaching *"the pupils."* Evangelical Sunday School leaders are united in believing that their great task is to indoctrinate boys and girls, men and women with the great revealed truths of the Word of God and apply them to life. This new generation of leaders has discarded the antibiblical naturalistic and humanistic philosophies which were basic to the principles and methodology of "liberal" religious education. They now are in the process of building a new concept of the Sunday School's educational task which is true to the Bible. The natural result is a new generation of pupils who sing with the Psalmist: "O how I love they word, O God; it is my meditation all the day. Thou through thy commandments hast made me wiser than mine enemies."

Evangelism has been restored to its rightful position in the purpose of the Sunday School. Again it is being bravely said, "The purpose of the Sunday School is to *win souls to Christ*, teaching them the Word of God and training them in Christian character and service." Evangelical leaders equate education and evangelism as the twin objectives of the Great Commission and zealously promote them simultaneously. This is resulting in three things: (1) Enrollment and attendance are climbing in schools which have caught the vision. The largest and most rapidly growing schools in America and abroad are of the strictly evangelical type. (2) People are being saved every Lord's Day as a result of the teaching of strictly Bible lessons. Every Bible lesson contains an "evangelistic emphasis" which enables the teacher to pin-point his instruction to win souls for Christ. (3) The churches fortunate enough to have Sunday Schools like this are reaching out in their communities, constantly touching new lives for Christ. They are known as alive and "on the job," and as churches that act as though Christianity is a vital, full-time business.

Spiritual power has been restored to the whole Sunday School operation. One of the reasons for this lies in the fact that the leaders in this new movement believe that the educational process involves crisis, conflict, and choice. This crisis involves the pupil's personal and individual acceptance of Jesus Christ as Lord and Saviour, his repentance, his obedience and his infilling by the Holy Spirit. If this is a truly valid experience it produces a regenerated and reborn person — a new creature in Christ Jesus. The old "progressive" educational philosophy was wedded to cold educational propositions, to methods and to programs which are purely naturalistic and intellectual in concept. They imparted no warmth and divine passion. They recognized no possibility of that spiritual influx by which God through the Holy Spirit breathes new life into the pupil. The evangelical concept gives spiritual dynamic for Christion growth, sharing and victory. In this new movement which is sweeping the land the Sunday School is being thought of as a divine institution with divine oversight, a divine program and a divine mission. Therefore it is bebecoming a dynamic spiritual power "winning souls to Christ, teaching them the Word of God and training them in Christian character and service."

Somewhat related to the Sunday School program is NAE's Commission on Youth. As at present constituted, this Commission is concerned primarily with the expressional activities of youth at the local church level.

In the beginning, however, NAE was concerned with a much broader concept of service to the youth of America.

Youth for Christ was sweeping the nation and all of its national leaders were active in the affairs of the NAE.[11]

They saw the crying need to combat juvenile delinquency and realized the inadequacy of most local church youth programs. Breaking with tradition such YFC leaders as Torrey M. Johnson, Robert A. Cook and Billy Graham organized popular Saturday night evangelistic mass meetings and packed the largest auditoriums of the land with eager youth bent on winning others to Christ. In the college and university field men like C. Stacey Woods were challenging students through Inter-Varsity Fellowship.[12] Early issues of *United Evangelical Action* were filled with articles and promotional material for these undenominational youth agencies.

The 1943 Constitutional Convention set up a Committee on Youth Evangelism headed by George Kendall with the purpose in view of coordinating existing evangelistic-type youth agencies, setting up regional youth offices as clearing houses for community activities, and the like.[13] At first the idea was welcomed and considerable enthusiasm developed for such a program. In 1945 a National Youth Conference was held in connection with the Chicago NAE Convention with Torrey Johnson as chairman.[14] The gathering was composed of youth leaders from a wide variety of organizations. By the time of the Minneapolis Convention in 1946 denominational youth leaders were becoming more vocal in the affairs of the Conference. An NAE-affiliated organization known as Evangelical Youth, Inc., was set up with the Rev. Ralph W. Harris as president and an NAE Commission on Youth was created.[15]

Denominational evangelistic-type and interdenominational youth leaders, while friendly to the undenominational agencies and cooperating enthusiastically in many of their programs, were committed to an educational approach to the youth problem through organizations related to the local church and operated under church supervision. It soon be-

11. Cf. early issues of *Youth for Christ magazine.*
12. Cf. Chapter VII, "A New Day in Evangelical Education," p. 82.
13. NAE Convention Report, 1943, p. 38.
14. NAE Convention Report, 1945, pp. 7-10.
15. NAE Convention Report, 1946, pp. 69-72.   Chairmen of the NAE Commission on Youth since its creation in 1946: the Revs. Ralph W. Harris (1946-48), H. K. Sheets (1948-50), J. Ronald MacDonald (1950-52), Val E. Hauck (1952-53), H. K. Sheets (1953-55), Gunnar Hoglund (1955-   ).

came evident that both types of youth work could not well be served by a single Commission in an inter-church body composed largely of denominational representatives.

With utmost good will both parties came to agree that the Commission on Youth should be developed to serve denominational and interdenominational youth groups.[16] In this area the Commission is of increasing value to youth leaders and organizations. It is a clearinghouse for common problems, the development of effective methods of youth work and inter-church programs, and is functionally related both to the National Association of Evangelicals and the National Sunday School Association.

16. *UEA*, April 1, 1955, p. 20.

XI

THE DEFENSE OF RELIGIOUS LIBERTY

From the beginning of this new movement deep concern was felt for the preservation of the American doctrine of Separation of Church and State, religious freedom, and freedom of speech, and for an effective evangelical Christian testimony in the nation's capital.

At St. Louis the Policy Committee recognized the fact that certain relations with the Government must be established and maintained. In their report, adopted by the Convention, there were paragraphs on "Relations with the Government" and on "Preservation of the Principle of Separation of Church and State" which proposed that these matters should "be left directly in the hands of the Executive Committee and the Executive Secretary for the present, asking them to take such actions from time to time as the exigencies" of the situations might demand.[1]

At the Constitutional Convention in Chicago the Committee on Policy and Fields of Endeavor elaborated on the need for united evangelical action in "War Services," "Moral Welfare and Social Service," "Separation of Church and State" and advised the Executive Committee to "designate" someone "to represent the interests of this Association at Washington."[2]

Dr. J. Elwin Wright visited Washington in the summer of that year (1943) and after conferring with evangelicals in the District of Columbia secured a suitable location at Kellogg Building, 1422 F Street, N. W., a half block from the Willard Hotel and near the U. S. Treasury Building and the U. S. Department of State.[3] On September 13 the office was formally dedicated. Participating in the event were Dr. Harold J. Ockenga, Dr. J. Elwin Wright, Song Evangelist Homer Rodeheaver, and members of the Washington Committee: Hon. Erwin H. Linton, the Revs. C. E.

1. *Evangelical Action* (1942), pp. 111, 112.
2. *UEA*, July 1, 1943, p. 5.
3. *Ibid.*, September 10, 1943, p. 1.

Hawthorne and John Ballbach, William Bond, Irwin W. McLean, C. Vernon Hill and George Kendall.

It was agreed that the new "director of affairs" in the capital address himself first of all to services for the missionary agencies affiliated with the NAE, secondly, to War Service activity, certifying chaplaincy applications, services to evangelical soldier centers, and third, to survey work in connection with the NAE Committee on Education. At first the burden of the work fell upon Dr. Wright, but soon the Association discovered a young man of wide experience and capabilities, the Rev. Clyde W. Taylor, pastor of Central Baptist Church, Quincy, Mass. He had been a member of the faculty of Gordon College of Theology and Missions and had served three terms in Colombia and Peru as a missionary of the Christian and Missionary Alliance. Mr. Taylor became Secretary of Missions in the summer of 1944 and later was placed in full charge of the Washington office.[4]

Eventually circumstances and experience clarified the functions of the Washington office. World War II finally came to a close and the need for War Services almost disappeared. In its place came the need for a permanent Commission on Government Chaplaincies and the establishment of liaison with the Pentagon to handle defense, draft, and other problems related to the clergy and full-time Christian workers. The Committee on Education, although requiring some services in Washington, soon realized that its orbit lay in other areas. Under Dr. Taylor's leadership there began to emerge a philosophy of evangelical relations with the government which he has stated somewhat as follaws[5]:

Evangelicals possess a dual citizenship. Paul said in Phil. 3:20 that "our citizenship is in heaven" and again in Phil. 2:15 that we are "the sons of God, without rebuke, in the midst of a crooked and perverse nation among whom shine ye as lights of the world." We are citizens of both heaven and earth.

Earthly governments are ordained of God to do certain things. They are to control and direct the environment in

4. *Ibid.*, August 15, 1944, p. 3.
5. Dr. Taylor's views concerning evangelicals and public affairs were well expressed in his address, "Citizens of Heaven and Earth," delivered before the Winona Lake (Ind.) Bible Conference in the summer of 1954 and broadcast over Radio Station WMBI Chicago. See *UEA*, February 1, 1955, p. 3 ff.

which we live. They are to guarantee to men the rights and freedoms that are God's gifts. Governments fail when they conceive of these rights and freedoms as granted by men. They may, however, demand respect, enforce the laws, regulate society for the benefit of all. God gives specific instruction as to the Christian's relationship with his government. On the other hand in working out the relationship of religion and government we find abuses prevalent, even in the USA.

First, there are the efforts of the Roman Church to promote Church-State union with the Church dominant. This is best seen in the many efforts of the Roman lobby in Washington to secure federal aid for parochial schools; to get federal funds for Roman Catholic hospital building, and to participate as a Church in USA politics.

Another abuse is the effort of the agnostics, atheists, and misguided zealots who misinterpret separation of Church and State, to take all religion out of government, to take Christ's teachings, ideals and witness out of government. This they say is necessary to keep the church out of government. They seem to take for granted that it is possible for Christians to live in a nation and yet be restricted in the exercise of their faith and testimony in their daily occupation in government.

A third violation is caused by minorities in the name of freedom of religion abusing their rights to restrict the majority. We see the same agnostics, anti-religionists, and in a few cases those of the Hebrew faith opposing the distribution of the New Testament to students on the grounds that it is a sectarian book. This has been carried so far in most public schools that anything regarding Christianity is considered controversial and is ruled out of order by teachers. The study of and comment on any part of the Bible is in most states taboo.

Another minority abuse comes in the management of the public school systems. The Roman Catholics, while sending their own children to Roman Catholic parochial schools, seem to feel it their obligation to run for election to state and city school boards. Blind, indifferent Protestants help elect them and then mourn when the school system deteriorates under their management.

A different type of abuse in Church-Government relations comes through the activity of religious lobbies. There are a number of such lobbies registered in Washington and each one supposedly acts only to safeguard violations of its own convictions. In the main this is true. However, some lobbies are occupied in seeking special and generally illegal appropriations of funds for schools, hospitals and other basically religious activities.

There are abuses committed by Communists and Socialists in the government. The well-documented seditious advance of this subversion into government frightens serious minded Americans, as it indicates how easily they can lose their most precious earthly possessions.

There is also that abuse which by promoting government ownership of resources, industry and property would make US citizens wards of the state, placing them economically on the dole. Such a government by absolute control of the people grants or denies God-given freedoms and produces a nation of fatalistic or indifferent citizens.

Evangelicals live in this world and have a testimony to give and a duty to perform as citizens which cannot be shirked. As Christian citizens they can be, as was the Apostle Paul, *transformers* by spiritual processes but can also be *reformers* through active Christian citizenship.

In a republic such as the USA Christian citizens, if aroused to their duty, have enough strength to elect godly men to office. They, with Christian convictions voiced through the polls and to their representatives, can accomplish the unbelievable, but the great inertia of the average American often dominates the Christian and he fails to act because he is not sufficiently aroused.

There are, however, encouraging signs across the nation. Largely through the influence of the National Association of Evangelicals, under the leadership of evangelical men, many are already alert to the serious conditions in the nation. The Washington office of the NAE is a "watchman" in the nation's capital. Using the *United Evangelical Action* magazine as its official organ, the NAE has published Dr. Taylor's "Capitol Report" for years. Legislation bearing on church and evangelical activity around the world is reported. Evangelicals are urged to influence their Congressmen for the right.

The separation of Church and State is watched. Threatened violations are published. Cooperation is given through the Washington office with other like-minded groups in this field until today such violations are instantly detected and protested. A new respect is growing in the minds of those who propose to violate this basic doctrine.

Every division of government that has bearing on the American way of life is being watched by evangelicals. The Department of State with its great diplomatic service and its control over the movement of USA citizens is not to be neglected. Abuses are bound to occur in such a large agency. Discrimination sometimes takes place and a voice of protest is needed for the correction and control of any subversive action on the part of department representatives overseas. If need be evangelicals must apply the pressure for what is right to counterbalance the influence of the Roman hierarchy and other forces that constantly exert their maximum influence for their own interests regardless of the legality of their action. Government needs strong support to resist such pressures.

Evangelicals, as never before, are stepping into the breach and helping to furnish a moral conscience for the nation. The law of expediency has so taken control of the thinking of many leaders that God's moral law and what God may think of actions receive little attention. The result is that any act in the government interest is condoned. Evangelicals are beginning to assert their testimony against ungodly relations with militant atheism. Unless they let their voice be heard, their influence felt, a pagan conscience will prevail.

In this area of endeavor, evangelicals live in a shrinking world where the affairs of their brethren in Christ become their concern when their liberties are restricted. Evangelicals must not only appeal the case to Heaven, they must *act* when able to do so. The greatest weapons in this combat are diplomacy and the press. During the past ten years great strides have been made by evangelicals in maintaining such relations with the Department of State that every violation of religious freedom may effectively be called to the government's attention. Where it involves US citizens, they request action and generally get it. Where it involves American interests, the State Department does what it can within its legal field of action. The press is an even greater weapon. Slowly evangelicals around the world are becoming more active in keeping the Washington office informed when they are persecuted or discriminated against. Slowly the American press is showing its willingness to print the news and public opinion is being moulded. Evangelicals have just started to use it in the defense of God's children. Evangelicals have the convictions and the means to exert great influence if they will shake off their traditional lethargy in such matters.

Much can be accomplished by reform, by vigilance, by using influence, letting the evangelical voice be heard, but to evangelicals there is still a better way. The better way is *transformation* with every Christian a transformer, being careful, however, to remember that this is not exclusive of *reformation*. Both methods may be used at once. Of course, in the Apostolic Church there was only one road open, that was *transformation* by saturation-evangelism. Amidst persecution and every form of violent opposition the Christian — everyone a witness, a personal missionary — went everywhere telling the Gospel. This was declared illegal but they obeyed God and pressed on. It took three hundred years, but the Gospel won. It took the Empire.

The twentieth century Christian in America has two ways open to serve His Lord and nation. He has a franchise, a moral responsibility before God to use his earthly citizenship for God's glory. Americans are a self-governing people. Either Christians who love the Lord are going to take Christ into the political life of the nation or the increasing infiltration of Roman Catholic power will take over. The Christian conscience is a dynamic that will take evangelical laymen into the political life of local governments. Evangelicals have demonstrated this time and again and have cleaned up local corruption.

Evangelicals do not want the Church in politics. They believe that only its members are US citizens. When the Church enters politics, it degenerates into another political lobby. The Church has a responsibility to inculcate in its members their responsibility as citizens and build the morality and ethics that control their lives through Christ.

In an increasing number of communities across the nation organized Christian lay leadership groups are promoting united evangelical action. This encourages evangelicals to take part in political life and run for office. These groups also supply evangelicals with information about candidates for office in ample time before city, county, state, and national elections so that they know the record, standing, and qualifications of each candidate regardless of party. Such groups expose corrupt political machines by giving the facts about the candidates who are machine controlled.

In 1944 the Commission on Chaplaincies was set up with Dr. Harold J. Ockenga as its first chairman, operating through the Washington office.[6] The Commission now represents NAE denominations for which it is the official endorsing agency in the appointment of chaplains for the Army, Navy, Air, Veterans' Administration and the Army Reserve. In November 1953, the Rev. Douglas G. Scott was called as the first full-time secretary of the Commissions. He is recognized on an equal basis with the representative of the National Council of Churches in all matters pertaining to Protestantism in the government chaplaincy picture.

In 1948 a Committee on Christian Liberty was set up to be the official liaison body between the NAE Board of Administration and the Washington Office in matters pertaining to public affairs. Dr. Frederick C. Fowler was made chairman. Associated with him were Mr. Frank Gigliotti, the Rev. Douglas G. Scott and Dr. Clyde W. Taylor. The Committee made its first report at the Chicago Convention in 1949. The Indianapolis Convention advanced the Committee to Commission status and changed its name to the Commission on Evangelical Action. It now speaks for the NAE in official pronouncements which are drafted under the leadership of its chairman in close cooperation with Dr. Taylor and NAE's headquarters office. Dr. Fowler is still chairman of this important body.

The National Association of Evangelicals soon came to be recognized by the Congress and other government agencies as having a right to express the views of a considerable sector of Protestantism on conferences, investigations, or opinionnaires affecting legislation or government policy in areas of morals or religion.

As an example, on November 8, 1949 Dr. Stephen W. Paine represented the NAE in the historic National Conference on Human Rights, sponsored by the Department of State, and presented the evangelical Christian point of view with regard to civil rights.[7] Mrs. Franklin D. Roosevelt had just stated the case for the framers of the Declaration of Human Rights to be laid before the United Nations

6. Designated at first as "Commission on Army and Navy Chaplaincies," the Commission on Chaplaincies has been headed by the following chairmen: Dr. Harold J. Ockenga (1944-46); the Revs. Hubert T. Spence (1946-49), Douglas G. Scott (1949-55), and O. L. Harrup (1955-   ).
7. *UEA*, December 15, 1949, pp. 3, 4.

Assembly, when Dr. Paine arose. In measured and impressive tone he said:

From what has been said here thus far, one would perhaps get the impression that the group is unanimous in its support of that part of the Declaration of Human Rights which deals with the social and economic rights of man, and that the group is unanimous also in feeling that these should be included in the International Covenant from which they are thus far omitted. I should like to get into the record the fact that, knowing the constituency of the National Association of Evangelicals as I do, I feel confident in saying that they would not at all concur in this feeling concerning the statement of social and economic rights.

Our objection would strike at the underlying assumption of this entire Declaration of Human Rights. It begins with the assertion that man has a certain "inherent dignity and inalienable rights." We believe this is an erroneous point of beginning.

The founders of our nation started, not with certain rights *inherent in man*, but described man's rights as given by God, saying that man is endowed by the Creator with certain inalienable rights.

We realize, of course, that the authors of the Covenant and the Declaration had to consider their constituency of widely varying shades of belief; but, nevertheless, the basic assumption in their Declaration is definitely different from that of our founding fathers.

Our forefathers went on from man's divinely-given rights to the premise that governments get their rights from the people, from the consent of the governed.

The Universal Declaration goes on from its start and sets forth a situation where the individual apparently owes his rights to the grant of the government. For example, twice in the Declaration, namely in Article 14, part 2, and in Article 29, part 3, the rights outlined are not enforceable if and when they run counter to the policy of the United Nations.[8] In this way the Declaration sets the United Nations above the rights of the individual and implies that these rights originate with the UN and are maintained by its sufferance. Our constituency of evangelical church people would, I am sure, deem this an in-

8. Article 14, Part 2: "This right may not be invoked in the case of persecutions genuinely arising from . . . acts contrary to the purposes and principles of the United Nations."
Article 29, Part 3: "These rights and freedoms may in no case be exercised contrary to the purposes and principles of the United Nations."

version of the correct viewpoint — the one held by the early leaders of our nation.

Now, the declared social and economic rights as outlined simply go on and reinforce the picture of government as the big father upon whom the individual is dependent. Consider Article 22, where the individual is seen as dependent upon the state for "social security" and for "the economic, social and cultural rights indispensable for his dignity." Or scan Article 23 in which man looks to the state for "the right to work" and for "just and favorable conditions of work and for protection from unemployment."

Incidentally, in this same Article, part 4, we read, "Everyone has the right to form and to join trade unions for the protection of his interests." But, by implication, this means forced unionization, for nothing is said of an individual's right to stay out of a union, if he desires. Hence, part 4 is an implied abridgement of part 1, which says, "Everyone has the right to work."

Again in Article 25 the state is seen as guaranteeing the right to an adequate standard of living: "including food, clothing, housing, medical care, and necessary social services, and the right to security in the event of unemployment, sickness, disability, widowhood, old age, etc." I feel sure that I can rightly report the constituency of the National Association of Evangelicals as feeling that this sort of thing is socialistic, that it leads in the direction of statism, and that our members would be opposed to having our country adopt any covenant which would attempt to enforce these principles.

The voice of religious and political liberalism was supreme throughout the Conference. Without the National Association of Evangelicals there would have been no open stand for the orthodox Christian viewpoint. Dr. Paine's view is now widely accepted by a very considerable sector of American Christianity and is a decided factor in the reluctance of the Congress to accept the Declaration of Human Rights in its present form.

The effectiveness of the work of the Washington office is well illustrated in two notable achievements in the field of religious liberty.

Roman Catholics had stoned missionaries of the Churches of Christ in the little town of Frascati, Italy. This was one of scores of similar incidents which had been accumulating and which had been well documented by the Washington office. Conditions seemed favorable to united evangelical action and, upon the advice of the Commission on Christian Liberty, it was arranged to call a gathering of representative Protestant leaders in the Wardman Park Hotel on the afternoon of January 17, 1950. All representatives of the NAE Commission were present. All the major news agencies were represented.

As a result of the conference the following letter was drafted and addressed to the Prime Minister of Italy, His Excellency Alcide de Gasperi:

The recent incident in Frascati concerning the Church of Christ Evangelists from Texas, stoned by Roman Catholics, has alarmed the Protestants of America. This is not the first incident of its kind in Italy since the end of the war. On numerous occasions we have been compelled to plead with your Government to intervene for the protection of our Protestant brethren. It is becoming increasingly difficult to understand why such incidents are tolerated, when according to your Constitution full Religious Liberty is a part of the law. Not only does this violate your own Constitution but is in direct disregard of Article 15 of the Peace Treaty.

To cover the inexcusable Frascati incident, the Italian Interior Minister has charged that the "activities of the American Protestants in Italy were unwittingly aiding the cause of Communism"— as though it would be proper to stone Communists. It is unfortunate that your Government should stoop to name calling in an attempt to hide the real issue. The issue involved is the Freedom of Worship in Italy. Protestants are strongly opposed to Communism; for we oppose all totalitarianism, ecclesiastical as well as civil.

We respectfully urge that your Government take action to avoid any repetition of the Frascati incident. This would necessitate a thorough investigation to the end that those who were responsible for inciting the incident be punished, and proper visas granted to our brethren.

We further respectfully urge that your Government produce evidence that Protestants are helping the cause of Communism, or, retract its charge.

We further respectfully urge that your Government issue a public statement regarding its stand concerning Freedom of Worship and that all local police be instructed to carry out the law and trace all incidents to their instigators so that they may be punished.

If such disregard of religious freedom continues, we shall be forced because of numerous requests, to present this matter to the Congress of the United States and to the United Nations to the end that the Peace Treaty be no longer violated. Questions that are being asked in America are:

1. Does the Italian Government, or does it not, expect to sincerely abide by the Peace Treaty?

2. Is the Italian Government unable to carry out its promises for Religious Liberty?

3. Is the local priest who incites riot responsible to the Italian Government or the Vatican?

4. Is the Italian Government a true Democracy or is it controlled by the Vatican?

5. Should aid be continued to a country whose Government does not respect her Peace Treaty?

6. Is the Italian Government aware of the autocratic position of the Vatican as stated in *La Civilta Cattolica* of April 1948: "The Roman Catholic Church convinced through its divine prerogatives of being the only true church must demand the right of freedom for herself alone . . . In some countries, Catholics will be obliged to ask full freedom for all, resigned to being forced to co-habitate where they alone should rightfully be allowed to live. The Church cannot blush for want of tolerance."

We sincerely trust that this will clarify the issue concerning the welfare and freedom of our Protestant brethren in Italy and that we will not have to go beyond this letter.[9]

This communication bore the official national endorsement of the NAE and was supplemented by the signatures of many Protestant leaders as individuals. An appointment was made with the Under Secretary of State in charge of Western European affairs. The project was discussed pro and con. Documentation was presented the State Department covering the Frascati incident and other similar happenings giving evidence of murders, stonings, and other infractions of religious liberty in Italy which constituted a violation of the guarantees in the Italian Constitution and the Treaty existing between the USA and Italy. It was requested that the NAE letter be transmitted to the Prime Minister of Italy through USA diplomatic channels. A letter to the Hon. Dean Acheson, Secretary of State, was presented which read as follows:

9. *UEA*, February 15, 1950, pp. 3, 4.

We are submitting herewith a copy of an open letter that is being sent to His Excellency Alcide de Gasperi, Prime Minister of Italy, through the courtesy of our State Department. This action, taken at the conference of National Protestant Leaders called together by the National Association of Evangelicals Committee on Religious Liberty which met in the Wardman Park Hotel January 17, 1950, is also the official action of the entire constituency of the National Association of Evangelicals in America, of the American Committee on Religious Liberty in Italy, and of the Christian Churches of North America.

Would you, on our behalf, convey this letter to His Excellency Alcide de Gasperi, Prime Minister of Italy?

We would also appreciate the continued interest of our State Department in maintaining a close watch over the compliance of the Italian Government with the Peace Treaty that they have signed.[10]

The Department of State was also apprised of the fact that if NAE's demands were ignored, action would be taken through the Congress to have the USA treaty with Italy annulled and to halt all financial aid to that country. The general public opinion at that time was such that a move on the part of the NAE might have had serious implications for foreign relations.

In addition to the presentation of the protest to the State Department the matter was officially brought to the attention of His Excellency, the Ambassador of Italy to the USA.

In every instance the representatives of the NAE were graciously received and assurances of the full cooperation of the respective government officials was promised. This incident marked the opening of channels through which the NAE has been able to render immense aid not only to its immediate constituency but to other Protestant agencies both in and out of the National Council of Churches.

At the same time another serious threat to the principle of Separation of Church and State was creating widespread concern in America. President Franklin D. Roosevelt had, as a war emergency move (December 23, 1939), appointed Mr. Myron C. Taylor as his personal envoy to the Vatican. For many years strong Roman Catholic influences in America had sought to establish formal diplomatic relations between the USA and the pseudo Church-State on the Tiber. Mr. Taylor returned to the USA soon after Mr. Roosevelt's

10. *Ibid.*, p. 8.

death in 1945, but on May 3, 1946 President Truman re-appointed him as his personal envoy.

When the war ended it was assumed by many naive evangelicals that the relationship would be discontinued. Mr. Taylor returned to Washington at about the same time the evangelicals were in their historic (1950) Wardman Park Hotel conference. Political observers were predicting that diplomatic relations with the Vatican were to be continued.

The whole matter of Envoy Taylor's representation at the Vatican was discussed and, as in the cases of approving the message to Alcide de Gasperi, there was also unanimous approval of a resolution to be sent to President Truman, not only insisting upon the recall of Mr. Taylor, but also requesting the complete dissolution of that mission:

> RESOLVED THAT, since the Protestant forces in America have seen no evidence to indicate that the appointment of Myron Taylor as the President's Special Envoy to the Vatican is either legal or of value to the American Government; but, to the contrary, his complete ignorance of even the religious bodies of Italy that came to light when he confessed to a committee in Rome that he had never heard of the Waldensians, a Protestant body active in Italy for centuries before the Reformation, causes serious question of his personal qualifications; and THAT, now that his inability to solve or make any effort to solve the problems arising from Roman Catholic persecution of American and Italian Protestants in Italy is evident;
>
> WE, therefore, again insist on the dissolution of the alleged American legation at the Vatican and the immediate recall of its head, Myron Taylor, Special Envoy of the President.

Arrangements were made to present the resolution to President Truman. Less than two hours after the resolution reached him, the White House released a statement to the effect that Mr. Taylor's "resignation" had been accepted.

It was later revealed that arrangements for the return of Mr. Taylor to Rome had been completed and certain programs had been outlined.[11] More than that, Mr. Taylor himself had asserted on Monday (January 16) that he was *not resigning and that he was returning to Rome.* Two days later the White House said that his resignation had been ac-

11. *Ibid.,* p. 4.

cepted. It may well be assumed that the NAE was fortunate in handling its resolution to the White House at this particular time. It appeared that enough additional pressure had been applied at the psychological moment to bring signal victory to the long effort made by Protestant bodies all over America to terminate this unholy alliance with the Vatican. In view of this, the following release was sent out to the press on January 19:

TAYLOR RESIGNS AS ENVOY TO THE VATICAN

Partial victory for the forces of evangelical Christianity was won this week when President Harry Truman accepted the resignation of Myron Taylor as his special envoy to the Vatican. Mr. Taylor has held the office under both Roosevelt and Truman administrations, despite the repeated and vigorous protests of all the principal evangelical denominations in America. The protests have sprung from the feeling that the maintenance of an envoy to the Roman Catholic Vatican state is a violation of the biblical and democratic concepts of separation of church and state.

The announcement of Taylor's resignation followed on the heels of a protest meeting called at the Wardman Park Hotel, Tuesday, January 17, by the Commission on Christian Liberty of the National Association of Evangelicals, and attended by a number of outstanding national Protestant leaders.

"Apparently our protest climaxed the long series of demands by Protestants that this unholy relationship between our government and the Papacy be terminated," commented Dr. Frederick C. Fowler, Commission Chairman.

"That something brought about a change in plans is indicated by the fact that, as late as Monday, Myron Taylor maintained that he would *not* resign his appointment to the Vatican," continued Dr. Fowler. "From other sources we have learned that his return trip was already planned. After our meeting on Tuesday, Mr. Taylor, for undisclosed reasons and in complete variance with his statement forty-eight hours earlier submitted his resignation, and it was accepted by the President."

Dr. Fowler concluded by saying, "While this *is* a victory, it is only one battle in a war. No plans have been announced to replace Mr. Taylor, but it may be confidently expected that enormous pressure will be exerted by the Vatican to bring this about."

Dr. Clyde W. Taylor, National Association of Evangelicals' Secretary of Affairs in Washington, stressed, "In order to counteract Catholic pressure, Christian leaders and their constituents should send wires and letters at once, congratulating President Truman for accepting the resignation and urging him to completely dissolve the mission to the Vatican."

Also sent the same day was the following letter to the President of the United States:

Dear Mr. President:

On behalf of the entire constituency of the National Association of Evangelicals we wish to congratulate you on the acceptance of the resignation of Myron C. Taylor as the representative to the Vatican.

We fully comprehend the difficulties involved in making this decision. We are also firmly convinced that great effort will be made to persuade you, as President of the United States, to appoint a successor. However, the great Protestant majority of America would urge you to completely terminate this mission and make permanent our traditional democratic principle of keeping church and state separate.

We all have complete confidence in our Ambassador to Italy, the Honorable James Dunn, and we are convinced that through this natural diplomatic channel all such affairs can be adequately channeled.

As a postscript to this incident, it should be recorded that the NAE figured largely in blocking the next political *coup d'etat* of the Vatican in this diplomatic battle. Because of continued Roman Catholic pressures on the State Department and the President, Mr. Truman on October 20, 1951 announced that he had appointed General Mark W. Clark as full-fledged ambassador to the Vatican. A diplomatic pipeline had been maintained *sub rosa* ostensibly to promote the cold war against world Communism. Now under guise of a "mobilization of the spiritual forces of the world" in the ideological conflict Protestants seemed to have suffered final defeat in their long fight.

The NAE immediately took up the gauntlet. On November 1, *United Evangelical Action* magazine carried a comprehensive study of the whole USA-Vatican story with an expose of the political aspirations of Rome. This was re-

printed and distributed by the hundreds of thousands.[12]
The Commission on Evangelical Action sponsored and promoted hundreds of mass meetings and caused hundreds of
thousands of petitions to be sent to Washington from
churches, religious organizations, conventions, regional associations, etc. Again the Washington office, cooperating
closely with Protestants and Other Americans United,
brought pressures on the press, the Senate Foreign Relations Committee, President Truman, the Congress, and
other agencies of government in Washington. Because of
the rising tide of public opinion, General Clark in January
1952 announced his decision not to accept if appointed.
Mr. Truman then withdrew his nomination and although
he indicated he might make another in deference to the
will of the people, he never did.

Protestants across America for years had sought an
answer to Knights of Columbus newspaper and magazine
propaganda for the Roman Catholic Church. This widely-
known frateral order had carried paid advertisements which
cleverly discredited Protestantism in the eyes of the reading public. No Protestant agency seemed to have the answer. In 1955 the NAE Commission on Evangelical Action
prepared a similar series of advertisements based on the
idea that the best answer to Roman Catholic propaganda
was the Gospel message of salvation as presented in the
Holy Scriptures. The ads were written in the language of
"the man in the street" and carried such headings as
"Strange Tales About Protestants," "Who Wrote the Bible
Anyway?" "To Which Church Did the Apostles Belong?"
"Protestantism: Key to Democracy," "Who is a Christian?" "Don't Protestants Believe in Confession?" "Why
Protestants Go to Church," "Was Mary the Mother of God?"
"Faith of our Fathers," etc. The ads make the specific
suggestion that the reader attend a Bible-believing Protestant church of his own choice. A coupon request for a
free pamphlet on the theme of the ad is being used by thousands. The advertising is usually sponsored by local church
groups and appears once a week. A series of thirty is
available.

Relations of the NAE with the United States government
reached an all-time high in cordiality in 1953 when, on July

12. *Shall America Bow to the Pope of Rome?* by James DeForest
Murch (1951).

2, a delegation from the National Association of Evangelicals was received by President Dwight D. Eisenhower at the White House.[13] The President discussed with NAE leaders the need for a moral and religious base for the guarantee and perpetuity of our American freedoms and affixed his signature to a document which called for a national reaffirmation of faith in God, the Author of man's freedom, repentance from sin and a new dedication to the task of bringing freedom to the world. Participating in the interviews were Dr. Paul S. Rees, Dr. R. L. Decker, Dr. Clyde W. Taylor, Dr. Frederick Curtis Fowler, Dr. James DeForest Murch, Senator Frank Carlson, Representative Walter K. Judd, Mr. Herbert J. Lorber, Mr. F. O. Masten, Mr. Charles E. Kellogg and Mr. James Powell-Tuck.

Since then the press, the radio, business and labor leaders — in fact, all major factors in American public life have become increasingly aware of the voice of evangelical Christianity. It is repeatedly heard in the nation's capital through the NAE's Office of Public Affairs. The record shows a vital expression of opinion on —

Indian affairs — pleas for religious liberty for non-Catholic Indians.

Civil rights — maintenance of the freedoms promised the individual citizen by the Bill of Rights of the Constitution.

Public schools — opposition to Federal aid and control; preservation of rights for Bible reading and distribution; released time for religious instruction.

Immigration — the preservation of reasonable limitations on the type and number of immigrants to be admitted to American citizenship. Immediately after the close of the War the Washington office processed over 1,000 Displaced Persons from Europe who desired to become citizens of the USA.

Liquor — encouragement of legislation restricting the advertising, sale and manufacture of intoxicating liquors for beverage purposes.

Salacious literature — advocacy of the outlawry of the sale and distribution of obscene and pornographic books and magazines.

Communism — encouragement of investigations of subversive activities, anti-Communist propaganda and the

13. *UEA*, August 1, 1953, p. 1 ff.

enactment of legislation protecting the nation and its citizens from the menace of Communism.

Statism and Fascism — opposition to governmental regimentation and bureaucratic controls.

Practically every phase of national well-being which involves morality and religion has been dealt with by the Commission on Evangelical Action and the NAE's Office of Public Affairs.

It is the conviction of evangelicals that the voice of God must be heard in the affairs of the nation and that His providential aid must be sought if He is to continue to preserve the liberties and happiness of its people. It is to this end that the NAE concerns itself with public affairs.

XII

EVANGELICALS AND HUMAN WELFARE

Evangelicals, as a whole, have always been interested in the social implications of the Gospel. They give primacy to the saving power of the Gospel in the life of the individual and hold the chief concern of the church lies in the supernatural and spiritual realm. In their best tradition, however, evangelicals have been leaders in the application of the principles of Christianity to every aspect of life.

The eighteenth century Evangelical Revival in Great Britain under the Wesleys saw not only fasting, prayer, Bible study and revival but special ministries to those in prison and a strong stand against slavery in the Empire. The evangelicals of that time did far more for the masses than did the "liberal" elements in the Anglican church. J. Russell Bready in his book, *This Freedom — Whence?* piles the evidence mountain high in proof of this thesis.

During the "Great Awakening" of the early 1800's in America there was revival but there was also the inauguration of inter-church cooperation through the World Evangelical Alliance with consequent organization for reform by social action. In 1826 the American Society for the Promotion of Temperance was organized and became the forerunner of the Prohibition movement. Evangelicals were in the forefront of the battle to write into the law of the land the Christian attitude toward intoxicants. The injustice of slaveholding was recognized by the great majority of evangelicals and in the War Between the States thousands of them gave their life's blood to bring freedom to the Negro in America.[1]

Evangelicals have a social conscience but they revolt at the idea of using the temporal power of the church to force world revolution according to any humanly-devised plan. They are particularly fearsome of such man-made ideas which have no adequate theological foundation.

1. *A History of American Revivals* by Frank G. Beardsley (1912).

153

While admitting the social and political implications of their Christian convictions they believe that this relationship must forever rest on the meaning of the content of the biblical revelation. They are certain that men who are not thoroughly biblical in their views on God, creation, man, sin, redemption and the church are incapable of guiding Christian thought and action in these fields.

Dr. C. Gregg Singer, then of Salem College, dealing with this issue in *United Evangelical Action,* reminded his readers that Reformation leaders

> were in agreement that the Church must not have secular power as had been claimed by the Medieval Papacy, but they also insisted that government as a divine institution was bound to enforce divine law and that the Church must exercise a moral influence in political affairs. While Church and State operate in different spheres, and while the spiritual realm is superior to the temporal, these differences are not of such a nature that these two institutions were not mutually dependent and could act without reference to each other.

Dr. Singer concluded,

> If evangelicals will formulate a philosophy of social action on the basis of an orthodox theology, once again the Church will become the mighty force for righteousness in the nation and a mighty testimony to the full orbed Gospel of Jesus Christ. Nothing less than such a testimony is adequate for the cultural crisis which has overtaken the western world. Christians will then have a more biblical perspective of the needs of humanity and of the policies which our nation must follow if it is to remain true to its divine purposes and functions. . . . They will see that there is a Christian social justice for an industrial age and they will be able to speak with authority in such matters in a way in which the liberals could never speak because their concept of social justice was not based upon the revealed righteousness of a sovereign God.[2]

At the time of the advent of the National Association of Evangelicals there was widespread criticism of the FCCCA because of its continued meddling in social and political affairs.[3] (See Chapter III, pp. 44-47.) The leadership of the Council was thoroughly committed to the Rauschenbusch interpretation of the Social Gospel and was unquestionably majoring in mundane matters.

While the new NAE called the churches back to the primacy of Gospel preaching for individual salvation and placed renewed emphasis upon the supernatural and the spiritual,

2. *UEA,* January 1, 1949, pp. 5-7.
3. *The Case Against the Federal Council of Churches* by Chester A. Tulga (1948), *The Ecclesiastical Octopus* by Ernest Gordon (1945), and *Death in the Pot* by J. Elwin Wright (1944).

it is significant to note that one of its first concerns was for "Moral Welfare and Social Service." The Committee on Policy and Fields of Endeavor reporting to the Constitutional Convention on May 7, 1943, said: "The policy of this Convention has been to outline general principles which will form the basis of fellowship and action for its members. It is obviously necessary that the same procedure be followed when dealing with the subject of moral questions."[4] In the same report there was set up a program of "War Services" through which evangelicals might minister in the name of Christ to the thousands of men in the armed services. There was intimation of the need for relief to those in foreign lands which had been devastated by World War II.

At the Columbus convention in 1944 a "Commission for Post War Relief" was authorized. Accordingly two meetings were held at the Bankers Club in New York City at which details were formulated and discussed looking to the immediate establishment of European relief work.[5]

The first meeting in New York, held on June 21, was attended by the following persons: Mr. Philip A. Benson, president of the Dime Savings Bank in Brooklyn; Mr. John G. Becker, president of Bible Magazine, Inc.; Mr. A. Herman Armerding of the New Jersey Stoker Corp., Newark, N. J.; Dr. Donald Grey Barnhouse of Tenth Presbyterian Church, Philadelphia; the Rev. J. J. Hiemenga, Christian Reformed Church, Paterson, N. J.; the Rev. William H. Nagel, executive secretary for the Northwest Region of NAE, Portland, Oregon; Mr. Robert F. Nelson, vice-president of the Arma Corporation of Brooklyn; the Rev. I. V. Neprash, executive secretary of the Russian Missionary Service, Philadelphia; the Rev. Nicolas Nikoloff of the Assembly of God, North Bergen, N. J.; Mr. Erling C. Olsen of the Fitch Investment Service, New York City; the Rev. A. C. Snead, foreign secretary of the Christian and Missionary Alliance, New York City; Dr. David Toong of the Chinese Students' Christian Association in North America, New York City; Dr. J. Elwin Wright, field secretary of NAE; and Mr. K. Paul Yphantis of the Greek American Missionary Association, Boston.

Several others attended the second meeting held on August 15. These included Bishop L. R. Marston, president

4. *UEA*, July 1, 1943, p. 5.
5. *Ibid.*, September 1, 1944, p. 1.

of NAE; Mr. J. Willison Smith, Jr., secretary of NAE; the Rev. Torrey M. Johnson of the Mid-West Bible Church in Chicago; Mr. Torrey Mosvold, president of Neptune Shipping, Inc., and the Rev. Clyde W. Taylor, secretary for Missions of NAE.

Mr. Philip A. Benson, formerly president of the American Bankers' Association, accepted the national chairmanship of the Commission. A strong and representative group of industrialists and leaders in church and mission work made up the membership of the Commission.

At the 1945 Chicago convention the "War Relief Commission" was officially recognized as an NAE-related agency and became a permanent part of its ever-enlarging service program. Offices were set up in New York City at 536 West Forty-sixth Street and in Philadelphia at 2124 Lincoln Liberty Building, government approvals were secured, a processing program was set up, and warehouse and dock facilities were secured in cooperation with the Salvation Army. Mr. Frank D. Lombar, an experienced businessman, took over the task of perfecting the organization and promoting its interests throughout the nation.[6] Soon appeals began to bring thousands of pounds of clothing and food from all parts of the nation. The Commission was literally swamped with relief goods long before the Allied governments were ready to use them. Liberal gifts of money likewise proved the hearts of evangelicals could be touched by the physical needs of the world. A unique feature of evangelical relief, however, was that every gift of clothing was to contain a Gospel tract and that everything was to be presented to the needy in the name of Christ.

After five years of emergency "War Relief" it became apparent that there would always be a need for an organization of this type. Accordingly the name was changed to "World Relief Commission." Mr. Lombar in his report to the Indianapolis Convention in 1950 said:

> During the past five years the gifts of evangelical Christians in America for relieving the suffering of their brethren in other lands has amounted to a total of

6. With executive committee approval the NAE War Relief Commission had begun in a limited way in 1944. On January 1, 1945, with Mr. Frank D. Lombar as executive director, it became a full-time operation. Its first Convention-elected personnel was chosen at Chicago, May 1-3, 1945. NAE Convention Report, 1945, p. 32.

$526,000.00 — more than one hundred thousand dollars a year. More important than the hundreds of lives saved from starvation is the revival of a Gospel testimony and the saving of a Christian witness — all the result of work by this Commission.

Our brethren in other lands still need our help and the brethren in this country seem both willing and able to help them materially and spiritually. These unfortunate brethren are still too poor to buy, too proud to beg, and too honest to steal. How else can they get the bare necessities of life unless we, who have so much, share God's plenty to us with them? Or shall we bring this work of Christian mercy and evangelism to a close? Perhaps Paul's injunction to the Galatian Christians is our answer: "And let us not be weary in well doing; for in due season we shall reap, if we faint not. As we have therefore opportunity, let us do good unto all men, especially unto them who are of the household of faith."[7]

With the war in Korea in 1950 the program was expanded. A West Coast processing and shipping office was opened. Central receiving agencies were established in various sections of the country. Cooperative relationships were set up with the large Central Mennonite Relief agency in which several NAE denominations participated. Upon the retirement of Mr. Lombar in 1955 the Commission elected Mr. Wendell L. Rockey to carry on as its Director.

Literally millions of dollars worth of food, clothing and money have gone out to bless the needy in the name of Christ because of the evangelical conscience in "moral welfare and social service."

In the field of business and industry the National Association of Evangelicals has furnished Christian leadership of the first order. Dr. Irving E. Howard, writing in *Christian Economics*, credits evangelicals with pioneering in the development of industrial chaplaincies.[8] That great Christian layman, Mr. R. G. LeTourneau, whose earth-moving machinery is to be found around the world, after experimenting in "shop meetings" for a number of years, in 1941 employed a full-time industrial chaplain, the first of the kind in America. This man programmed regular religious services and instruction classes in the far-flung factory system of the LeTourneau industries. The 1944 NAE con-

7. NAE Convention Report, 1950; *UEA*, May 1, 1950, p. 16.
8. *Christian Economics*, March 8, 1955.

vention in Columbus, upon the advice of a number of evangelical manufacturers, set up a Commission on Industrial Chaplaincies.

The Commission had its first meeting in the LaSalle Hotel, Chicago, in October of that year.[9] Numbered among the membership of the new body were Mr. A. Herman Armerding, president of the New Jersey Stoker Corporation of Newark, N. J.; Mr. Walter W. Block, president of the Quaker Stretcher Co. of Kenosha, Wis.; the Rev. Don R. Falkenberg, director of the Bible Meditation League, of Columbus, Ohio; Mr. Samuel A. Fulton, president of the Fulton Co., Milwaukee, Wis.; Mr. John E. Mitchell, Jr., of the John E. Mitchell Co., Dallas, Tex.; Mr. Torrey Mosvold, of the Neptune Shipping, Inc., New York City; Mr. Robert F. Nelson, executive vice president of the Arma Corporation, Brooklyn, N. Y.; and Mr. Rollin M. Severance, president of the Severance Tool Industries, Inc., Saginaw, Mich. All members were present or represented by associates with the exception of Mr. Fulton, who was occupied with a meeting of the Gideon Cabinet at Elkhart, Ind. Mr. Armerding was chosen chairman. Shortly thereafter a full-time director was chosen in the person of Mr. Ernest L. Chase, a well-known consultant in public relations.

The *Christian Century*, amazed at this venture of evangelicals into such a field of endeavor, carried an editorial "Are the Evangelicals Being Taken for a Ride?" It expressed the fear that this move might be "an attempt of employers to use the office of the ministry to keep the workers docile under substandard wages (in 1945!)." Had the editors of this "liberal" journal known the sincere motives actuating both the leadership of the NAE and the business men they could not have written in this vein.

An important contribution was made in this field under the leadership of Mr. Chase. Classes and courses for the preparation of ministers in this specialized field were provided for theological seminaries and Bible colleges. For a time a placement bureau was maintained. Eventually experience proved that industry, cooperating with ministerial training schools, could satisfactorily meet all needs without further guidance from the NAE. The industrial chaplaincy idea continued to grow. Today there are hundreds of men engaged in such ministries under various designa-

9. *UEA*, November 1, 1944, p. 1.

tions and industry is finding that with "God as its Partner" it can solve many of its management-labor problems and make a real contribution to the Church and the Christian community.

An interesting evangelical experiment in labor welfare is the Christian Labor Association.[10] Although it has no connection with the NAE as such, the CLA has frequently cooperated in its Social Action programs. The CLA was organized by a group of workers in the Christian Reformed Church under the leadership of Joseph Gritter. It is recognized by the National Labor Relations Board and other Federal and State labor agencies as a bona fide representative of evangelical thinking in this field.

The Christian Labor Association believes in regard to—

Wealth: A more even distribution of wealth is necessary for the welfare of society.

Employer-Employee Relations: Employees should have a larger share in the control of the production and of the distribution of the goods which they have helped to produce.

Class-Conflict: Complete cooperation between employers and employees should be based on the biblical conception of equality, liberty and brotherhood.

Sin: Sin is the underlying basis of all discord between employers and employees.

Collective Bargaining: All working people should be members of labor organizations of their own choosing, and such organizations of workers should have the right of representation in the bargaining process.

Labor Strike: Labor problems should be solved through cooperation, mediation and arbitration, and a strike sanctioned only as a last resort.

Wages: The workingman has a right to demand that the actual profits of industry should be considered in the determination of wages, in so far as this is consistent with a safe margin of business capital-forming and capital turn-over.

Obligations of Employees: The workingman has obligations towards his employer as well as to society at large, including the duty to be a steward of the abilities, capacities, and the wealth entrusted to his care.

Sunday Labor: No "unnecessary work" should be performed on Sunday; that is, work in which material

10. *Ibid.,* October 15, 1946, p. 9.

gain for the employer (and to a lesser extent for the employee) is the only consideration.

Legal Workingday: State and federal legislations are necessary for the establishment of the eight-hour workingday as the legal workingday.

In 1947 one of the outstanding theologians of the new evangelical movement startled evangelicals with a small but dynamic volume entitled *The Uneasy Conscience of Modern Fundamentalism.*   Dr. Carl F. H. Henry said forcibly:

> What is almost wholly unintelligible to the naturalistic and idealistic groups, burdened as they are for a new world order, is the apparent lack of any social passion in Protestant Fundamentalism.   On this evaluation, Fundamentalism is the modern priest and Levite, by-passing suffering humanity.
>
> The picture is clear when one brings into focus such admitted social evils as aggressive warfare, racial hatred and intolerance, the liquor traffic, and exploitation of labor or management, whichever it may be.
>
> The social reform movements dedicated to the elimination of such evils do not have the active, let alone vigorous, cooperation of large segments of evangelical Christianity.   In fact, Fundamentalist churches increasingly have repudiated the very movements whose most energetic efforts have gone into an attack on such social ills. . . .
>
> In a company of more than one hundred representative evangelical pastors, the following question was proposed: "How many of you, during the past six months, have preached a sermon devoted in large part to a condemnation of such social evils as aggressive warfare, racial hatred and intolerance, the liquor traffic, exploitation of labor or management, or the like — a sermon containing not merely an incidental or illustrative reference, but directed mainly against such evils and proposing the framework in which you think solution is possible?" Not a single hand was raised in response. . . .
>
> The failure of the evangelical movement to react favorably on any widespread front to campaign against social evils had led, finally, to a suspicion on the part of non-evangelicals that there is something in the very nature of Fundamentalism which makes a world ethical view impossible.   The conviction is widespread that Fundamentalism takes too pessimistic a view of human nature to make a social program practicable.

This modern mind-set, insisting that evangelical super-
naturalism has inherent within it an ideological fault
which precludes any vital social thrust, is one of the most
disturbing dividing lines in contemporary thought.   In
the struggle for a world mind which will make global
order and brotherhood a possibility, contemporary spec-
ulation has no hearing whatever for a viewpoint which
it suspects has no world program.   It dismisses Fundamentalism with the thought that, in this expression of
the Great Tradition, humanitarianism has evaporated
from Christianity.[11]

In 1951 a Forum on Social Action was included in the program of the NAE national convention.[12]   By courtesy of
the Commission on Evangelical Action the Forum occupied
the Commission's allotted time.   As an outgrowth of the
interest generated in these historic sessions a permanent
Commission on Social Action was set up in the NAE with
Dr. Henry as its chairman.   Among the issues discussed at
Chicago that year were the Politico-Economic Problem,
Labor Relations and Race Relations.

Concerning   the   Politico-Economic   Problem,   it   was
pointed out that three relevant views are possible: (1)
Christianity is not wedded to any specific politico-economic
view, although some are more desirable than others; (2)
Christianity is wedded to capitalism of some type, to private
property, to free enterprise, to the profit motive; (3) Christianity is wedded to a non-capitalistic view (perhaps socialism).

President Fowler of the NAE, vice chairman of the All-
American Conference to Combat Communism, pointed out
that Russia was taken over for Communism by 20,000
party Communists, and that there are today in the United
States 55,000 Communists.   Dr. Fowler, while urging the
importance of combating Communism in the interest of the
American way of life, urged also the necessity of distin-

11. *The Uneasy Conscience of Modern Fundamentalism* by Carl F.
H. Henry (1948).

12. *UEA*, May 1, 1951, pp. 14-16.   The report on this conference is
used at length for two reasons: (1) Historically, this was the first
time that a deliberative inter-church body of evangelicals had realistically faced modern social problems in the light of Holy Scripture,
and (2) the discussions reflect evangelical thinking in the areas concerned.   The views expressed are not to be considered in any sense
the official views of the National Association of Evangelicals or its
Commission on Social Action.

guishing Christianity from democracy as it is customarily defined today, and insisted that our nation is a republic.

Dr. Gordon H. Clark, professor of philosophy at Butler University, emphasized that the Scriptures are the only rule of practice, and must determine this subject of politico-economic alignment, also. Christianity is wedded to no form in the sense that Christians are obligated to obey all governments except when civil disobedience, about which the Bible says little, is based on a conflict between the divine and human will. Dr. Clark stressed the noteworthy absence from the New Testament of social reform and political action, and the concentration, instead, upon the gift of repentance as the cure for the problems of morality. With righteousness as the central issue, the Christian can favor some politico-economic views, oppose others. Dr. Clark referred to the confiscation of gold in 1933 as a Communistic trend, declared that the income tax, first proposed by Marx, is an essential part of Communism. He too urged caution in defending merely democracy, which can be as totalitarian as any dictatorship. Emphasizing the corruption of man, he said increased power should not be put into the hands of corrupt officials, for this brings totalitarianism, which persecutes Christianity. He reported that Jesus condemned the socialist who did not put his money out at interest, commended the capitalist who did and spoke against the communistic view in the principle: "To him that *hath* shall be given . . ."

Dr. J. Edwin Orr, world evangelist and author of a dissertation on the social influence of the 1858-59 revival in Great Britain, pointed out, with regard to identifying Christianity and the American way of life, that Canadians would have to regard as treason any such demand, and we should be cautious of putting the matter thus, on biblical ground. He criticized *laissez faire* (unrestrained) capitalism, for exploitation of the poor and of the misery of others as condemned by the Bible; on the other hand, man is entitled to a just return on his investment, and free enterprise is not wrong. Dr. Orr spoke first of the social impetus derived historically from the evangelical movement. The first trade union was formed by evangelicals as a protest against low salaries; Lord Shaftsbury worked for social reform; evangelicals introduced the workmen's compensation act, penal reforms, and made slavery impossible by buying out the slave runners. Dr. Orr then spoke of the movement to

Christian Socialism in Great Britain, pointing out that the Labor party, founded by a believer, has two wings, the Marxist and the Christian. The majority of British people, including the Christians, favor socialized medicine, he reported, but the movement is throttling free enterprise and initiative.

Dr. John W. Bradbury, editor of the *Watchman-Examiner* (Northern Baptist), spoke briefly on collectivism, declaring that it is social action on the part of the group, is as old as the patriarchal family and was their economy (cf. Joseph in charge of the granaries), was practiced in the initiation of Christianity when everything—probably due to an emergency—was held in common, and has been a vital topic of Christian practice through the Christian ages. He asserted that the exploitation of millions of people for power is the curse of *laissez faire* capitalism.

The discussion proceeded by questions from the floor, after which the chair pointed out that the issue had not been directly faced as to whether there is something inherent in the collectivistic view which does violence to the biblical demand upon the believer, *i.e.*, whether biblical Christianity must oppose itself to the drift toward socialism no less than to communism. It was pointed out that the NAE at its 1950 convention had already adopted a resolution supporting private property.

Regarding Labor Relations three viewpoints were presented by spokesmen for labor. Mr. Joseph Gritter of Grand Rapids, Mich., secretary of the Christian Labor Association of the United States, pressed the viewpoint that the biblical principles which employers and employees must heed can be met only in an organization of believers, so that the laborer can be unfailingly true to Christ and God's will in labor only by a Christian union. He outlined the principles of his organization, with its objection to Sunday labor, its approval of a fair margin of profit but not of exploitation and excess profits, its opposition to slow-downs, unfair impositions on employers, excessive demands, yet emphasized that men should share in the fruit of their labor through old age insurance of some form (social security pension). In such an organization, conflicting interests become mutual and communal interests. But above all, men serve God by the labor of their hands, and a sound emphasis deals with human beings as both spiritual and physical creatures, disregarding neither soul nor body.

The Rev. C. W. Boyer of Dayton, Ohio, secretary of the committee on industrial relations for the Mennonite Brethren in Christ, pointed to the big stick in collective bargaining as the reason that his people could not participate, and abjured the spirit of retaliation in all human relations. He asserted that his approach and that of Mr. Gritter's organization had much in common, but emphasized opposition to any coercive method to compel an opponent to do good, whereas the Mennonite approach is to love an opponent to do him good. Mr. Boyer pointed out that the AFI has advised its groups to respect the Mennonite view against union obligations, and that during labor-management disputes it permits Mennonite workers to continue without picketing, as neutrals.

Mr. Homer Humble, of Mobile, Alabama, ninth vice-president of the International Brotherhood of Pulp, Sulphate, and Paper Workers, AFL, pointed out that the AFL is composed of independent labor unions federated for protection, and that local unions retain complete autonomy and are not subject to overhead dictation. He declared a cleaning up of both management and labor is needed, and that the labor movement should be the practical right arm of evangelical Christianity. He held that the evangelical approach to labor should be friendly, with an interest in souls but also in bodies and physical needs; he pointed out the collusion of Catholicism abroad with great wealth. He declared that Christ was against special privilege and for the downtrodden.

The representative of management was Mr. John Bolten, Sr. of the Bolta Company, in Lawrence, Mass. Mr. Bolten said there have been sins on both sides, and that management was once most guilty, but now labor is the culprit. He declared that the word security is a Marxist term not used by Christ. Referring to Ephesians 6, regarding the relationship of servants and masters, he declared that his responsibility is to God rather than to labor, and that Christian management is to consider its work a stewardship which carries a responsibility commensurate with one's authority. The tensions in industry he traced to a breakdown in America of the laboring man's spiritual life and of the American home, so that there is a tendency to seek a total security for life by way of compensation in the economic area.

During the discussion, Dr. Clark took exception to statements that Christ identified Himself with labor; he replied that our Lord stirred up no class strife and that the Bible specifically declares that God is the God of Abraham, although Abraham is one of the wealthiest men in the Bible. The discussion also concerned the merits of specific Christian labor organizations and the secular alternatives. Mr. Gritter emphasized that the neutral organizations divide religion and daily life, and are not bound to the Word of God. Mr. Humble replied that one need not subscribe to union obligations to be a member of AFL, that a man can witness better in a non-separatist organization, and that the separatist organizations are fore-doomed to failure or ineffective labor action.

The final forum was on the problem of Race Relations. Dr. Henry pointed out that despite the immense Roman Catholic propaganda concerning a welcome to the Negro, Catholicism had attracted only 500,000 American Negroes in unimpressive contrast with the much larger number identified with Protestant denominations. Rev. Gilbert James said that two thirds of the world's population is colored so that the whites are the minority, and the problem may yet turn into the white problem. Erwin Wedel, national director of the Pioneer Gospel Mission to Negroes, said that Negroes have comparatively no opportunity to attend Bible institutes and Christian colleges in the North, and that this throttles the training of evangelical Negro leadership, which can do effective indigenous evangelical work among its own people. Dr. Roy S. Nicholson, president of the General Conference of the Wesleyan Methodist Church and a native of South Carolina, was asked to speak for the viewpoint that class distinction cannot be swiftly overthrown, and that evangelism can be accomplished in the face of segregation. Although not speaking for all Negroes, the Rev. William Houston, one of the Negro delegates to the NAE convention, took the position that a violent overthrow of segregation would furnish only a temporary solution, and that the attack on the problem must be pressed jointly with a spiritual solution. Dr. George A. Turner, professor of English Bible at Asbury Theological Seminary, took the ground that there is no Christian segregation and that evangelicals are obliged to press the case against segregation simultaneously with evangelism.

At the conclusion of the sessions, a summary of the week's activities was given by Dr. Henry and it was learned that throughout the week a representative of the State Department had attended as an observer, and he was asked for comments. He remarked that this earnest discussion of social problems by evangelical leaders was in his opinion one of the most significant movements on the horizon and that the spirit in which the participants had shared their differences and the earnest concern for spiritual solution was gratifying. The delegates, without exception, voiced the opinion that the work of the forum must be extended, and voted to recommend the appointment of a committee to carry forward the work.

Dr. Henry observed that the big agreement of all participants was that in contrast with the liberal gospel the effective attack upon social problems could come only through an emphasis on what liberalism conceals—the substitutionary redemptive death of Christ for sinners. Secondly, he pointed out that evangelicals who begin at this point will not agree, therefore, on the content nor strategy of Christian ethics at many points, and inquired whether an evangelical, who defines social problems and proposes a solution in the same terms in which liberalism does, is actually performing evangelical social action. He pointed out further that during some of the panels competing issues had not been focused as sharply as desirable, and inquired whether the time had now come for evangelical teachers of Christian ethics and social science to move in and carry forward a more technical approach to these problems from the theoretical side.

The Convention created a separate Commission on Social Action, naming able and distinguished evangelicals, who were to arrange for the panel discussions for the next year when, in accord with the desire of the Chicago meetings, action would be given to the issue of church and state, war and peace, and more time to the political economic issue.[13]

While there is still much to be accomplished before evangelicals' "uneasy conscience" is assuaged in the field of Social Action, nevertheless their critics cannot justifiably accuse them of quiescence in this field.

13. In 1956 Dr. S. Richey Kamm succeeded Dr. Henry as chairman of the Commission.

The Evangelical Welfare Agency is rendering an effective social service.[14] It had its origin in the city of Chicago in 1950 when evangelicals became aware of the fact that the Roman Catholic Church was about the only distinctly religious agency cooperating with the Juvenile Court in the placement of foundling children for adoption. A study of the situation revealed that the same was true in placing orphans for foster care, in cases of juvenile delinquency, and in the care of the destitute. A few concerned individuals got together for prayer and study, seeking the leading of the Lord.

After canvassing the situation thoroughly the group made application to the Illinois Department of State for a license to operate in this field. The Department, aware of the fact that similar attempts of this kind had ended in failure, required that the group incorporate and affiliate with some national body which would guarantee stability for the future. Application was made to the Midwest Region of the National Association of Evangelicals and thus was provided the required backing in the sight of the state and nation. The connection proved mutually satisfactory. In May, 1950, the State of Illinois chartered the Evangelical Welfare Agency. It immediately went to work caring for children assigned to its care by the courts. In the first two years the EWA in Chicago cared for about one hundred and twenty-five children in foster homes and placed many babies for adoption. The offices and budget of the EWA soon outgrew the Midwest Regional offices and now operates as a self-supporting unit of ever-increasing proportions. Pittsburgh, Los Angeles, and other cities called for advice in setting up similar agencies and now the idea is spreading throughout the nation. Dr. Harold L. Lindquist has given valuable leadership in this important development. The reorganized Social Action Commission is now providing guidance to other groups desiring to set up agencies similar to EWA. Such agencies will affiliate with the NAE through the Social Action Commission for a national pattern of welfare work.

If there ever was a day when evangelicals were concerned only with evangelization, that day has passed. It is true that the Apostle Paul and other early church leaders did not organize Social Action agencies to oppose slavery,

14. Promotional brochure, Evangelical Welfare Agency (1955).

gladiatorial combats and other social sins of the day. The church in those days was largely an "underground" organization and was not free to give its testimony in the forum. In the Old Testament, however, the prophets declared God's will with respect to all aspects of government and community life. Evangelicals in this day are increasingly conscious of the fact that preaching alone or mere loyalty to an orthodox theology will not absolve them from moral responsibility in the area of citizenship. They believe that salvation begins, but does not end with the individual's transformation; that new life in Christ demands new attitudes and relationships with all men. They realize that the Saviour commanded His followers to watch as well as pray, to work as well as watch and to *occupy* until I come." While having no tolerance for a liberal theological position nor toward atheistic humanism in church or state; while repudiating merely humanitarian ends or the ultimacy of "the kingdom of God on earth" the evangelicals of nineteen hundred and now are humanitarians in the very best sense of that term, and are aggressively concerned in building a better world by the Christian methods of enlightenment, persuasion and exemplification.

XIII

THE EVANGELICAL PRESS

From the beginning of the National Association of Evangelicals for United Action at St. Louis, its leaders recognized the necessity for a journal which would be a voice for evangelical Christianity in America, promoting the interests of the new association and keeping evangelicals informed concerning trends in religion and society.

Accordingly, a modest four page 10½ x 14½ "bulletin" titled, *United Evangelical Action,* made its appearance on August 1, 1942 bearing the name of the Rev. John A. Huffman as editor. It was published irregularly until the time of the Constitutional Convention in the spring of 1943.

In the issue of May 4 an optimistic announcement was made concerning enlargement. The NAEUA Executive Committee authorized the editor to formulate a definite editorial and business policy for a "national newspaper covering the entire field of evangelical journalism." The plan envisioned a weekly with a financial underwriting of $10,000 per year, growing support from subscribers, advertisers and conservative business men, with a big public launching at the coming Constitutional Convention.

Early in this convention the Executive Committee appointed a Publications Committee of three, headed by Dr. Walter Vail Watson, of Buffalo, N. Y., to consider the proposals. A "model" issue in eight-column, eight-page newspaper format (dated June 1) was distributed and Dr. Harold J. Ockenga presented the plea for the expanded journal at the Convention. Some 3,600 annual subscriptions at $1.00 each were received on promise to pay at a later date. The response must have been disappointing and the committee, faced with the stern realities of financial limitations and journalistic technicalities, took no definite action on a future program.

Dr. Watson in the next issue of *United Evangelical Action* intimated that the committee was under fire because of delays in producing the weekly "newspaper covering the entire field of evangelical journalism." However, he was not discouraged. He said, "But there has been no lack of direction in the minds of the men whom God has raised up to lead us. With so many showing such a vital interest from so many divergent groups of evangelicals, it is imperative that the movement must take form and develop under the guidance of the Holy Spirit." He saw the new journal as "something unique in religious journalism"— promoting the movement, of course, but "informing its readers of trends and accomplishments in all areas related to the areas of united action" carrying "definitive articles of great variety of authorship and emphasis" and a news coverage second to none in the religious field.[1]

This noble vision was not immediately realized. The newspaper limped along with irregular publication dates. The name of the first editor disappeared from the masthead. In January 1944 the publication office, which had been functioning in Canton, Ohio, was moved to Boston, Mass., where Dr. J. Elwin Wright and Dr. Ockenga gave such time as they could spare from their busy lives to editorial supervision. In August 1944 the unwieldy newspaper format gave way to the more popular tabloid style. The names of assistants to Dr. Wright appeared at intervals—Mr. Charles W. Campbell, Dr. Charles G. Chilton, the Rev. Gerald E. Richter. The publication began to issue regularly twice a month on the first and fifteenth.

Realizing that the time was long past due when the NAE should produce an official organ which would be a real credit to the organization and the cause which it represented, the Executive Committee issued a call (July 1, 1945) to Dr. James DeForest Murch, of Cincinnati, Ohio, long associated with the Standard Publishing Company in varied capacities and widely recognized as an author and editor of distinction, to become its editor. Offices were moved to Cincinnati and with the issue of August 1 *United Evangelical Action* appeared in standard magazine format.

Today the journal is recognized far and wide as an important "voice of Evangelical Christianity in America." It is:

Informative — providing up-to-date and comprehensive news service on evangelical concerns, persons, and events.

1. *UEA*, July 1, 1943.

Educative—defining and interpreting trends and movements in the whole religious world. Articles dealing with orthodoxy, neo-orthodoxy, modernism, liberalism, secularism, naturalism, apostasy, worldliness, formalism, ecumenicity, communism, socialism, internationalism, racism and every modern concern appear in its columns.

Propagative—sowing propaganda for the evangelical faith and united evangelical action.

Constructive—concerning itself primarily with the common tasks of evangelicals and the upbuilding of the kingdom of God.

Servicive—using its columns to advance the aims and programs of the NAE and its affiliated organizations and all agencies advancing the evangelical cause in general.

Productive—yielding results in a thousand ways to the glory of God.

Religious leaders, colleges, seminaries, national and regional religious organizations, and the religious and secular press subscribe for it and frequently refer to it. Reprints of its leading articles and editorials have reached hundreds of thousands beyond its circulation and it is constantly quoted in college and seminary seminars, and in official gatherings of denominational and inter-church organizations.

The aggressive journalism of *Action* magazine has been marked by some very interesting accomplishments. In 1952 when President Truman appointed an American envoy to the Vatican, the editor produced a special edition carrying a feature article, "Shall America Bow to the Pope of Rome?" which gave the whole authentic story of USA's diplomatic dealings with the Vatican and stated the case for the American principle regarding Church and State. It was a journalistic "scoop" of the first order. Reprints were used by the hundreds of thousands in the Protestant campaign which effectually halted the President's venture.[2] In 1952 when the National Council of Churches launched its Revised Standard Version of the Bible, *Action* magazine was the first religious journal in America to print scholarly views of evangelical scholars pro and con, an objective achievement which called forth words of appreciation from

2. *Shall America Bow to the Pope of Rome?* by James DeForest Murch (1952).

many of the religious leaders of the nation.[3] The journal
was instrumental in encouraging a movement of evangelical
scholars to achieve a more satisfactory translation which
might be of general acceptance by all Protestants.   This
movement is now in the developmental stage.

Features of major interest in a given year included: (1)
a drive to get recognition of evangelicals on the Voice of
America, a government operated worldwide radio propaganda agency in the cold war with Russia, (2) a series of
articles on religious persecution in Italy, Colombia, and
Spain, (3) another on "Seven Crucial Issues Confronting
American Protestantism," (4) a campaign against the
publication and sale of pornographic literature, (5) widespread distribution of critiques of the National Council of
Churches[4] and the World Council of Churches[5] which give
the commonly accepted evangelical view of these great
inter-church organizations, and state the apologetic for the
existence of the National Association of Evangelicals and
the World Evangelical Fellowship.

In controversial matters it should be borne in mind that
United Evangelical Action does not speak officially for the
NAE unless pronouncements are specifically designated as
official.   Every issue carries the statement: "All editorials,
sermons and articles appearing in *Action* magazine represent the personal views of the authors.   They do not neces-
sarily reflect the policies of the NAE, of its constituent
groups or the conviction of their individual members." This
permits the widest possible expression of thoughtful
opinion, stimulates considered action and promotes evangelical progress in all fields of endeavor.   Dissenting views
of all issues are given a fair hearing in the "Readers Say"
department.   The journal has thus earned a reputation for
balance and fairness which reflects credit upon the NAE
and the evangelical cause in general.

One of the many services which *Action* magazine renders
evangelical leadership is its Annual Book List.   The Evangelical Book Committee[6] was set up in 1945.   The NAE had
begun to realize that "liberal" philosophies had so infil-

3. *UEA*, issues Sept. 15, Oct. 1, Oct. 15, Nov. 1, Nov. 15, Dec. 1,
1952; Jan. 1, Jan. 15, 1953; articles by Dr. Oswald T. Allis, Dr. J.
Harold Greenlee, Dr. Frank J. Neuberg, and Dr. James DeForest
Murch.
    4. *The Growing Super-Church*, James DeForest Murch (1952).
    5. *The Coming Great Church*, James DeForest Murch (1955).
    6. NAE Convention Report, 1945.

trated the religious book field that the average reader needed capable guidance in his reading. The first committee, headed by Dr. Carl F. H. Henry, then a professor in Northern Baptist Theological Seminary, consisted of twenty-seven intellectual leaders whose literary attainments qualified them to evaluate current literature and recommend certain books (1) as to their doctrinal soundness and (2) as to their significance to evangelicals. This service has been provided annually without break since 1946.

A by-product of this venture has been the Evangelical Book Club, a privately-owned service which selects a "Book of the Month" and lists each month new volumes coming from the presses of evangelical publishers. It now numbers some 2,000 ministers and evangelical leaders in its membership.

Probably one of the most significant by-products of the publication work of the National Association of Evangelicals has been the Evangelical Press Association.

The Associated Church Press, though not officially related to the National Council of Churches, has long been considered the professional service organization of Protestant journalism. In common with all such organizations it has been under "liberal" leadership and its programs reflected liberal thought and guidance. At the time the NAE came upon the inter-church scene the conventions of the ACP had little to offer in the technical field and were majoring in Social Gospel propaganda.

At the first convention of the National Sunday School Association in Chicago, October 1947, the editor of *Action* magazine met informally with a group of editors of evangelical journals to discuss the possibility of setting up a distinctly evangelical press association. No action was taken. The seed sown there, however, took root and the following year in Cincinnati on October 10 in the editor's office of *Action* magazine another group of editors including Dr. Louis H. Benes of the *Church Herald*, Dr. J. H. Walker of the *Evangel* and Dr. Carl L. Howland of the *Free Methodist* met and decided to proceed with a formal call to be issued all evangelical editors of record. Accordingly on May 6, 1948 editors of some thirty-five denominational publishing houses met in Chicago. Choosing Dr. Murch as chairman, the group set up a temporary organization under the name Evangelical Press Association, appointed a Constitution Committee, and called a Convention for April 4-6, 1949, to set up a permanent organization.[7]

The Constitutional Convention opened in the Lakeview Covenant Church, Chicago, on Monday evening with Mr. William F. McDermott, former religious editor of the *Chicago Daily News* and widely-known publicist, speaking. The work sessions were held in the Electric Club with special conferences for editors of general denominational, Sunday School, missionary, youth and children's publications. There was also a session devoted to the problems of religious publishers.

It was agreed that the field of evangelical publishing has a different base and outlook from any other. Secular standards and methods must be adapted, adjusted and converted to fit evangelical needs. Furthermore, the liberal slant of the ACP rendered its program inadequate for evangelicals. The only possible solution to meet the needs of evangelical journalism was a new organization which could provide a forum for the exchange of ideas and discussion of problems, develop an evangelical program and offer the best of technical advice for the improvement of the product.

A Constitution and Bylaws was adopted with the Statement of Belief of the National Association of Evangelicals as the theological basis of membership. After prayerful and thoughtful discussion it was unanimously agreed, however, that the EPA should not be NAE related. The principles of freedom of the press, freedom of speech, wider evangelical coverage and denominational responsibility were determining factors in the discussion.

The Purpose of the Association as set forth in the Constitution is as follows:

> The purpose of the Evangelical Press Association is to promote the cause of evangelical Christianity and to enhance the influence of Christian journalism by providing Christian fellowship among the members of the Association, by rendering practical assistance and stimulating mutual helpfulness among them, by encouraging high ethical and technical standards in the field of Christian journalism, and by suggesting concerted and timely emphasis on important issues.

7. Documentation of EPA historical resume in author's files, including personal letters, memoranda, minutes of committee meetings and convention sessions, brochures and other printed matter.

Officers elected were Dr. James DeForest Murch, editor of *United Evangelical Action*, president; Dr. Robert Walker, editor of *Christian Life*, secretary, and Dr. Martin Eriksen, editor of the *Baptist Standard*, treasurer.

Since that time of formation, the Evangelical Press Association has grown with real life and vitality. Membership numbers nearly one hundred, representing publications of many denominations and publishing houses with a combined circulation approaching 4,000,000. A very successful and interesting convention has been held each year in the last week of January. These conventions have been especially marked by the solid and helpful information which is given in lectures and in demonstrations by outstanding and recognized authorities in the field of journalism and editorial activity. Sectional meetings to explore the problems and interests of specialized publications are also a feature of each convention, and the emphasis is constantly on the practical presentation of information and "know-how" which will be essentially helpful to the members when they are back at work.

Sectional groups are now organized to cover the following fields of religious publication: Youth Publications, Denominational and General Publications, Periodical and Book Publishers, Sunday School Publications.

The business of the EPA is administered under an official Constitution and is largely carried on during the yearly convention. During the interim, administration is by a Board of Directors consisting of the President, Vice President, Secretary, Treasurer and two Advisory Members.

Membership in the EPA is by publication, not by individual. Publications may be represented by as many workers as desired at the EPA conventions, but each publication is allowed only one vote in business sessions. Press-membership cards are issued by the EPA to all member publications, and additional cards are supplied to member publications for as many workers as requested.

At the 1954 Convention a Code of Ethics was adopted which is a guiding light for evangelical publications:

The primary function of Christian publications is to advance the work and witness of Jesus Christ in the world. Our first responsibility is faithfulness to the truth and will of God as it is expressed in the Bible, which we accept as the infallible revelation of God, our only authority for faith and conduct. This dedicates Christian journalism to serve the highest welfare of mankind.

As our secondary responsibility we recognize our duty to serve the "principles, purposes, and policies" of the cause or organization our publications represent.

I

The freedom of Christian publications to publish the truth and to set forth the principles contained in the Word of God must be zealously guarded. Christian publications should be honest and courageous in all their presentations. Sincerity, truthfulness and accuracy should characterize all Christian publications.

II

Readers of Christian publications have the right to expect that news items and articles published are written truthfully. Those responsible for the publication must exercise the utmost care that nothing contrary to the truth is published. It is the privilege, as it is the duty, of a Christian publication to make prompt and complete correction of its own serious mistakes of fact or opinion, whatever their origin.

III

Christian publications are conscious of their duty to protect the good name and reputation of others. Should it become necessary at any time to engage in controversy for the defense and maintenance of the truth, care should be taken to present opposing views honestly and fairly.

IV

Christian publications do not publish any material except with consent of the authors or owners. The editing of the articles should not change the thoughts expressed by the author, without consultation with, and permission of, the author. Articles published in other magazines should not be reproduced without first receiving permission. Such articles should receive proper acknowledgment. Whenever previously published material is used, care should be taken to ascertain and acknowledge — if possible — authorship and source.

Some hundred evangelical journals are now members of the Evangelical Press Association.[8]   There has been an

8. Among the journals which now hold membership in the EPA are the following: *The Alliance Weekly, The Banner, The Baptist Record, The Bible Advocate, The Bible Expositor and Illuminator, The Bethel Witness, Brethren Missionary Herald, Call to Prayer, CBMC Contact, Christian Home and School, Christian Leader, Christian Life,*

amazing improvement in the style and content of all the participating magazines during the years. Each year plaques are awarded editors of journals showing the greatest technical progress and making the best contribution in the field of religious journalism.

Christian Medical Society Journal, The Christian Witness, The Christlife Magazine, Christ's Ambassadors Guide, Christ's Ambassadors Herald, The Church Herald, Church of Christ Advocate, Conquest, Conservative Baptist, Contact, The Covenant Weekly, The Covenanter Witness, Church of God Evangel, DeWachter, El Heraldo de Santidad, Eternity, Evangelical Beacon and Evangelist, The Evangelical Christian, Evangelical Visitor, The Free Methodist, The Free Will Baptist, Good News Broadcaster, The Gospel Banner, The Gospel Call, Gospel Gleaners, Gospel Herald, Gospel Light Press, Healing, Illinois Observer, Israel My Glory, Light and Life Evangel, The Lighted Pathway, Message of the Open Bible, The Mission Post, The Missionary Banner, The Missionary Broadcaster, Missionary Monthly, Missionary Tidings (Winona Lake, Ind.), Missionary Tidings (Circleville, Ohio), The Missionary Worker, The Moody Church News, NSSA's Link, Our Sunday School Counsellor, Pentecostal Evangel, Pentecostal Holiness Advocate, Power, Salvation, The Sower, The Standard, The Standard of Holiness, Sunday School Herald, The Sunday School Journal, Sword of the Lord, Team, Teen Time, Today, Trowel and Sword, Truth on Fire, The United Brethren, The United Evangelical, United Evangelical Action, The Wesleyan Methodist, The Wesleyan Missionary, The World Challenge, World Conquest, World Vision News, The Young Ambassador, The Young Calvinist, Youth Compass, Youth for Christ Magazine, Youth in Action, Youth's Visitor.

XIV

WORLD EVANGELICAL FELLOWSHIP

The same basic considerations which brought the National Association of Evangelicals into existence and made it a factor of importance in the religious life of America caused evangelicals of other nations to desire similar organizations through which they might have fellowship and united action on the basis of a common faith.

The NAE had no desire to expand into an international body. Its leaders felt that it was conceived and should be maintained as an American organization to meet and to serve the peculiar needs of the USA. The Association had repeatedly declined to admit into its membership petitioning groups in Latin America and Europe. American evangelicals, however, had a deep interest in the welfare and the encouragement of their brethren of like faith throughout the world. They made available to others information and aid which enabled them to set up autonomous fellowships in their respective lands.

There also grew up a particularly friendly relationship between the NAE and the World Evangelical Alliance of Great Britain (Chapter I). The doctrinal position of the Alliance was still that of its founders in 1846. It stood foursquare on the divine inspiration of the Bible, the depravity of human nature, the incarnation and atoning work of Christ, justification by faith, the work of the Holy Spirit, the immortality of the soul and the eternal punishment of sinners. The leaders in Great Britain were of firm evangelical faith. There was, however, considerable infiltration of liberalism in the Continental European branches of the Alliance. The British organization itself was beginning to be in danger of atrophy. It was merely perpetuating itself on its endowments and its traditions. There was little activity save for the promotion of the Universal Week of Prayer which had been observed without break ever since it was instituted in 1846.

In 1946, the centennial year of the WEA, the NAE sent
Dr. J. Elwin Wright to London bearing the greetings and
good wishes of American evangelicals to their British
cousins.[1] It was the beginning of a beautiful friendship. A
new generation of WEA leaders yearned for the day when
their organization with its noble history might see a re-
birth of evangelistic activity and a real world movement
of evangelicals commensurate with the needs of the new
day. Dr. Wright and British leaders proposed that an
unofficial meeting of evangelicals be held at Clarens,
Switzerland, in 1948 to consider prayerfully the establishment of a world fellowship. Dr. Wright was commissioned
by the NAE to make the preliminary arrangements as
"Secretary of International Cooperation for the National
Association of Evangelicals."

The year 1948 was notable in world church affairs for
the year of the founding of the World Council of Churches
in the city of Amsterdam. It early appeared that the evangelicals of the world would not be happy in the fellowship
of the Council.[2] There was liberal opposition to the adoption of a basis of faith which recognized the Bible as the
inspired, authoritative, and infallible Word of God and
Jesus Christ as God and Saviour. There was also evidence
that the new Council would sacrifice the distinctly Protestant and evangelical testimony which was so dear to the
hearts of the NAE and the WEA constituencies. The
predominant politico-social emphasis in the pronounce-
ment of its "liberal" leadership prior to Amsterdam was
also exceedingly distasteful to evangelicals.

The Clarens Conference met August 7-10 in St. George's
School in an atmosphere of expectancy.[3] The gathering
was opened in a devotional service led by Dr. R. L. Decker,
president of the NAE. Dr. A. H. Oussoren, pastor at Middel-
burg, The Netherlands, was elected chairman. There were
eight members of the NAE Board of Administration pres-

1. Dr. Wright's visit was preceded by exploratory conversations
between Dr. Harold J. Ockenga and Mr. John Bolten, Sr., unofficially
representing American evangelicals, and Dr. Martin Lloyd Jones,
successor to Dr. G. Campbell Morgan in Westminster Chapel, and
other British brethren. *UEA*, January 1, 1947, p. 12. NAE Convention Report, 1948, p. 14.
2. "An Evangelical Charter," issued by the World Evangelical
Alliance on the occasion of its One Hundredth Anniversary; *Evangelical Christendom* (1946) ; *Amsterdam, 1948: An Evangelical View
of the World Council of Churches* by James DeForest Murch.
3. *UEA*, September 15, 1948, pp. 3, 4.

ent. The Honorable H. M. Gooch, general secretary of the WEA, and other leaders of the British organization were present. Almost all European nations were represented.

It was agreed that before any attempt at world organization, national fellowships should first be set up where no such bodies already existed and that existing alliances or associations should be encouraged. A committee of five was elected to prepare for a convention in the summer of 1949. A guide for the formation of associations of evangelicals was adopted as follows:

In all its activities the Association should spread the Gospel on the basis of the adopted Declaration of Faith. The Association in no way desires to supplant or duplicate the churches or existing evangelical societies and agencies. It is to be devoted to that which is of general interest; it aims at coordinating the efforts of the various churches and organizations and doing what individual churches and other organizations can not do separately, in:

1. Creating unity among the believers.

2. Serving as a center of information and coordination of evangelical activity.

3. Representing evangelicals before Governments, especially evangelical minority groups whose religious liberty is threatened.

4. Informing the NAE in America of real needs in Europe.

5. Advising as to the equitable distribution of funds which may be sent from America for relief and other forms of evangelical united action such as: (1) Evangelization; (2) Printing and distributing evangelical literature; (3) Training Christian workers in Europe for places in other parts of the world where there is need for evangelical workers speaking European languages.

There was a certain lukewarmness in some quarters to the development of a new organization at the world level. There was no meeting held in 1949. Dr. Wright, more than any other person or organization, was responsible for keeping the flame alive.

At the 1949 convention of the NAE in Chicago some thirty evangelical organizations were represented at a luncheon in the Congress Hotel which was designed to further the interests of evangelical cooperation at the world level.[4] Dr. Stephen W. Paine presided. A committee of three, consisting of Mr. H. J. Taylor, chairman, Mr. Donald MacDonald, and Mr. Charles M. Dean, was set up which proved to be the forerunner of the NAE Commission on International Relations.[5]

With new developments in the British organization the situation became more favorable for "follow through" from Clarens. Lt. General Sir Arthur Smith and Mr. Roy Cattell of the WEA now began to move to the foreground. They brought a new faith and vision to their British constituency and vast encouragement to all concerned.

Accordingly an "International Conference" was called together by the World Evangelical Alliance at Hildenborough Hall in March, 1950.[6] It was followed in September of the same year by a similar gathering in Boston, Massachusetts. Each conference served in its own way to resolve problems and to clarify thinking. Boston endorsed the findings of Hildenborough almost *in toto* and there was remarkable unanimity in the ultimately emerging views at Boston.[7]

The outstanding decisions and recommendations at this stage of the development were:

1. That the times and the circumstances of evangelical endeavor demand the formation of an international evangelical organization. This organization should be named the "International Association of Evangelicals."

4. NAE Convention Report, 1949, pp. 51-53.
5. A Committee on International Relations was officially set up by the 1949 NAE Convention in Chicago, April 19-22. It consisted of Dr. R. L. Decker, chairman, Dr. Leslie R. Marston, Dr. William H. Rutgers, Dr. Clyde W. Taylor and Dr. J. Elwin Wright.
The Committee was elevated to Commission status by the 1950 NAE Convention in Indianapolis, April 18-21. Personnel: Dr. Harold J. Ockenga, chairman, Miss Elizabeth M. Evans, secretary, Mr. A. Herman Armerding, the Rev. Frank Birch, Mr. Ernest Blombach, Mr. John Bolten, Dr. R. L. Decker, Dr. Theodore H. Elsner, Mr. E. Joseph Evans, Dr. Howard W. Ferrin, Dr. Billy Graham, Mr. B. J. Heetderks, Dr. Bob Jones, Jr., Dr. L. R. Marston, Miss Henrietta Mears, Dr. J. Palmer Muntz, the Rev. Earl P. Paulk, the Rev. Noel Perkin, Dr. Paul S. Rees, Dr. John R. Rice, Mr. William Rottschaffer, Dr. Henry H. Savage, Mr. Clifford F. Smith, Dr. Oswald Smith, Dr. Louis Talbot, Dr. Clyde W. Taylor, Mr. H. J. Taylor, the Rev. Emo F. J. Van Halsema.
Dr. Ockenga has continued to act as chairman since 1950.
6. *UEA*, April 1, 1950, pp. 17, 18.
7. *Ibid.*, October 15, 1950, pp. 3-6.

2. That a statement of faith, unequivocal in its stand on the Word of God and historic evangelical Christian doctrine, should be made the basis of the new Association. It was voted unanimously to appoint a committee to study, discuss and formulate such a statement. The chairman suggested Mr. F. Roy Cattell of Great Britain, Dr. Howard Ferrin of the USA, and Dr. G. A. Hadjiantoniou of Greece. Each was elected by popular vote.

3. That there should be no power at the center which would dictate to the various national organizations, but that each should run its own affairs in full autonomy.

4. That the objectives of this international body should be: (1) To witness to evangelical and historic Christianity, (2) to encourage and promote fellowship among evangelicals, and (3) to stimulate evangelism and promote united evangelical action in every sphere of life.

5. That every country should develop its own evangelical organization in the way it saw fit. It might be an incorporated organization or a rather loosely knit fellowship. The only essential requirements should be that the organizations or associations subscribe to the statement of faith of the international association and that they be representative of the whole area involved.

6. That only delegates to the "International Association" who came from properly organized national groups be recognized. Encouragement would be given for unofficial observers or auditors to attend but only organized areas would be permitted to vote.

7. That a constitutional convention be held in Holland in 1951 (probably in August).

8. That there be an interim Executive Committee formed, composed of Lt. General Sir Arthur Smith, Dr. J. Elwin Wright, Dr. A. H. Oussoren, Mr. F. Roy Cattell, and Dr. Clyde W. Taylor.

9. That every country be invited to appoint a corresponding secretary who would be informed of the progress of events from time to time throughout the year and would inform this Executive Committee of the suggestions and decisions of the evangelicals of that country.

10. That an interim committee meeting be held in Holland between January 20 and 24, 1951, for the purpose of setting up the details of the coming international constitutional convention.

11. That an outline draft of the constitution be made by a committee consisting of: Dr. A. H. Oussoren of The Netherlands, Prof. Roger Nicole of France, Dr. Howard

W. Ferrin of the USA, and Miss Betty Hu of China. This
first draft was to be sent to the corresponding secretary
of each national organization for study and suggestions.
It was to be discussed and amended by the interim committee in its January meeting and prepared in final form
for presentation to the constitutional convention.

12. That three delegates be sent by each national organization or fellowship and qualified to vote in the constitutional convention. The interim committee was to
consider carefully the application of each country for
participation in the constitutional convention and decide
whether the country was entitled to official representation. The committee was also to decide upon the method
of voting at this convention.

13. That the Boston conference ratify and approve the
action of the Hildenborough conference in asking His
Highness Prince Oscar Bernadotte of Sweden to serve
as Honorary President of the interim executive committee and that a message of greeting and thanks for
his acceptance be sent him by the secretary.

14. That the World Evangelical Alliance and the National Association of Evangelicals continue, at least until the January meeting in Holland, to work in conjunction with each other in notifying their contacts in various countries of the formation of this new international
body and of the desire that they shall form national
groups and participate in the constitutional convention
in 1951.

15. That Dr. J. Elwin Wright and Dr. Clyde W. Taylor be authorized to make a globe-encircling trip to
acquaint leaders in various countries with the purposes
of the international association and encourage the formation of autonomous organizations in those lands.

16. That world evangelicals were not yet ready for
representation at the United Nations, but that it would
be of value to think ahead and have concrete information
and convictions about such representation for consideration at the constitutional convention in 1951. It was
agreed, however, that unofficial observers should keep all
informed of what might be of particular value to evangelicals in maintaining Christian liberties and should
provide the United Nations with information as to the
evangelical position.

17. That evangelical missionary organizations should
make the indigenous church of each country self-supporting and self-sustaining as rapidly as possible. Furthermore, that proper representation of the national church

in the three voting delegates from each country be provided even where the missionaries must still play major roles in the evangelization of these countries.

18. That the program of the Universal Week of Prayer, begun by the World Evangelical Alliance over a hundred years ago, should be furthered by the new international association.

Matters now began to move speedily. Woudschoten (near Zeist), a noted meeting place for international gatherings in the Netherlands, was chosen as the site for the Constitutional Convention. Saturday, August 4, 1951 was set as the convening date.

The times served to emphasize the necessity of some sort of cooperative evangelical fellowship of an international character. The remnant of orthodox Christians in the world cried out for some outward realization of their essential oneness in the Lord Jesus Christ and the dissolution of the misunderstandings and prejudices which divided them. They were conscious of the need for presenting a united front to Communism, Romanism, Liberalism, Paganism, Atheism and other enemies of the "faith once for all delivered." They were beginning to realize that liberty in the propagation of the Gospel as they proclaim it hung by a slender thread in a changing world situation and that such liberty could only be preserved by united evangelical action.

Russia was behind an "iron curtain". Czechoslovakia, Bulgaria, Hungary, Rumania, Poland, Yugo-Slavia and Albania were in her grip, making evangelical worship and the propagation of the gospel hazardous or impossible. China was fast closing; Korea was in grave jeopardy. Indo-China, Burma, India and Malaya might be next. Africa was seething with Communism. South America was in ferment.

In such a state of world chaos, spiritual isolationism was starkly seen as a sin against God and Christian brethren. To fail to join hands with all believers for the completion of the common task of world evangelism could only increase the terrible cost in property and lives which might be paid as world forces would strike against God and His Church.

There was deep disappointment concerning developments within the World Council of Churches.[8] It had failed to adopt as a basis of fellowship the absolute minimum of

8. *Amsterdam 1948* by James DeForest Murch.

fundamental evangelical Christian doctrine. It had admitted to its membership and leadership a host of "liberals" committed to subversive doctrines. Millions of evangelicals in the WCC were without a voice and many of them were eager for some effective means of keeping their testimony strong and clear.

While the conviction of definite need for united evangelical action at the world level had grown with the years, the road to Woudschoten was beset with many conflicts and disappointments. A certain sector of American evangelical life had early withdrawn from the main stream of the new evangelical movement. It seemed to be the settled policy of "The American Council of Christian Churches" never to cooperate with anything which it did not originate and to brand as heretical that which did not conform to its *modus operandi*. Other bodies which had expanded from the home base in America to positions of some influence internationally were unable to see beyond their own restricted horizons and failed to realize their obligation to the whole church in a time of world crisis.

This lack of complete evangelical unanimity in America posed a dilemma for the united evangelicals in lands across the sea who were to a large degree dependent upon America for financial and moral support. If they turned toward fellowship with those who were represented by the NAE they might be branded as compromisers of the faith and threatened with ostracism. If they turned in the other direction they feared they might be misunderstood. In one country about a hundred missionaries committed themselves to cooperation with a small international body of evangelicals. There are 1,400 other thoroughly evangelical missionaries who refused to do so, but hesitated to move in any direction or to advise their native churches to move. Nevertheless plans for the new world evangelical organization went on. Its leaders had great faith that eventually all obstacles would be overcome.

The specifications of the new organization as they began to emerge indicated that it would be big enough and broad enough to include every true evangelical in all the world who desired to avail himself of its fellowship and aid. On the other hand it would be as narrow as He who is the Way, as the Holy Scriptures which are the Word of God, and as the Church which the Blest Redeemer built. It would bear malice toward none and have charity for all. It would be a united testimony for "the faith once for all delivered;" a haven of evangelical fellowship made rich in a common faith and Lord; and a medium through which evangelical conviction might be translated into effective united evangelical action.

Representatives of over twenty nations finally met in Woudschoten for the history-making Constitutional Convention.[9] On August 4 preliminary meetings were held. On Sunday, services were held in the chapel and were truly international in character. Morning worship was conducted by Dr. Frederick Curtis Fowler of the USA, president of the National Association of Evangelicals of America and an inspiring address was given by Director F. Heitmuller of Hamburg, Germany. In the afternoon Lt. General Sir Arthur Smith, chairman of the Conference, presided and a masterly address on the unity of the true Church was given by the Rev. J. R. W. Stott, M.A., Rector of All Soul's Church, Lamgham Palace, London. The evening session was devoted to reviews of earlier post-war conferences which paved the way for Woudschoten, at Clarens, Hildenborough, and Boston.

On Monday, messages of greeting were received from the Princess Wilhelmina of The Netherlands, Prince Bernadotte of Sweden, and President and Madame Chiang Kai Shek of Free China, and reports were given by national leaders of the different countries represented.

By Wednesday the convention was ready to act. After a full and frank discussion of the project, by an overwhelming majority the delegates voted in favor of the formation of a world fellowship for evangelical cooperation. The delegates were greatly moved by the speech made by the Rev. Paul Das of India, in which he pleaded for evangelical Christians in the West to extend the hand of fellowship to the younger groups of the Orient. The proposition for the formation of the Fellowship was moved by Dr. Fowler, seconded by the Rev. Paul Das. Many of the delegates spoke warmly of the project and after the vote had been taken, the Conference proceeded to consider the suggested Constitution. In the preamble to the Constitution, the members of the Fellowship declared their purpose to be:

1. Honoring God and His Word.
2. The furtherance of the Gospel.

9. *UEA*, September 1, 1951, pp. 5, 6.

3. The defense and confirmation of the Gospel.

4. Fellowship in the Gospel.

Those who joined the Fellowship were committed to acceptance, without mental reservation, of the statement of faith that was incorporated in the Constitution, but complete autonomy was recognized for every constituent national or area-wide body within the Fellowship. The members undertook to embark upon a program of mutual helpfulness in the propagation of the Gospel, in the defense of Christian liberties, and in all other matters of common concern.

The Fellowship was to consist of such national autonomous evangelical groups as might from time to time be elected and other groups all of which would be required to subscribe annually to the Statement of Faith of the World Evangelical Fellowship, as follows:

I. The *Holy Scripture*, as originally given by God, divinely inspired, infallible, entirely trustworthy; and the supreme authority in all matters of faith and conduct.

II. *One God*, eternally existent in three Persons, Father, Son, and Holy Spirit.

III. *Our Lord Jesus Christ*, God manifest in the flesh, His virgin birth, His sinless human life, His divine miracles, His vicarious and atoning death, His bodily resurrection, His ascension, His mediatorial work, and His personal return in power and glory.

IV. The *salvation* of lost and sinful man through the shed blood of the Lord Jesus Christ by faith apart from works, and regeneration by the Holy Spirit.

V. The *Holy Spirit* by whose indwelling the believer is enabled to live a holy life, to witness and work for the Lord Jesus Christ.

VI. *Unity in the Spirit* of all true believers, the Church, Body of Christ.

VII. *The resurrection* of both the saved and the lost: they that are saved unto the resurrection of life, and they that are lost unto the resurrection of damnation.

According to the national situation, it was visualized that individuals, societies, church congregations, denominations of various kinds, would be admitted to membership in the Fellowship.

The name of the particular national or area-wide group would be decided by the group itself, but the overall body would be known as the World Evangelical Fellowship. Each country would be called upon to ratify the proposals made at the conference. Only the most important matters affecting the Fellowship were to be incorporated in the Constitution, matters of detail being dealt with in the by-laws.

The Conference gave its attention on Thursday to the consideration of outstanding points in the constitution and by-laws. It was agreed that the charter-members of the newly formed World Evangelical Fellowship should consist of those national organizations which should ratify the actions of the Woudschoten Conference by accepting the Constitution in its various provisions.

The matter of the relationship of the Evangelical Fellowship to other Christian organizations was fully discussed. It was agreed that there could be cooperation with other Christian bodies that are true to the accepted Statement of Faith of the Fellowship. Each autonomous group in membership of the World Evangelical Fellowship would maintain its testimony by only inviting to its platform speakers who accept the statement of faith of the Fellowship.

A proposal was made by the German delegation that interim arrangements be made for the eventual setting up of Commissions for Evangelism, Missions, Literature, and Christian Action. This resolution was carried unanimously. It was agreed to appoint interim chairmen to facilitate this action.

The Committee of Nominations brought forward a proposed slate of officers and Interim Committee members, and the following were elected: President, Lt. General Sir Arthur Smith of Great Britain; Treasurer, Mr. John Bolten, Sr., of the USA; Members-at-large: Dr. Clarence W. Jones of Ecuador; Pastor F. Heitmuller of Germany; Dr. Harold J. Ockenga of the USA; Dr. A. S. Guruswamy of Ceylon; the Rev. K. Hiraide of Japan; Pastor M. Zilz of Germany.

With hearts full of gratitude to God the Conference unanimously said:

> After these days in which the Lord has been pleased to bless and unite us in such a gracious manner, we deeply feel that we must humble ourselves before Him for all the shortcomings of the past. We praise Him for the new vision He gave us and the closer bond by which we shall be greatly strengthened in our common task.

With one heart we dedicate our lives afresh to Him who redeemed us by His blood out of every people and nation, to make us members of His own Body. We pledge ourselves to consecrate all that which we are and have to the glory of His name, the sanctification of His people, and the salvation of lost souls. May He help us by His grace until He comes again.

To the evangelical world it sent out this message:

The World Evangelical Fellowship, in recognition of the unity in the Body of Christ of all who love our Lord Jesus Christ in sincerity, affirm their unity in the Spirit with, and express their fraternal greetings to all our brethren in Christ the world over, whether individuals, churches or societies, who hold "like precious faith" with us. The hour has truly come when all the born-again Bible believing Christians should unite in order to strengthen their fellowship in the Body of Christ, to bear wider witness to His infallible Word, and to better evangelize the world until He comes. We look to Him that we might be enabled "to speak the truth in love with all lowliness and meekness, endeavoring to keep the unity of the Spirit in the bond of peace."

The intervening years between Woudschoten and the first full-fledged convention under the Constitution at Clarens, Switzerland in 1953 were filled with intense activity.[10]

At St. John's school overlooking Lake Geneva evangelicals saw July 27-31 the realization of the vision which had come to them in this identical spot five years before.

Some two hundred delegates and visitors from thirty lands attending the opening session heard Dr. Paul S. Rees, head of the USA delegation, call for a mid-century revival throughout the world.

The first half of the current century, said the American evangelical leader, has been marked by the challenge of Communism which has halted Christian missionary advance, one of the most severe economic depressions in history, the full flower of apostasy in the churches largely due to "liberal" theological infiltration, and a menacing materialistic state of mind throughout society in general.

Dr. Rees said that evangelicals faced the tremendous spiritual potential of the second half of our century with a surfeit of bickering, division and aloofness. He urged a re-

10. *Ibid.*, September 15, 1953, pp. 17-19.

pentant and humble waiting before God for His clear word for our day, quite possibly the word "Revival." He reminded his listeners that revival always comes from God and is not primarily the result of organization or high-powered advertising.

Preceding Dr. Rees' address the conference had been formally opened by Lt. General Sir Arthur Smith, WEF president, who made it clear that all those present were on business for Christ and in all things should exalt His name.

Six national evangelical organizations were received into full membership at the first business session — Singapore, Hawaii, Switzerland, Germany, France, and Holland. Seven had previously been received: Evangelical Fellowship of Ceylon, Gospel Workers Fellowship of Cyprus, Evangelical Alliance of Great Britain, Evangelical Fellowship of India, Japanese Association of Evangelicals, Taiwan (Formosa) Evangelical Fellowship, and the National Association of Evangelicals (USA). In addition, the following were granted "associate" membership: The Evangelische Contact Comité of Belgium, The Evangelical Fellowship of Cuba, The Evangelical Brotherhood of Greece, The Evangelical Alliance of Greece, The Chinese Foreign Missionary Union (Indonesia). Other applications were received. Terms of membership were broadened at Clarens to include "consultative members" and "individual members." Contacts had been established which were being cultivated with care.

WEF commissions were functioning:

The Commission on Evangelism supplied an exchange of speakers for conferences in mission lands. In several instances it aided national units in the establishment of educational institutions for the training of native leadership. Its basic policy as stated at Clarens was "to speed the complete evangelization of the world, by working through national units wherever they exist. National units, in turn, shall work through the national churches and not institute independent and free-lance projects." Regional conferences majoring in evangelism were planned in the various continents during the triennium.

The Commission on Christian Action set up machinery to deal with the problem of religious liberty in Roman Catholic and other countries where full freedom is denied those who wish to preach the evangelical Gospel message. The Commission established the relations to implement more effectively its crusade for universal religious freedom.

The Commission on Missionary Cooperation set up media for completing surveys and compiling statistics on evangelical mission work in all parts of the world. Machinery was perfected for dealing with governments in lands where evangelical missionaries are serving.

A world evangelical literature program to challenge Red Communist propaganda was being mapped by the *Commission on Literature*.

Said Chairman Clyde W. Taylor:

> With the development of large scale literacy programs throughout the backward areas of the world, a great change is taking place in missionary techniques. Many new millions are now able to read and Communism is literally flooding Africa, Asia, South America, and other areas with millions of books and pamphlets filled with revolutionary and anti-Christian propaganda.
>
> There is an imperative necessity for a new strategy which will send forth millions of copies of evangelical Christian literature to meet this Red Challenge and to convert millions to Christ. Already our evangelical missionary literature program in America is well past the planning stage. We are now well started on the international level.

The WEF plan calls for Committees on Literature in all areas where national Fellowships are functioning, each with a member on the International Commission. In other lands committees will be appointed.

Surveys will be made in each country. Spanish surveys have already been completed involving every Spanish-speaking nation. Catalogs include listings of all literature available, the types needed for more effective propaganda, spiritual education of Christians and texts for use in educational institutions. All findings are to clear through the International Commission of the WEF.

Cooperating publishing houses, of which there are scores, will print literature according to a carefully prepared schedule and act jointly in the distribution. Basic materials will be prepared in English and adapted, translated, and printed by nationals in their own respective areas. Approved translation committees will be set up by national groups, or in case of the broad languages, such as German, French, Spanish, Portuguese and Italian, by cooperating committees to which any evangelical publishers or writers may be referred for translations of their works.

Central bookstores have already been opened in some lands; others are planned.

The attitude of Protestants toward the Holy Bible was recognized as the basic cause of the current separation of "liberals" and "evangelicals" at national and world levels, when the Fellowship discussed the matter of Christian unity at Clarens.

As an outgrowth of these discussions an international theological study conference was planned under WEF auspices, at which the "revelation and inspiration of the Holy Scriptures" was to be the chief issue to be considered.

With the encouragement of the Executive Committee of the WEF a *theological discussion* group was set up with Dr. Carl F. H. Henry convening the meetings. Participating were theologians from England, Belgium, France, Switzerland and the United States. As a result of their findings assignments were made for the preparation of an international bibliography of evangelical publications since 1925 in the field of revelation and inspiration. Long range plans were made for the meeting which should last for ten days and bring together about twenty-five evangelical theologians from Continental Europe, Great Britain, the United States and possibly Asia. This group would consider the issuance of a Manifesto to the Christian world, in view of recent theological tendencies; would discuss papers and research reports prepared in advance by a temporary committee; and would consider the subsequent issuance either of a symposium or a volume concerned with this area of Christian knowledge.

Another forward step taken in the closing sessions was the setting up of an *International Radio and Television Committee* which will attempt to correlate the activities of hundreds of evangelical broadcasters around the world, looking to a more comprehensive and effective coverage of the globe with the saving message of the Gospel. Some of the strongest short-wave radio stations in the world are now owned and operated by evangelicals affiliated with the WEF.

Lt. General Sir Arthur Smith of London, England, was re-elected president of the Fellowship for the ensuing triennium.

Vice Presidents chosen were: Direktor Heitmuller of Germany; the Rev. A. P. Guruswamy of Ceylon; and Dr. Paul S. Rees of Minneapolis, Minnesota, USA. Mr. John Bolten of Lawrence, Massachusetts, was elected treasurer.

Other members of the Executive Committee appointed were: the Rev. K. S. Hiraide of Japan, the Rev. C. Chao of Singapore, Dr. Everett Cattell of India, the Rev. J.

Savage of South America, and Pastor J. Bordreuil of France.

Commission chairmen were announced as follows: Dr. Harold John Ockenga of the USA, Evangelism; Dr. Rene Pache of Switzerland, Literature; Dr. Clyde W. Taylor of the USA, Missions; and the Rt. Rev. Hugh Gough of Great Britain, Social Action. These men will also serve as members of the Executive Committee.

It was unanimously agreed that a new central world headquarters office would be opened in the immediate future with a new secretariat. In the interim the two joint secretaries, Mr. A. J. Dain of London, England and Dr. J. Elwin Wright of Boston, Mass., USA continue to serve.

Switzerland was favored as the site of the new world headquarters, but final choice was to be made later by the Executive Committee. Both London and Washington were favorably mentioned in this connection.

The final public session was held in Lausanne, July 31, where an audience of some 600 greeted The Rt. Rev. Hugh Gough, Lord Bishop of Barking and Dr. Paul S. Rees, president of the National Association of Evangelicals, the speakers. A deep spirit of consecration prevailed in the closing moments.

The world gathering of evangelicals at Clarens, Switzerland, fully justified the faith of those who had through the years envisioned a global association for Christian action. The World Evangelical Fellowship is now definitely functioning under the blessing of God and gives promise of great accomplishment in the days ahead.

The WEF is the answer to those who are seeking a sound basis for evangelical Christian cooperation and action at the world level. The Fellowship stands foursquare for the fundamental doctrines of the Christian faith as expressed in the Word of God. It refuses to compromise with quasi-Christian forces. It seeks the motivation, the direction, and the power of the Holy Spirit of God in its every endeavor. It is dealing with the problems of the hour. It is small wonder that the movement is gaining ground so rapidly.

To some casual observers it might seem that the Fellowship is "too little and too late" to deal seriously and effectively with the vast issues which confront Christendom. Such an estimate fails to see the spiritual plus. A similar estimate might have been made of the 120 followers of

Christ before Pentecost. They had little in culture, wealth, and influence but when endowed with the Spirit of God they became a force which literally turned the world upside down. It is not by might nor by power but by my Spirit, saith the Lord of Hosts.

The only question as to the outcome of the events at Clarens has to do with the quantity and quality of the consecration and the faith of the evangelicals of the world. God is abundantly able, not only to protect and preserve His people, but to use them mightily to bring revival and restoration and advance the world around.

XV

MARCHING ALONG

The rapid expansion of the National Association of Evangelicals in every area of inter-church cooperation from 1942 to the present hour is one of the most significant developments in the recent history of American Protestantism. The NAE has had every mark of the guidance and blessing of God.

During this period beginning with the leadership of such men as Dr. Harold J. Ockenga and Dr. J. Elwin Wright, literally hundreds of outstanding evangelical leaders have figured in the development of NAE's far-flung organizational life. Particular recognition must go, however, to the presidents and the executive secretaries of the Association proper. These are the men who imparted the vision, mapped policy and program, counselled with boards and committees, implemented the directives, sought financial undergirding and "sold" the NAE to the vast potential evangelical constituency across the nation. The chronological story of the NAE can well be told in terms of their administrations.[1]

Dr. Harold J. Ockenga (1943-45), pastor of the historic Park Street Congregational Christian Church, Boston, Massachusetts, saw the preparatory work done, the Statement of Belief drafted, the Constitution adopted, and the blueprints drawn. The first offices were opened in Boston, Massachusetts under the direction of the executive director, Dr. J. Elwin Wright. The nation was canvassed from coast to coast in regional conferences and mass meetings. The Washington office was opened. Commissions began to function. Much of the story of these years has already been told in other chapters. Everywhere Dr. Ockenga's intellectual and spiritual capacities were recognized and it was with full confidence that evangelicals accepted his lead-

1. Data arranged under the administrations of the presidents and executive directors of the NAE may be verified in the annual printed reports of the annual conventions from 1943 to 1950 and the convention reports appearing in *United Evangelical Action* magazine.

ership in this crucial formative period. Together with Dr. Wright he shaped basic philosophy, organization, policy and program and left the stamp of his guiding hand upon the Association for all time. Conventions in Chicago in 1943, in Columbus, Ohio, in 1944 and in Chicago in 1945 recorded the achievements of his administration.

Dr. Leslie R. Marston (1945-47), Bishop of the Free Methodist Church and former president of Greenville College, succeeded Dr. Ockenga. He brought to the NAE a leadership characterized by deep piety, virile orthodoxy and spiritual power. His experience in ecclesiastical administration was invaluable to the Association. Under his term of office rapid growth continued. The National Sunday School Association was organized and began to function. Education received a new impetus through the developing program of the Commission on Education. Plans were laid for research and study which eventuated in the noteworthy report of the Commission on Philosophy of Christian Education. The official journal, *United Evangelical Action*, was revamped and offices were opened in Cincinnati, Ohio. Conventions were held in Minneapolis, Minnesota, in 1946 and in Omaha, Nebraska, in 1947. At Omaha it was noted that thirty denominations with 1,300,000 communicants were then members of the Association, together with a service constituency of another 3,000,000. The Washington office had served seventy mission boards in some way or other. Commissions were actively functioning in the fields of Army and Navy Chaplaincy, Education, Evangelism, Foreign Missions, Home Missions, Industrial Chaplaincy, Radio, War Relief, and Youth.

Dr. Rutherford L. Decker (1946-48), pastor of Temple Baptist Church, Kansas City, Missouri, was third president. Like his predecessors he had been identified with the NAE from its beginnings and had a keen grasp of its principles and objectives. His aggressive leadership encouraged continued expansion. Headquarters offices were moved from Boston to Chicago in order that operations might be carried on more effectively from the heart of the nation. The National Association of Christian Schools came into being with offices also in Chicago. The National Sunday School Association, also located here, began to issue its outlines for the Uniform Bible Lessons. Contacts with lay leadership were established. The Women's Fellowship and the

Laymen's Advisory Council were organized.[2] About this time Dr. Wright, who had served so faithfully as executive director from the beginning, saw the necessity of developing evangelical cooperation at the world level. Contacts had been established with the World Evangelical Alliance in Great Britain and evangelicals in other lands were calling for a new world organization. Under the burden of this new concern, Dr. Wright asked to be relieved of his executive duties and was made, first, Assistant to the President, and later, Secretary of International Cooperation. In his report to the 1948 convention in Chicago Dr. Wright said:

> The NAE has come a long way in these short five years. We have proved that Christians of strong convictions and diverse backgrounds can meet and work together without compromise and yet with mutual love and respect for each other. We have proved that there are many areas in which we may cooperate without infringing on the work of the churches or embarrassing them by unauthorized pronouncements.

Dr. Wright pointed out that national headquarters offices of the NAE are maintained in Chicago. Regional offices are maintained in Boston, Minneapolis, Portland, and Los Angeles, with full-time directors. Seven offices for specialized work are maintained — War Relief in New York City; Purchasing and Transportation, also in New York City; Chaplain Counselors for Industry, Newark, N. J.; Publication, Cincinnati, Ohio; National Sunday School Association, Chicago; National Association of Chris-

2. The Evangelical Women's Fellowship was organized in May 1948 for the purpose of creating a means of fellowship for Bible-believing women supporting the National Association of Evangelicals. It is directed by an NAE-appointed executive committee of nine, five of whom fill the offices of president, first and second vice-presidents, secretary and treasurer, and four others who represent different geographical sections of the USA and differing church affiliations. The president is automatically a member of the NAE Board of Administration. EWF has chapters in local communities. It promotes projects in harmony with the general policy of the NAE. Its national presidents, in order of succession, have been: Mrs. Leslie R. Marston (1948-51), Mrs. Theodore H. Elsner (1951-54), Mrs. Merrill C. Tenney (1954-).

The Laymen's Advisory Council was organized in May 1948 to "make available to the NAE the experience, counsel and influence of the Bible-believing laymen of America." It enlists members and provides financial aid for the NAE. Its chairmen have been: Mr. Seth Rohrer (1948-50), Mr. Gene Gillis (1950-51), Mr. Harry J. Burkema (1951-54), Mr. Kenneth S. Keyes (1954-).

tian Schools, Chicago. Local committees maintain offices in such centers as Philadelphia and Chicago.

In closing, Dr. Wright said:

The battle for spiritual unity among believers is still in its early stages. The accumulated prejudices of generations do not easily give way to understanding, unselfish consideration of all groups within the evangelical framework, and appreciation of the gravity of the issues which all of us face in common. There is, as yet, *insufficient* emphasis upon . . . those doctrines which we hold in common and *too great* emphasis upon our differences in secondary matters.

A paramount need of the Church today is the wise and statesmanlike leadership of men who will rise above petty bickering over differences that cannot be helped by argument. We need an all-out crusade for the unity for which Christ prayed before He went to the cross. It must, however, be a unity based on the Gospel if it is to succeed.

Evangelical cooperation has made amazing progress in these short years. There is no excuse for discouragement, but, on the contrary, every cause for rejoicing and optimism. But, with the passing of the days must come an increasing conviction of the urgency of our mission. Upon our hearts lies heavily the burden of the task before us. The time is short. Let us not use it for secondary objectives. "The night cometh when no man can work."

So brilliant had been the leadership of Dr. Decker that he was prevailed upon to resign his pulpit in Kansas City and to become full-time executive director of the NAE. For several years he endeavored to direct administrative affairs from Kansas City with varying success. In 1948 Dr. Decker was listed as Acting Executive Director. It was not until 1952 that he came to Chicago in the capacity of full-time Executive Director. Meanwhile, Dr. Wright and Dr. Clyde W. Taylor gave much of their time to administrative matters in the national headquarters office.

Dr. Stephen W. Paine (1948-50), president of Houghton College and outstanding leader in the Wesleyan Methodist Church of North America, succeeded Dr. Decker. Dr. Paine had rendered distinguished service in the field of policy and parliamentary procedure and had expertly guided the course of the Commission on Education, as it had expanded to include elementary, secondary, and collegiate services

to evangelical educational institutions. His administration
stressed "inter-church cooperation without compromise"
and dealt wisely with the thorny problem of "separation"
which had become a divisive issue among evangelicals themselves. Dr. Paine's guiding hand helped to keep progress
on an even keel and encouraged a deeper sense of fellowship and cooperation among NAE's constituent members.
New regional offices were opened. Three radio networks
gave recognition to the NAE and allocated national broadcasting time on a sustaining basis. The emergency War
Relief Commission was reorganized on a permanent basis
and became the World Relief Commission. Conventions
were held at Chicago in 1949 and in Indianapolis, Indiana,
in 1950. At the latter it was indicated that some seventy
independent evangelical boards, conferences and institutions were members of the NAE. The outreach of the Association as a vital influence in evangelical life continued.

Dr. Frederick Curtis Fowler (1950-52), pastor of the
Knoxville Presbyterian Church (USA), Pittsburgh, Pennsylvania, was NAE's fifth president. He had rendered
distinguished leadership in the field of religious liberty
and evangelical action. Working closely with the Washington office he was well and favorably known in government
circles. Under his administration (with conventions in
Chicago in 1951 and 1952) the Association dealt aggressively with problems of church and state and the subversive
encroachments of atheistic communism. This was a time of
grave national and international crisis which culminated
in "police action" in Korea. NAE spoke boldly the evangelical testimony for the times and was heard with respect
and honor. The Commission on Social Action held its first
national forum. The Commission on Philosophy of Christian Education issued its notable report, *Christian Education in a Democracy*. A Commission on Stewardship was
created. The NAE participated in the constitutional conference of the World Evangelical Fellowship and had a
large part in framing the structure of this organization.

Dr. Paul S. Rees (1952-54), pastor of the First Covenant
Church (EMCA), Minneapolis, Minnesota, was elected to
the presidency at the 1952 Chicago convention. Dr. Rees,
a strong advocate of evangelical inter-church cooperation,
was widely and favorably known for his radio, literary
and evangelistic accomplishments. His church had long
been a bulwark to evangelical cooperation in the Upper Mid-

west. Great prosperity and prestige came to the NAE under his guidance. The Cincinnati convention in 1953 was the Association's largest. The presence of Evangelist Billy Graham attracted nationwide attention. Here were consummated plans which led to Dr. Rees' later close association with Dr. Graham in England, Scotland, and elsewhere. The Evangelical Foreign Missions Association reported expansion to serve one-third of the Protestant missionaries in the world field. Its purchasing office showed gross sales approaching $1,000,000. The National Religious Broadcasters said its members spent some $6,000,000 annually in national network contracts to get the Gospel out to the nation. A delegation of NAE leaders was received at the White House by President Dwight D. Eisenhower. The National Sunday School Association swept the land with its program of "revitalizing the American Sunday Schools" with new metropolitan, state, and regional organizations springing up everywhere.

But with the coming of the Cleveland convention in 1954 came internal crisis. Overexpansion without proper concern for financial needs had plunged the Association into serious fiscal difficulties. The headquarters office was without an Executive Director and an adequate staff and several of the regional offices were leaderless. Dr. Rees furnished magnificent spiritual and practical leadership in the crisis. An emergency committee headed by Dr. Wm. H. Lee Spratt, pastor of the Lorimer Memorial Baptist Church, Chicago, stepped into the breach. A special meeting of the Board of Administration was called. The response was wonderful in this time of testing and gave proof of the essential solidarity of the Association. A new sense of faith in and dependence upon God came upon the entire leadership.

Dr. Henry H. Savage (1954-56), pastor of the First Baptist Church (CBAA), Pontiac, Michigan, was persuaded to assume leadership of the Association in the midst of this critical period. Only his great love for NAE and his strong conviction that it had "come to the Kingdom for such a time as this" caused him to make the many sacrifices entailed. His great congregation released him from many of his responsibilities so that he could counsel, plan, pray, and work with the brethren at headquarters as they sought to meet the emergency. The Rev. George L. Ford, who had served the Northwest Region as executive director and

had only recently assumed similar duties in the Southwest
Region, had been called to become "associate executive director" of the National Association. He proved to be God's
man for the task.

Financial retrenchment was ordered. New budgets were
drafted. A "charter plan" was initiated for all regional
offices. *Action* magazine was reduced in size and its budget
integrated with that of the central office. Commissions
were put on a self-supporting basis. A drive for funds to
reduce the deficit was undertaken by a group of evangelical
laymen. Headquarters offices were moved from Chicago to
Wheaton, Illinois.

By the 1955 Chicago convention a balanced program began to emerge and a new spirit of optimism had again per-
vaded the leadership. The regional program was soon expanded, with offices in seven areas. It was clear that the
Association had become top-heavy at the national level and
that its organized life needed to be extended to local communities across the nation. Scores of new community associations of evangelicals began to come into being, each with
a program of service for the pastors and laymen in the
local churches.

As a result of the crisis of 1953-55 the NAE is stronger
than ever before in its history and is rebuilding on sure
foundations that reach into every geographical area of the
USA and that enlist whole armies of new leadership at
local levels. The second Cleveland convention (1956) was
the most deeply spiritual of all NAE's great national gatherings. It equalled the best in attendance. The simultaneous
meetings of commissions and associated agencies were the
largest ever. The Commissions on Home Missions and Evangelism were merged to form the Commission on Evangelism
and Church Extension. A new Commission on Spiritual
Life came into being. All reports were superlatively
good in every area of service and activity. NAE was
marching along again.

Dr. Paul P. Petticord (1956-   ), president of the Western Evangelical Seminary, Portland, Oregon and former
conference superintendent of the Evangelical United Brethren Church, stepped up from the vice-presidency to become
president at Cleveland. Dr. Petticord had furnished excep-
tional leadership during the dark days of 1953-55. He had
been active in the affairs of the Association since its inception, particularly in the Northwest Region. There is

every indication that he will add new distinction to the long list of noble leaders (or "servants of God," as they might prefer to be called) who have served so well in days gone by.

It has been a great record. All who have had a part in it would say that it has been achieved "not by might, not by power" but by the Spirit of God working through dedicated men.

As the National Association of Evangelicals stands today (1956) it numbers in its membership forty complete denominations, individual churches from forty other denominations, and many Bible institutes, colleges and seminaries, ministerial fellowships, evangelistic organizations, youth groups, benevolent institutions, as well as individual Christians. The actual membership of the NAE proper exceeds 2,000,000. There is a service constituency through its commissions and affiliated agencies of more than 10,000,000.

The actual official membership by denominations and associations is as follows:[3]

Assemblies of God	400,000
Association of Fundamental Ministers and Churches	1,000
Brethren in Christ Church	6,000
Christian Church of North America, Inc.	18,000
Christian Union	15,000
Church of God (Cleveland, Tenn.)	200,000
Church of the United Brethren in Christ	20,500
Churches of Christ in Christian Union	10,500
Congregational Methodist Church	12,500
Church by the Side of the Road	2,000
Conservative Congregational Conference	10,000
Elim Missionary Assemblies	5,000
Evangelical Free Church of America	30,000
Evangelical Mennonite Brethren Church	2,000
Evangelical Mennonite Church of North America	2,000
Evangelical Methodist Church	20,000
Evangelistic Tabernacles	2,000
Free Methodist Church of North America	51,000
General Six-Principle Baptists	280
Grace Gospel Evangelistic Association	1,000
Holiness Methodist Church	1,000
International Church of the Foursquare Gospel	88,000

3. Official listing by NAE Headquarters Office.

International Pentecostal Assemblies 5,000
Krimmer Mennonite Brethren Conference 2,000
Mennonite Brethren Church of North America 15,000
Missionary Bands of the World, Inc. 250
Missionary Church Association 7,000
Missionary Methodist Conference 2,000
New England Fellowship of Evangelical Baptists 2,000
National Association of Free Will Baptists 400,000
Ohio Yearly Meeting of Friends 7,000
Open Bible Standard Churches 27,000
Oregon Yearly Meeting of Friends 6,500
Pentecostal Church of God of America 45,000
Pentecostal Holiness Church 45,000
Primitive Methodist Church of the USA 12,500
Reformed Presbyterian Church of North America 5,000
United Fundamentalist Church 1,000
United Holy Church of America 27,000
United Missionary Church 10,000
Wesleyan Methodist Church of America 35,500

Conferences of Denominations:

Advent Christian Church, Massachusetts
Conference 5,000
Advent Christian Church, New Hampshire
Conference 1,200
Baptist General Conference of New England 3,000
California Conference of the United Brethren
in Christ 600
North Central District of the Pilgrim
Holiness Church 5,000
Pacific Northwest Conference of Evangelical
United Brethren Church 11,000
Western Conference of Evangelical
Congregational Church 3,000

All major denominations in America (Baptist, Methodist, Presbyterian, Lutheran, Christian, Congregational, etc.) are represented by many individual ministerial or local church memberships in the National Association of Evangelicals. The 21,000,000 American Protestants in the denominations outside the National Council of Churches find in the NAE their most effective instrument in time of need.

Among the denominations officially served in the NAE's service constituency are The Lutheran Church (Missouri

Synod), The Church of the Nazarene, The Christian and Missionary Alliance, The Conservative Baptist Association of America, The Baptist General Conference of America and many others that might be mentioned.

The NAE is a voluntary association of evangelical churches, denominations, organizations, and individuals for united evangelical action. It is not a council of churches. It does not seek the union of churches. It has no means of exercising control over its constituent members. Essential services are rendered in every major field of Christian activity and its testimony for the fundamental doctrines of the evangelical Christian faith is increasingly effective.

The national headquarters office is located at Wheaton, Illinois. Other offices are maintained at Washington, D. C.; New York City, N. Y.; Boston, Mass.; Williamsport, Pa.; Cincinnati, Ohio; Detroit, Mich.; Chicago, Ill.; Minneapolis, Minn.; Wichita, Kans.; Portland, Ore., and Los Angeles, Calif.

Commissions and affiliated agencies operate in the following fields:

Evangelism — A constant nation-wide evangelistic emphasis is being encouraged by the Commission on Evangelism and Church Extension. The Commission does not promote evangelistic campaigns, believing that this is the distinctive task of the churches, but it inspires, encourages and educates for evangelism by all means at its command. The Commission acts as a clearing house for voluntary united action among evangelical home mission boards and boards of church extension.

Higher Education — This Commission has had a tremendous influence in building and perfecting the higher educational program of the evangelical cause. Accrediting, textbook needs, classroom techniques, administration, business management, public relations, etc., are some of the areas of service.

Sunday School — This work is carried on through the National Sunday School Association with offices in Chicago. Evangelical Sunday School teachers and leaders by the thousands participate in the Association's activities at national, state, and local levels.

Christian Day Schools — Evangelicals have aroused conscience on the necessity of Christian-based education for the boys and girls of this generation. The National Association of Christian Schools has aided hundreds of communities in setting up Christian Day Schools to meet growing needs, providing teacher training, placement, and other services.

Publications — *United Evangelical Action,* the official news magazine of the National Association of Evangelicals, is issued twice a month and reaches evangelical leaders in all parts of the nation and throughout the world. It endeavors to promote the work of the National Association and its affiliated agencies and has often been the medium through which evangelical action has produced effective results in national life. Books and brochures are produced as needs arise.

Foreign Missions — Voluntary united action among evangelical mission boards and missionaries is expedited through the Evangelical Foreign Missions Association. Its office in Washington promotes better public relations; deals with diplomats of all nations; arranges passports, visas, and other legal matters; etc. The purchasing office in New York City serves missionaries as well as churches and ministers in America.

Laymen's Advisory Council — Evangelical laymen are manifesting a growing interest in the development of the National Association of Evangelicals and its allied agencies. To channel this interest and make it most effective the Laymen's Advisory Council has been formed with chapters in a growing number of areas.

Women's Fellowship — Evangelical women are forming auxiliaries for cooperative effort in all sections of the nation where the NAE is organized. They hold regular meetings and support such projects as child evangelism; hospitals; homes for girls; work with shut-ins, the aged, cripples, and incurables; world relief; evangelism among unsaved women at all social levels; etc.

Evangelical Youth — The Commission on Youth Work and Evangelical Youth, Inc., serves as a clearing house for voluntary united action among the youth agencies of denominations which are members of the NAE. Basic standards have been adopted; evangelical methodology has been devised; conferences are held for inspiration and education.

Evangelical Action — This Commission, through the Washington office of the NAE, keeps a finger on the pulse of the nation and when necessary makes vocal the evangelical view on governmental and social matters. One of the objectives is the sponsoring of positive Protestant advertising in newspapers and magazines across the country.

Radio-TV Broadcasting — The NAE Commission on Radio and the National Religious Broadcasters, Inc., have within their constituency most of the larger evangelical broadcasting interests in America. When the industry planned to eliminate "commercial" religious broadcasts it was NRB which "saved the day." Today it is having similar influence in holding the line for evangelical broadcasters in television.

Government Chaplaincies — This Commission represents the constituent denominations of NAE in providing evangelical chaplains for the armed services. It answers hundreds of inquiries each year and endeavors to see that evangelical bodies receive due recognition in all matters pertaining to government chaplaincies. Its standing with the office of the chief of chaplains is of the highest quality.

World Relief — Beginning with aid to Europe's needy millions following World War II, the World Relief Commission has sent food and clothing worth many millions of dollars to all parts of the world. Its New York office is constantly sending aid to German D.P.'s, orphan children, and hospital cases; to the needy of Southern Europe, notably in Yugoslavia and Greece; to Korea and other Oriental lands where the need is so great.

International Relations—The Commission on International Relations was largely responsible for the organization of the World Evangelical Fellowship in 1951. Through its office in Boston it maintains contacts with other evangelical organizations throughout the world and promotes projects of mutual benefit among the various autonomous evangelical organizations affiliated with the WEF.

Social Action — This Commission seeks to apply social teachings of the Holy Scripture in practical life situations. Evangelical welfare associations are being encouraged throughout the nation.

Stewardship — Various promotional activities serve to increase giving to the Lord's work. Annual reports indicate that member denominations rank in the topmost brackets in per capita giving among American Protestant bodies.

Spiritual Life — This Commission provides programs for observance of the World Week of Prayer and the World Day of Prayer. Throughout the year periods of special emphasis are observed to promote prayer for revival and the development of spiritual life in the churches.

As the new evangelical movement looks to the future it finds a new world — a world far different from the one in which it was born. History moves swiftly these days and with the strange atomic discoveries promises to move even more rapidly in the future.

Basically, of course, the eternal things never change. God, Christ, the Holy Spirit, are the same yesterday, today and forever. Man is the same sinful creature Christ came to save. The great fundamental doctrines of the Holy Scriptures and the Church of Jesus Christ remain in all their pristine grandeur and relevance to the ultimate purposes of God.

The impact of a relentless Communism has changed the political and geographical face of the earth. It is a totalitarian system masquerading under the guise of socialism. It has an inherent consistency based on dialectical materialism. It hates God and is committed to a stark antichristian pragmatism. Man is hideously distorted into an economic digit, a creature of the state. There is growing evidence of the fact that this world menace may well eventuate in Armageddon.

As ever-resourceful Roman Catholicism continues its relentless warfare against Protestantism — open where it has temporal power, underground where the use of force is impossible. While in some respects Communism and Romanism are diverse, they are both systems of power. Both are absolutist. Both have concepts of freedom which are capable of enormous abuse.

Some evangelicals harbor the illusion that there is yet a possibility that the National Council of Churches of Christ in the USA may be amenable to changes in its doctrinal basis, structure, and policies which would permit the NAE constituency to join in one great Protestant inter-church organization.

When the earliest moves were made toward the merger of the major Protestant inter-church agencies (1940) and the blueprints were being drawn for the Federal Council's successor corporation there was a time of great heartsearching among evangelicals. They hoped that the leaders of the new enterprise would approach the problem of Protestant inter-church cooperation in humility and prayer, seeking the leadership of the Holy Spirit and taking into their counsels truly representative men from the more than 30,000,000 evangelicals within and without the old Council. Had they done this there might have been a disposition to move toward a more biblical viewpoint, a more evangelistic program and a more democratic organizational structure.

But the old "liberal" leadership of the FCCCA, which dominated the planning conferences, ignored evangelicals and made it clear that they were thoroughly committed to the old policies. It soon became evident that there was no hope for rapprochement between the two camps. When the National Council of Churches was organized[4] in Cleveland, Ohio, November 28 - December 1, 1950, the leaders of the National Association of Evangelicals were more certain than ever that they had been called to the Kingdom "for such a time as this." They were convinced that the NAE was to be in the days ahead the only effective advocate of that type of inter-church cooperation in America which believes that unity and cooperation lie primarily in the realm of faith; that the deity of Christ and the authority of the Holy Scriptures must forever be upheld and that the basic principles and liberties inherent in historic Protestantism must be preserved and perpetuated at all hazards.

This viewpoint has persisted throughout the great majority of the NAE's constituency from that day to this.[5] History gives abundant evidence of the fact that institutions are seldom converted. The NCC is the fulfillment of the hopes of many for a powerful institutional answer to Roman Catholicism at the national level. It is no longer distinctly Protestant. Doctrinal considerations are of little importance. The NCC has prestige, money, and intelligent liberal leadership within a growingly efficient and effective organization. Evangelicals accept this situation realistically and pursue their original course — cooperation without compromise — with growing evidence of the blessing of God.

During the brief lifetime of the National Association of Evangelicals theological liberalism has undergone tremendous changes. Classical liberalism is *passe* — the liberalism which evangelicals fought to the death in the first half of the twentieth century. The *Christian Century*, "liberalism's" chief journalistic advocate, was finally forced to admit it in a devastating series of articles by its foremost pundit, Dr. Charles Clayton Morrison.[6] While the apparent

4. *Christian Faith in Action* (1951).
5. *The Growing Super-Church* by James DeForest Murch (1952).
6. *Christian Century*, June 7, 14, 21, 1950.

thesis of the series was Liberalism's advance, Dr. Morrison admitted:

First, that much of liberal thinking had been shallow, premature and, in a large measure, erroneous.

Second, that the original liberalism which caused such havoc in the Christian world foreclosed its own case, crystallized prematurely before all the facts were in and reached conclusions which it now holds dogmatically. While this liberalism is considered *passe*, it still exists as a monument to its utter failure.

Third, that there is a new liberalism which rejects the conclusions of the old liberalism and that, therefore, the forces of liberalism are divided.

Fourth, that the liberal tendency to give science the final word as to the nature of the universe and to shift religious interest from the cosmology of the Bible to the ethical teaching of Jesus is erroneous. It is now clear that the enduring substance and essence of Christianity is not to be found in its ethic but rather in the nature of the cosmos and the meaning of human existence.

Fifth, that liberalism was premature and unwarranted in humanizing the Bible as a whole and in regarding the idea of revelation as having no realistic foundation.

Sixth, that liberalism was wrong in conceiving of Christianity as the religion *of* Jesus in contrast with a religion *about* Jesus. Such a religion can be little more than Judaism carried to its highest ethical and universal expression.

Seventh, that liberalism has been forced by the findings of competent scholarship to abandon the view that the writings of the Apostle Paul postdated the true literature of Christianity and that, therefore, his theology is an obscuration of essential Christianity as contained in the Synoptic Gospels.

Eighth, that liberalism was wrong in making its goal the "building of the Kingdom of God on earth" and in accepting the concept that all historical progress is "onward and upward forever." Furthermore, it erred in identifying the eschatology of the New Testament with "sheer obscurantism and escapism."

Ninth, that liberals now have some doubts regarding their doctrine that man is inherently good and that sin is an expression of his immaturity or ignorance or some maladjustment. They concede that some intelligent people believe in the doctrine of original sin.

Tenth, that liberalism's subservience to the dictates of human reason as it operates in science and philosophy is unfortunate and has resulted in its failure to discover the true nature of reality.

This undercurrent of criticism which runs throughout the three articles rises to its height at the conclusion of the series when the venerable pundit cries:

> Those who claim to have a sort of patent on liberalism have betrayed it. They have carried liberalism into a blind alley. In clinging to the earliest conclusions from modern science, biblical criticism, the psychology of religion and comparative religion, those who still wear the label of liberalism as a partisan badge are essentially dogmatists.

Dr. Morrison made it clear that he still considers himself a "true liberal." He is no evangelical. He is not even neo-orthodox, but as a "true liberal" recognizes an affinity with neo-orthodoxy's method and some of its conclusions. Dr. Morrison declared that liberalism is primarily a method and a movement which changes its doctrine as often as new discoveries of science, new dicta in philosophy, ever-changing human experience, and historical circumstances may require.

Evangelicals had won a battle, but the war is still on. The chastened liberals have surrendered none of their basic views; they have simply compromised them. Liberals still are in a free "search for truth" which will not admit guidance by an external authority such as the Holy Scriptures. Human reason is regarded as the perfect instrument which enables man to discover truth and it is also the final test of truth.

One noted compromise is neo-orthodoxy. Its very name indicates that it is a compromise. Neo-orthodoxy holds that God is transcendent, absolutely distinct from His creation and highly exalted above it in glorious majesty. It denies continuity between man and God and makes clear man's absolute dependency upon Him. It has restored the idea of special revelation as essential to man's knowledge of God. It gives due prominence once more to the idea of sin and strengthens the sense of sin. It restores salvation by grace through faith and makes clear that man cannot be saved by his good works. As Louis Berkhof puts it:

> In spite of the fact that the protagonists of the Theology of Crisis take issue with the subjectivism of the lib-

erals, that is, their practice of basing their whole theology
on their own subjective ideas, impressions, or experi-
ences, and that they appeal to an objective revelation of
God, this revelation has no permanent objective existence. It comes to man from time to time only in flashes,
in redemptive acts, which have no doctrinal content on
which man can construct his theology. Their view of
Scripture as a mere human product, containing myths
and legends and inaccuracies; their denial of the historical existence of Adam, and of the historicity of the story
of the fall and of the state of integrity; their restricting
the revelation of God in Christ to a few outstanding facts,
such as His death and resurrection; and their failure to
give a satisfactory explanation of the atonement — are
all very disappointing. Their interpretation of the truth
is still too much under the domination of philosophy.[7]

Another compromise of chastened liberalism is Christian
realism. John C. Bennett in his *Christian Realism* and
Walter M. Horton in his *Realistic Theology* set forth its
new type theology. It is predicated upon a resolute determination to face all the facts of life candidly and through
them to penetrate the solid structure of objective reality
in order to derive from it whatever ground there is for
courage, hope, and faith. It accepts the idea of special
divine revelation although it does not identify revelation
with the Bible as the infallible Word of God. It involves
a greater respect for the so-called "Hebrew-Christian tradition" and less dependence on the "Greek tradition" which
came to full flower in the Renaissance. Christian realism
involves a more "realistic view of man", refuses to believe
in his "inherent goodness" and his progressive advance
toward perfection by purely natural processes. These theologians go so far as to mention "original sin" although they
do not embrace the Scriptural doctrine.

All these views are basically liberal and represent a
strategic retreat to newly entrenched positions where more
subtly and (it is hoped) more effectively than ever the
orthodox, evangelical, biblical position may be attacked.[8]

7. *Recent Trends in Theology* by Louis Berkhof (1946).
8. The following books give conservative, liberal and neo-orthodox
views currently accepted in Protestantism: *Fifty Years of Protestant
Theology* by Carl F. H. Henry (1950); *The Study of the Bible Today
and Tomorrow*, by Harold R. Willoughby, ed. (1947); *Therefore
Stand* by Wilbur M. Smith (1945); *A Theology of the Living Church*
by L. Harold DeWolf (1953); *The Faith of the Christian Church* by
G. Aulen (1948); *Systematic Theology* by Louis Berkof (1941); *The*

There is another theology in the making which is the product of the ecumenical movement. Actuated by what seem to be the most plausible motives for a united church and using the vocabulary of orthodoxy, ecumenical theologians are busily engaged in devising a theology which will be acceptable to all who may be persuaded to participate in "The Coming Great Church." There is much said of the "sovereignty of Christ," indeed, a "Christological approach" is proposed to the solution of the theological problems posed by widely varying viewpoints. This may not in any way be synonymous with the law of the spirit of Christ and the apostolic doctrine of Christ as revealed in the Holy Scriptures. It would appear from preliminary statements of the leaders in this new movement that ecumenicity is the chief motivating factor, not the Holy Spirit-breathed revelation of the Christ of the New Testament. Such an approach could only result in a man-made "Christology" which would best serve the purposes of the ecumenicists. Walter M. Horton, in his book *Christian Theology: An Ecumenical Approach,* sets forth six theological positions represented in the ecumenical movement: (1) Catholic, (2) Conservative Protestant, (3) Liberal Protestant, (4) Radical Protestant, (5) Neo-orthodox, and (6) Anglican.[9] He then proceeds to seek a synthesis which will be acceptable to all shades of theological thought. Never was cooperation *with compromise* more charmingly sought. This ecumenical approach will have a winsome appeal to all who deplore the divided state of Christendom and seek an early end to its tragic quarrels.

What shall evangelicals do in this situation? Unquestionably they are living in a new day—a day with all the basic factors of life conditioned in their favor. There is not a day that passes without thousands of unheralded conversions from the ranks of liberalism to a more biblical Christianity. The whole wide world is waiting for some prophetic utterance of the eternal truth of God that will meet the need of the hour. This must come from men who are in close touch with the living Christ and hold the revelation of the Word of Life inviolate.

Christian Faith by J. Stump (1942); *Karl Barth's Church Dogmatics* by Otto Weber (1953); *Systematic Theology* by Paul Tillich (1951); *Christian Realism* by John C. Bennett (1941; rev. ed., 1947); *Realistic Theology* by Walter M. Horton.

9. *Christian Theology: An Ecumenical Approach* by Walter M. Horton (1955).

This is not the world in which "Fundamentalism" had its rise. That was yesterday's world. Today's world calls not for yesterday's approach to the problems of religion and life, but for new approaches, new emphases, new strategies. Christ is "the same yesterday, today and forever." Old truth — if it *was* truth, *is* truth and *will be* truth. God's plan of salvation is immutable. The true Church is indestructible. Our chief enemy is the same old Satan. Sin is unregenerate and man's inherent stumblingblock. But if we will study the history of the Church for some two thousand years we shall discover that in a changing world it has met new situations with new tactics. What is the strategy for our day?

If historian may turn prophet, he would say:

We need to lift our sights above old non-biblical concepts, accept the valid discoveries and worth-while advances of modern life and think, plan, and act accordingly. We need to abandon our isolationisms, provincialisms and traditionalisms which are obsolete and which might keep us from a realistic approach to the actual problems of men in our day and time.

We need to realize that the Christian world is in a state of flux. Many of the old lines which used to separate us have little meaning in a modern frame of reference. Men who were "liberals" yesterday are not so sure of their ground today as they face an atomic world and the possibility of the utter destruction of civilization and the human race. Evangelicals who were anti-cultural, anti-scientific and anti-educational yesterday are realizing the necessity of living effectively in a bigger, wider world than they even knew existed. While, as we have said, the great eternal facts and truths of Christianity are unchanging, men and institutions and science are changing and we must meet them, challenge them, and help them grow in the direction of God and the Gospel. We must not condemn sincere thinking and growing men or refuse to meet with them (because of some preconceived notions about them) and talk and pray with them and teach them.

We need to examine ourselves, not only to determine whether we are in the faith, but to see whether we are guilty of self-righteousness and pride. We need to humble ourselves and pray and seek the face of God in new and vital spiritual experience. We need a new endowment of the Holy Spirit and a new willingness to follow His leading.

We need to restudy the Bible itself. The dogmas and creeds of men, however noble and inspiring, however enlightening and strengthening, however purposeful in grounding our minds in fundamental doctrine, can never take the place of the Bible as the direct revelation of God and the infallible authority in all that pertains to faith and life. Fresh touch with the living, written Word can under God give evangelicals a new birth of freedom of thought and launch us upon a movement of such broad proportions that it can sweep the world.

We need to rise above all organizations of men in a bigger and broader fellowship, as big and as broad as the eternal Church of God. God has blessed some of us in our bold and uncompromising stand for the "faith once for all delivered" in the midst of doubt and apostasy. We have built great churches, great Bible institutes, colleges and seminaries, missionary enterprises that span the world, publishing houses, radio ministries and inter-church agencies that show every mark of the blessing of God. But if we are going to allow these works of our hands to bulk so large in our thinking as to cut us off from fellowship with others of like mind and heart, we are failing Him who made it possible for us to achieve great things for Him. We need to see today's religious problems from the viewpoint of God and be as big and as broad in our concerns as He is. Any barriers that we allow to keep us from having a love for mankind as wide as the love which our Lord Jesus Christ demonstrated on Mount Calvary should be pulled down *now!* Tomorrow may be too late in the schedule of God's plan of the ages.

We need to mobilize all our evangelical forces, endowments and personnel in the local churches, in inter-church agencies, in education, in evangelism, in journalism, in radio and television, in missions — in all fields and spheres of Christian service — for a movement of such proportions that God can take it and use it to the accomplishment of His ultimate purposes. This will call for the absolutely complete and unwithholding surrender of our intellectual, material, and spiritual resources and a wholehearted determination to match and exceed the highest and the best that liberalism, humanism and paganism have to offer.

Dr. Harold J. Ockenga at St. Louis in 1942 said that an organization of evangelicals should be launched which "will be the vanguard of a movement" which will have "repercussions in every phase of life" to the glory of God. That organization was realized in the National Association of Evangelicals, which has rendered and is rendering yeoman services in inter-church cooperation. But let us not lose the vision of Dr. Ockenga. Let us think of ourselves as "the vanguard of a movement" that shall achieve God's purposes in our time and literally "turn the world upside down" for Him.

If evangelicals cannot measure up to a vision, a dedication, a purpose, and a program superlatively adequate for our day, the God who gave us the torch of Faith two generations ago will take it from our hands and pass it to some new Company of the Saved who can and will carry it to victory.

INDEX

217